I'LL HAVE WHAT SHE'S HAVING

I'LL HAVE WHAT SHE'S HAVING

Behind the Scenes of the
Great Romantic Comedies

DANIEL M. KIMMEL

Ivan R. Dee Chicago 2008

Photographs courtesy of Photofest.

www.ivanrdee.com

Library of Congress Cataloging-in-Publication Data:
Kimmel, Daniel M.
    I'll have what she's having : behind the scenes of the great romantic comedies /
Daniel M. Kimmel.
        p. cm.
    Includes bibliographical references and index.
    ISBN-13: 978-1-56663-737-4 (cloth : alk. paper)
    ISBN-10: 1-56663-737-6 (cloth : alk. paper)
    1. Romantic comedy films—United States—History and criticism. I. Title.
PN1995.9.C55K545 2008
791.43'617—dc22   2008004705

791.43
K

Dedicated to the memory of my grandparents,

who lived two of the best love stories I know:

Leo and Rose Kimmel

Isadore and Alice Leibowitz

CONTENTS

I'LL HAVE WHAT SHE'S HAVING

INTRODUCTION

THE BIRTH of the talking motion picture is usually set on the night of October 6, 1927, when Al Jolson wowed the audience at the premiere of the movie *The Jazz Singer* by insisting, "Wait a minute! You ain't heard nothin' yet!" He was right, of course, more than anyone might have guessed. The "talkies" quickly became the art form of the twentieth century. All sorts of subsequent innovations—television, VCRs and DVDs, the Internet—have been built, in whole or in part, on the success of movies. Movies are now consumed in ways that Jolson's audience might never have imagined, such as via cell phones, but they remain a primary force in art and entertainment eighty years after the introduction of sound, with no sign of that changing anytime soon.

Students of film (and teachers) have long debated how to approach the body of work that's been produced. Should they consider the director as author of the film (or the *auteur*, as the French critics have it) and study the collected works of, say, Ingmar Bergman or Alfred Hitchcock? Should seriousness of purpose be the primary factor, so that *Citizen Kane* is in but *Abbott and Costello Meet Frankenstein* is out? Perhaps modern (or postmodern) approaches such as Marxism, feminism, or psychoanalysis should be applied to the works in order to uncover what they are "really" about? Or are the fans right, and movies are all just entertainment, meant to be consumed like cotton candy and then forgotten?

3

Each of these approaches has a certain amount of validity, including the notion that many movies were made primarily to entertain, not to be analyzed and explored. Indeed, until recent decades it was often difficult for people to study the films that they wanted to see, when they wanted to see them. Viewers were at the mercy of theater owners and TV stations. If you had access to a repertory house showing older movies, you were very lucky indeed. Now, with much of our film history available through video stores, Netflix, cable channels, or the local library, movie fans can organize their explorations and provide a context for their viewing. In a hosted film series or in a college film class, there's a reason for seeing a group of films and understanding them in a particular context. When you're on your own, there may be no rhyme or reason at all, just the serendipity of what happens to be on the shelves. This book hopes to provide an entertaining passageway into one of the most popular and long-lived film genres, the romantic comedy.

Across the decades, only the gangster film seems to have thrived as well as the romantic comedy. Other once-hardy genres like the western have largely faded, even if a handful of films in recent years have suggested there may be life in them yet. Other kinds, like science fiction or war movies, go in and out of fashion. The success of one type of film breeds a host of like-minded imitators while providing opportunities for others to break new ground. Ultimately audiences determine if a genre category of movie continues to speak to them. The musical was long out of fashion until the 2002 success of *Chicago*. This led to big-screen versions of *Rent*, *The Producers*, and *Phantom of the Opera*, but audiences weren't buying. It remains to be seen if the musical is making a comeback or not.

The romantic comedy remains a hardy perennial because all of us fall in love, hope to fall in love, or have fallen in love. The story of human coupling—why they get together, not what they do in private, which is the subject of another kind of movie entirely—captures everyone's interest. From the ancient Greeks to Shakespeare to Shaw, the foibles and foolishness of people in love has been a prime topic for storytelling. It's no surprise that it has drawn us to the movies as well.

*

The 1930s and early 1940s are often referred to as the "Golden Age" of Hollywood, and certainly of the romantic comedy. Several books on this kind of film focus solely on that era. This is because of the rise of what became known as the "screwball comedy," where the comedy was not parceled out to the Marx Brothers or Laurel and Hardy or other designated comic relief, but was handled by the romantic leads themselves. This book begins the discussion where it usually begins, just before the start of the "screwball" era, with the work of a man who was synonymous with sophistication in Hollywood, Ernst Lubitsch. The famous "Lubitsch touch," described herein, could pack volumes of innuendo into a raised eyebrow or a closed door without crossing the line into bad taste—before the advent of the Production Code, which for the next three decades would severely restrict what could be shown or said in the movies. A comparison of the two Lubitsch movies discussed in the following pages, *Trouble in Paradise* (1932) and *The Shop Around the Corner* (1940), makes one appreciate the slyness of the earlier film, released two years before the Code. Without really saying or showing anything, the characters are clearly sexual as well as romantic, and for Lubitsch there was really no reason to parse the two. The latter film, beloved by those who have seen it but not as well known, focuses much more on the romance. An illicit sexual entanglement occurs off-screen, with sad results.

For other directors, new to the screwball comedy, the Code restrictions were more of a challenge than a reminder of options no longer available. Frank Capra in *It Happened One Night*, Gregory LaCava in *My Man Godfrey*, and George Cukor in *The Philadelphia Story* were able to divert the sexual energy that could not be explicitly acknowledged into the crackling repartee of the film's witty scripts, as well as letting the glamorous stars be glamorous. It might be Katharine

Hepburn, succeeding in a Hollywood comeback after leaving town with the label "box office poison," who never looked as vital and radiant as she did in *The Philadelphia Story*. But glamour was in the eye of the beholder: for many female moviegoers, the height of sexiness was Clark Gable, in *It Happened One Night*, getting undressed for bed and revealing he wore no undershirt.

After World War II the romantic comedy did what film genres can often do when they are done well: use formula situations and stock characters to explore new and serious issues in code. This is a side of films not always appreciated by critics or moviegoers. It might have been difficult to address the paranoia of the cold war with the Soviet Union at the height of the 1950s Red Scare, but if we turned the Communists into aliens we could confront our fears in *The Day the Earth Stood Still*, *The Thing*, and *Invasion of the Body Snatchers*. Race and the new civil rights movement was an issue only a few filmmakers dared face directly, but turn African Americans into Indians, and westerns like *Broken Arrow* and *The Searchers* addressed racism in the 1950s where a more direct approach might have failed. The task of the postwar romantic comedies was to begin to question the assumed and assigned roles of men and women a decade or more before the feminist movement would put those subjects into mainstream discourse.

So we get *Adam's Rib*, arguably the best of the Spencer Tracy / Katharine Hepburn matchups, where as married lawyers on opposing sides of a case, the question of sexism (a word not yet coined) could be addressed within the conventions of a traditional "battle of the sexes." Likewise *Sabrina* gives us a conventional modern-day fairy tale where the poor chauffeur's daughter (Audrey Hepburn) ends up with the prince—or at least the wealthy son of the employer. Yet in considering whether such a match was appropriate, the film brought viewers to think about issues of class and gender that were only beginning to percolate into the public consciousness. (William Holden's dashing playboy ought to carry the day, yet it's Humphrey Bogart's stuffy businessman who becomes the romantic hero.) Later in the 1950s there would be movies like *Pillow Talk* and *Some Like It Hot* that didn't violate the moral standards imposed by the Production Code but acknowledged that women wanted and enjoyed sex, and that men could be unscrupulous in attaining their own gratification.

Of course these are movies where you can just sit back and enjoy while munching on your popcorn. Still, there's nothing preventing you from thinking as well, and the movies here are intended to be enjoyed on many levels, including as sheer entertainment. The romantic comedy primarily employs the tried-and-true plot of boy meeting girl, boy losing girl, and eventually boy winning girl. Yet *My Man Godfrey* makes sense only in the context of the Great Depression (as the dreadful 1950s remake demonstrated), and Doris Day's character fighting to retain her virginity, however misunderstood that plot device may be, reflects a change in attitude toward sex in the fifties and sixties that made her first appear daring and later seem to be a throwback. Genre formulas evolve over time, reflecting the eras when they were made. The couples in *It Happened One Night* and *When Harry Met Sally . . .* end up together, but the differences between the two films are at least as important as their similarities.

There's a curious gap in romantic comedy in the sixties and seventies, explored in more detail in this book's "Intermission," when this kind of film appeared to have run out of steam. It took a new generation of filmmakers, largely coming out of the world of television, to recreate the form for modern times. Woody Allen's *Annie Hall*, Steve Gordon's *Arthur*, Rob Reiner's *When Harry Met Sally . . .* , Garry Marshall's *Pretty Woman*, and Richard Curtis's *Love Actually* can all be critiqued as bringing a sitcom sensibility to the big screen. (So can Bobby and Peter Farrelly's *There's Something About Mary*, though the Farrelly brothers did not emerge from television.) What more recent romantic comedies suggest is that a happy ending is not always guaranteed, though the belief in the power of love remains strong enough that we continue to want these stories and hope for the best.

Critics unfamiliar with the history of romantic comedy are likely to fall into the trap of criticizing *There's Something About Mary*, or more recent examples like *The 40 Year Old Virgin* or *Knocked Up*, and claim that contemporary filmmakers have fallen short of the giants of the past. Once we had sophisticated romantic comedies, now we rely on vulgarity. What they forget is that genre films become gems only in retrospect. *It Happened One Night* may have been the first film to sweep the top Oscars (Best Picture, Best Director, Best Actor, Best Actress, and one of the screenplay awards), but some were shocked and appalled at the choice, and predicted the film would not be long remembered. Twenty-five years later, studio after studio turned down *Pillow Talk* as a throwback to a dead style—then rushed to catch up when it turned into a surprise hit. Richard Curtis got mixed reviews for his scripts for *Four Weddings and a Funeral*, *Notting Hill*, and *Love Actually* (the last of which he directed) because his characters are so smart and witty. Then someone like Judd Apatow is criticized for a movie like *Knocked Up* on the grounds that, in the old days, characters in romantic comedies were smart and witty rather than raunchy. Genre films are sometimes recognized for their achievements upon initial release, but more often it is only in retrospect that a movie given the back of the hand at first is recognized as a great western, a great *film noir*, or a great romantic comedy.

What follows are the stories of the making of fifteen of the great romantic comedies.

*

It's worth noting how these films were chosen. Various lists appear, from time to time, of the greatest movies ever made, or the funniest comedies ever, and so on. For the fan looking for classic films they may have missed, such lists can be useful. For the more serious buff they can be a kickoff for debate and discussion. Under no circumstances should they be considered the authoritative final word. Is *Citizen Kane* the greatest movie ever made? It's certainly one of them. Yet how would you quantify its "greatness" compared to, say, *Lawrence of Arabia* or *Singin' in the Rain* or *The Seven Samurai*? You can't. These films are so different and so uniquely brilliant that it's absurd to argue that, objectively, *Kane* is greater than *Samurai*. It's like arguing that da Vinci's *Mona Lisa* is "greater" than Picasso's *Guernica* or, for that matter, Beethoven's *Ninth Symphony* or Shakespeare's *King Lear*. All are towering artistic achievements. We needn't rate one higher than the other.

Such is the case here. A person who wishes to explore romantic comedy in the movies could do worse than see the fifteen films described in the coming pages. Some are, by overwhelming consensus, important achievements in the form. Anyone who wants to understand the romantic comedy simply must see such films as *Trouble in Paradise*, *It Happened One Night*, *Adam's Rib*, *Annie Hall*, and *When Harry Met Sally* . . . . Others included are well known to film buffs, historians, and critics but not often viewed by people looking for movies at the video store or on Netflix. Here's where my preferences and tastes come in.

In trying not to do the usual "weren't the screwball comedies the greatest?" book, which has already been done many times, only a few examples of them are presented here, notably *It Happened One Night* and *My Man Godfrey*. Missing are such great films as *Twentieth Century*, *The Awful Truth*, *Theodora Goes Wild*, *Easy Living*, *Nothing Sacred*, *Bringing Up Baby*, *Holiday*, *Ninotchka*, *His Girl Friday*, *The Palm Beach Story*, *The Lady Eve*, and many, many others.

Since the aim of the book is to tell the behind-the-scenes stories of how these films were made, that too was a factor in selecting them. Audrey Hepburn became an icon in *Roman Holiday*, but the story of the making of that film is essentially the challenge of shooting on location in Italy in the early 1950s. That's why the Hepburn film explored here was her next one, *Sabrina*, which tells us far more about how Hollywood worked, the impact of on- and off-screen romances, and how the filmmaking process may be a very different experience for the participants than for viewers of the finished product.

More recent films, made after the end of the Production Code in 1968, raise their own issues of sexual frankness as well as exploring matters that wouldn't have even been considered decades earlier. Woody Allen gets to question the anti-Semitism (real and imagined) of the non-Jewish characters in *Annie Hall*. Male sexual fantasies provide the subtext for movies like *Pretty Woman* and *There's Something About Mary*. The most famous moment of *When Harry Met Sally . . .* , the delicatessen scene, came out of a discussion over whether women ever fake their reactions during sex, with screenwriter Nora Ephron unable to convince director Rob Reiner until he began questioning women on his own. As you examine romantic comedies across the decades, it becomes obvious that while they clearly share plots, characters, and attitudes, they just as clearly reflect great differences that come out of the times and sensibilities that gave birth to them.

In the end, romantic comedies—like any film genre—are a lens through which we can see how *we* have changed over time.

ISN'T IT ROMANTIC?

"Well, all you need to start an asylum is an empty room and the right kind of people."—Alexander Bullock (Eugene Pallette) in *My Man Godfrey* (1936)

1

TROUBLE IN PARADISE

HISTORIES of the romantic comedy on film often start with *Trouble in Paradise*, and for good reason. Although it would not prove to be the model for future movies, as *It Happened One Night* would be, there is no avoiding the wit and charm of this 1932 film.

The most important name connected with *Trouble in Paradise* is that of its director, Ernst Lubitsch. Sadly forgotten today except by historians and buffs, Lubitsch is owed an enormous debt by every filmmaker and fan of romantic comedy. He was born in Germany in 1892, the only child of a conventional German Jewish family. His father was a tailor who owned a men's shop, a heritage that Lubitsch would make use of in subsequent films, most notably *The Shop Around the Corner*. He loved to appear in school plays and by age sixteen had announced he would pursue a career as an actor. His father was appalled.

"Are you crazy?" he asked his son. "Look at yourself. And you want to go on stage? If you were at least handsome—but with your face?"

When it became clear that Ernst was not a gifted salesman, he was relegated to the backroom as a bookkeeper. Eventually he moved along a dual career track. By day he was his father's bookkeeper, by night he would act in cabarets and music halls—wherever he could get a part. In 1913 he made the transition to film, where his comic gifts were quickly appreciated. After the success of his first two movies, the young Lubitsch was asked if he had any ideas of his own for his next comedy, and he suggested that of a klutzy clerk at a men's clothing store. *Die Firma Heiratet* (1914)—*The Firm Marries*— featured Lubitsch in the leading role, and it was such a success that he later repeated variations on the character in several more movies. Before the year 1914 was out, he began directing, much as—that same year—a young British music-hall comic named Charlie Chaplin was starting to do for the American comedy filmmaker Mack Sennett.

Over the next several years Lubitsch continued to act, but it was clearly directing that captivated him. By the time he left Germany for Hollywood in 1923, he was becoming known as the director not of slapstick comedies but of lush melodramas and historical romances: *Carmen* (1918), *The Eyes of the Mummy Ma* (1918), *Madame Du Barry* (1919), *Anne Boleyn* (1920), and many others. His success paved the way to Hollywood, where he made his debut in 1923 directing Mary Pickford in *Rosita*. Lubitsch would go on to make his mark as one of the great silent directors in such films as *The Marriage Circle* (1924) and *Lady Windermere's Fan* (1925). Had his career ended with the introduction of sound, he might still be remembered as one of the greats of the silent era. Already he was known for a sophisticated wit and what would soon become hailed as "the Lubitsch touch," the ability to convey ironic, sophisticated innuendo with the slightest of devices.

With the transition to sound in 1927, Lubitsch segued into a series of frothy romantic musical comedies, set in fairy-tale European settings. Many of them starred Jeanette MacDonald, Maurice Chevalier, or both, including *The Love Parade* (1929) and *The Smiling Lieutenant* (1931). These are delightful and charming, ripe for rediscovery by mainstream movie lovers. For Lubitsch, though, it was a string of films that eventually left him hungry for a project with substance, and that led him to *The Man I Killed* (1932), the only sound drama the director ever attempted. It is an anti-war film about a French soldier who is overcome with guilt for having killed a young German soldier during the Great War, and who goes to Germany to seek out the man's family. Although it achieved critical recognition, it was not the sort of film that depression era audiences wanted to see. Indeed, it was an experiment Lubitsch would not repeat.

Instead, after a brief sojourn in New York, where he contemplated a return to the stage, he came back to Hollywood. He made the charming trifle *One Hour with You*, the last of his musicals, then turned his attention to what many consider one of the most perfect romantic comedies ever produced, *Trouble in Paradise*.

*

We first meet Gaston Monescu (Herbert Marshall) in a deluxe hotel in Venice. He is planning an assignation with a countess (Miriam Hopkins) who believes him to be a wealthy baron. As we quickly

Director Ernst Lubitsch got away with a lot in the pre-Code days, including allowing two jewel thieves (Miriam Hopkins and Herbert Marshall) to be the romantic leads of this film.

learn, in a scene played with sophisticated wit and effortless speed, they are both frauds. In fact both Gaston and Lily, for that is her real name, are thieves, who are surviving the depression by robbing the idle rich. They are not only birds of a feather: in a scene that will not be quoted here since it must be seen to be believed, they slyly rob each other during a private dinner. It is more than two professionals showing off. They seduce each other with their skill, as when Lily returns Gaston's watch, noting that she has taken the liberty of resetting it to the proper time.

Lubitsch and screenwriter Samson Raphaelson now up the ante by moving the action to Paris. For audiences wondering how they themselves could make ends meet, this must have seemed sophisticated and fanciful, but any similarity to the real Paris is purely coincidental. Lubitsch, of course, knew the difference. "I've been to Paris, France, and I've been to Paris, Paramount," he said. "Paris, Paramount is better." There Gaston lifts the bejeweled purse of Marianne Colet (Kay Francis), the beautiful and wealthy widow who runs Colet et Cie, the renowned perfumers. Realizing he can get more money as a reward for returning it than he can for fencing it, he brings it to her pretending to have found it, and ends up getting a job as her personal secretary. As the story unfolds, two chief issues of plot arise. First, Gaston and Marianne quickly become attracted to one another. Where does this leave Lily? Second, Gaston—for all his charm and elegance—*is* a thief. How and when will he be exposed, and what will be the consequences?

The film ends in a cynical and wholly satisfying manner, and may surprise today's audiences, given that modern viewers probably don't know any of the principals and can't use the relative star power of the actors to anticipate the ending. In *When Harry Met Sally . . .* there are all sorts of clues that Harry (Billy Crystal) and Sally (Meg Ryan) will end up together, from the title to the fact that they are the two big stars in the film. How are modern audiences to compare Miriam Hopkins to Kay Francis, much less determine who is more equal to Herbert Marshall?

*

Of the three leads, Herbert Marshall may be the most familiar, at least to fans of vintage movies. He worked for director Alfred Hitchcock in *Murder* (1930) and *Foreign Correspondent* (1940). He appeared opposite Bette Davis in such films as *The Letter* (1940) and *The Little Foxes* (1941), and appeared in memorable forties fantasies such as *The Enchanted Cottage* (1945) and *The Secret Garden* (1949). Late in his career he was still working in science-fiction thrillers such as *Riders to the Stars* (1954) and *The Fly* (1958). At whatever age he played, his characters would be described as intelligent, cosmopolitan, and smooth. As the film historian Ethan Mordden put it, "MGM likes heroes who have been around the block; Paramount likes heroes who have been around the world."

It wasn't exactly a secret, but it might have surprised his fans to learn that Marshall had lost a leg in World War I. Both the actor and his directors contrived to ensure that it was never an issue in his movies. Watch, for example when he goes bounding up the stairs in *Trouble in Paradise*. The actor moves off camera and a double, his face away from the camera, takes his place, racing up the steps. By casting Marshall as Gaston, Lubitsch ensured that we would never question the character's skill or intelligence, nor the fact that two beautiful women would quickly and easily fall in love with him.

Miriam Hopkins was a star primarily in the 1930s and early '40s, though one can spot her on screen in the 1960s in movies like *The Children's Hour* (1962) and *The Chase* (1966). Her casting in *The Children's Hour*—the Lillian Hellman drama about two schoolteachers whose lives are ruined by rumors of a lesbian affair—may have been in part due to nostalgia. She had played one of the teachers in a much diluted 1936 version called *These Three*. Although not well known today, Hopkins had a number of notable starring roles, including *Trouble in Paradise* and *Design for Living* (1933) for Lubitsch and an Academy Award nomination for her turn in the title role of *Becky Sharp* (1936), an adaptation of Thackeray's *Vanity Fair*.

As for Kay Francis, even the biggest film buffs might have trouble instantly placing her. Only one other of her films is regularly screened these days, and the reason *The Cocoanuts* (1929) is shown at all is not because of her but because it's the first Marx Brothers film. She was a leading player in the 1930s and '40s, and even played Florence Nightingale in *The White Angel* (1936); but there's no question that her turn as Marianne in *Trouble in Paradise* is her most enduring screen performance. The film historian Jeanine Basinger, an admirer of Francis, admits that she "became a star *only* because of fashion and glamour. . . . Her career is absolute proof of the importance of clothes, makeup, and jewelry both on and off the screen."

Modern viewers are much more likely to recognize Lubitsch's supporting players. Edward Everett Horton and Charles Ruggles pop up in a variety of comedy roles from the thirties through the sixties. Horton was a voice actor for Jay Ward (*Rocky and Bullwinkle*) whose final film appearance was in 1971's *Cold Turkey*. Ruggles too worked steadily across the decades, though his best-remembered film today is probably *Bringing Up Baby* (1938), as a daffy sportsman sharing a memorable dinner with Cary Grant and Katharine Hepburn. In *Trouble in Paradise*, Horton and Ruggles play the comical and ineffective rivals for Marianne, with Horton's Filiba also being one of Gaston's past robbery victims who now can't quite place Madame's new secretary. Also on hand was C. Aubrey Smith, who usually played a stiff-upper-lip Brit, but here he is the pompous—and corrupt—executive at the perfume company who resents Gaston's prying inquiries.

Contemporary audiences were familiar with the players, and their casting made the exotic story easier to take. With such an array of British and American actors, though, this was clearly Paris, Paramount.

*

Before turning to the famous "Lubitsch touch" and why it makes *Trouble in Paradise* so extraordinary a film, one more person involved in its production deserves attention: the screenwriter Samson Raphaelson. Although writing in Hollywood has had its financial rewards, respect from the industry is not part of the package. Other writers might recognize outstanding work by their peers, but for the most part the director and producer and stars are the nobility of the movie industry. Among the creative talent, the writers are treated as hired hands, whose work can be rewritten without their permission or even their knowledge. A sardonic joke of the thirties—undoubtedly expressed by a screenwriter—told of a movie starlet who was so dimwitted that she thought she could advance her career by sleeping with the picture's writer.

But the good directors appreciated their collaborators, and some of the best writers—like Preston Sturges, John Huston, Billy Wilder, and Joseph L. Mankiewicz—eventually went on to direct, looking to protect their own words in the filmmaking process. In Samson Raphaelson, Lubitsch had a partner in whom he had complete trust. The story is told that Lubitsch was working on a scene for a film and made it clear that it had to be shot just so. Asked why, Lubitsch said he had no idea: "It is in the script, which is good enough for me. If I didn't have a reason, it would not have been there when Sam Raphaelson was writing it in the first place."

Raphaelson would already have a secure place in film history if he had never met Lubitsch. He had worked as a journalist and an advertising copywriter before hitting the big time on stage with that classic bit of twenties schmaltz, *The Jazz Singer*. It was the toast of Broadway with star George Jessel, and gained even greater fame when Raphaelson adapted it for the screen in 1927 for Al Jolson. *The Jazz Singer* was a huge breakthrough that transformed the film industry. Within two years silent movies were dead, with Charlie Chaplin proving to be the only holdout. (Chaplin's first all-talking picture would not appear until 1940, with *The Great Dictator*.) Fortunately, as the film industry found its voice, it desperately needed writers who could handle spoken dialogue instead of stilted speeches for title cards. Lubitsch, who had become a consummate visual stylist, needed someone who was good with words. They would prove to be one of the great Hollywood teams, collaborating on nine films, including *Trouble in Paradise* and *The Shop Around the Corner*.

As with many Lubitsch projects, *Trouble* began its life as a play or story from which he might choose to borrow very little at all. In this case it was a Hungarian play, *The Honest Finder* by Laszlo Aladar, Lubitsch thought little of it, telling Raphaelson, "No use reading the play, Sem. It's bad." What intrigued Lubitsch was doing a romantic comedy about a swindler. The play had been inspired by a Hungarian scam artist named George Manolescu, who had written his *Memoirs* in 1907. His fingerprints may still be seen on Herbert Marshall's character, whom Lubitsch named Gaston Monescu.

Raphaelson wrote Lubitsch a script etched with diamonds, as when Lily asks Gaston—who has been passing himself off as a baron—who he really is. Gaston replies, "You remember the man who walked into the Bank of Constantinople, and walked out *with* the Bank of Constantinople?" Lily realizes that Gaston is that man, and it's love at first sight.

Raphaelson and Lubitsch nearly had a falling out—over money, of course—when Raphaelson decided he was being taken advantage of financially himself. It's not clear whether Lubitsch was trying to deny Raphaelson his due or, more likely, had forgotten to follow through on promises made in good faith. In any case, Lubitsch knew how much he owed the writer in terms of making their films work, so he made sure Raphaelson was properly rewarded. They worked things out, and Raphaelson remained a frequent collaborator with Lubitsch until the director's final film, *That Lady in Ermine* (1948), which was completed by Otto Preminger when Lubitsch died. Years later Raphaelson was still singing Lubitsch's praises. It's interesting that he didn't try to take credit for Lubitsch's contributions, nor did he claim Lubitsch had taken credit where it was not deserved. It was a largely happy partnership. Here's Raphaelson describing how he and Lubitsch worked on their scripts:

"We met every morning. I didn't sit in a corner and write. There was a secretary in the room. We wrote it together, that's all. You couldn't trace it. If the problem was, 'How do we get into this scene?,' whoever finally found it wouldn't necessarily be the author of it because he might not have found it if the other hadn't said two other words before."

They'd hammer out the story and characters together, as well as the various visual elements the film would have and how a scene would play. Then Raphaelson would work out the dialogue. According to the writer, he had only one regret about this wonderful collaborative process: "I wish to God the tape recorder had been in existence in our time, to take it all down—it would have been wonderful to have an actual recording of these sessions—that would have been a great thing."

*

Once on the set, Lubitsch had a script that had been polished to a high sheen, and he had cast his actors with care. Edward Everett Horton appeared in five Lubitsch films, and—as did nearly everyone else in Hollywood—held him in high regard. "He always had an actor in mind. In no part of any Lubitsch picture did he have an actor who was not just right. You rehearsed a whole week on the picture without shooting anything at all. We rehearsed in the sets." According to Horton, the goal was to find out what Lubitsch expected of you, and then give it to him. "Just as soon as you could put yourself *en rapport*, you were very happy. He knew these actors very well, and he wanted something from them even they didn't know they had. He was a genius, you see. Just a genius."

As he ran the actors through their paces, it was amazing how much sexual innuendo Lubitsch could work into the film. In one scene it becomes clear that Gaston and Marianne have become lovers, but, of course, that could not be shown. So Lubitsch and Raphaelson constructed a series of moments focusing on clocks and doors that let us know exactly who was going where at what time. You didn't see anything—except for an exquisite moment where their *shadows* fall across a bed—but it was there all the same. In his approach Lubitsch showed equally exquisite timing. Two years later, when the new Production Code went into effect, a story about jewel thieves who get away with their crimes—as well as their game of musical bedrooms—would have been simply impossible to film. Even so, there were no complaints about *Trouble in Paradise* because Lubitsch was always in the best of taste. As the film historian Gerald Mast put it, "Lubitsch's art is one of omission. It is an art of 'not'—what is not shown, what is not heard, what is not said." Perhaps it was the European sensibility—albeit of Paris, Paramount—that made his films so different. As Mast noted, "Love in the Lubitsch world is nothing like LOVE in the traditional American, romantic film world. The usual separation in the American film is between LOVE and SEX. . . . For Lubitsch, LOVE and SEX are not opposites, but allies; the two passions are inseparable."

The romantic triangle is a standard structure for this type of comedy, but there's a problem. Usually the one who ends up on the outside has to become the butt of the joke. When in *The Awful Truth* (1937) Cary Grant's ex-wife Irene Dunne takes up with Ralph Bellamy, audiences are immediately clued in—from both the characters and the relative star power—that of course Dunne and Grant will end up together while Bellamy's character will be sent packing to Oklahoma. In *Trouble in Paradise* the dilemma is that Gaston has two different but equal worthies for his affections. Lily is a kindred spirit, his match in animal cleverness as a thief and equally able to pass herself off in social circles that ought to be beyond her reach. But Marianne is a different creature. She's a wealthy widow who turns down one purse for 3,000 francs as too expensive and then buys one for 125,000 because she thinks it's beautiful. She willfully plays the part of the society woman with no head for business, but does it with great purpose. Told by her board of directors that they should cut wages, she announces that she finds such discussions boring and she's much too busy—thus the wages will have to stay the same.

She is not at all naive at the ways of the world, and so when Gaston and Lily become employees with an eye to robbing her, it's equally clear that she sees the opportunity to take on Gaston as more than a mere personal secretary. When Gaston notes that her previous secretary must have been very happy in her employ, she answers, "Yes, too happy. That's why I had to let her go." What bounds were overstepped are left to the viewer's imagination.

Making Lily and Marianne true rivals adds spice and tension to the story, and Lubitsch and Raphaelson resist the urge to make the loser, Marianne, look ridiculous in the process. Instead we see that she is also at the apex of another romantic triangle, between Filiba and the Major, and both of *them* are utterly ridiculous. This double-triangle structure allows Marianne to end the film with her dignity intact, breaking off with Gaston on very nearly her terms. When he reveals the pearl necklace he has stolen for Lily, Marianne grandly gives it to him "with the compliments of Colet and Company." Since he has both spared her the scandal of having his identity revealed while in her employ *and* exposed the faithful company director (C. Aubrey Smith) as a fraud who has been ripping off the company for years, he has left her better off, in spite of the money and jewelry with which he and Lily have absconded.

Trouble in Paradise was not a big success upon its release. The film actually lost money, and perhaps the depths of the depression required a more populist vision than Lubitsch could offer. Over the years, though, the film has grown in reputation to the status of a bona fide classic, now awaiting rediscovery by modern audiences who need only to be directed to it. In the literature on film comedy, particularly romantic comedy, it is one of the most praised and discussed movies ever made. As William Paul notes in his book on Lubitsch, "The passage of time has produced a general reassessment of the film, with most critics now seeing it as firmly rooted in the Depression and a not too covert social criticism underlying much of the comedy."

For example, much is made of the opening where we hear a gondolier singing on the Venice canals—as romantic an image to start a film as any—only to discover that he is a garbage man making his rounds. Is this a moment deflating romantic pretensions, or is it, as the critic Richard Corliss argues, just the opposite: "What the scene actually shows is a man with a garbage can who turns out to be a romantic tenor. Although the filmmakers are robbing the upper classes of their expensive pretenses . . . they are also investing the working class—garbage men and con men alike—with romance and respect."

Which is it? In the end, does it really matter? Although we would not see the likes of such sophistication in romantic comedy after Lubitsch, the ability of the romantic leads to play together and play off of each other—to turn love into an act of improvisation—would become a model for many of the best romantic comedies to come. It is in the interplay of the characters that *Trouble in Paradise* may have exerted its most lasting influence on the genre. What would change is the way Hollywood would tell such stories, making romantic settings out of motels and garbage dumps as well as more elegant surroundings, but making most of the characters uniquely American instead of real or imaginary European sophisticates. With the advent of what came to be known as the "screwball comedy," Hollywood romance was about to undergo a revolution.

2

IT HAPPENED ONE NIGHT

IT WAS supposed to be punishment for Clark Gable and Claudette Colbert and make-work for Frank Capra. Instead it became one of the most beloved and honored romantic comedies of all time. *It Happened One Night* is a perfect example of the film that happened by accident. It wasn't supposed to make history, but it did. Because its romantic stars got belly laughs, the way romantic comedy would be done was forever changed. Every new film of the kind would owe a debt to this one.

The story begins with Frank Capra, the most successful director at Columbia Pictures—a "Poverty Row" operation, so that's not saying much—sitting in a barbershop in Palm Springs. He was leafing through a copy of *Cosmopolitan* and came across a story by Samuel Hopkins Adams entitled "Night Bus." It had to do with a runaway heiress and an inventor who meet by chance and, naturally, end up together. He had his screenwriting collaborator, Robert Riskin, take a look at the story. Capra and Riskin were currently at work on a project entitled "Lady for a Day." Both the director and the writer saw potential in the bus story.

So they had Columbia look into acquiring the film rights. As it happened, *Cosmopolitan* was a Hearst magazine, and MGM had first refusal on all stories in Hearst publications. (This was part of an elaborate preexisting deal in which Cosmopolitan Pictures—a vanity operation that publisher William Randolph Hearst had set up to produce films starring his actress paramour, Marion Davies—released their productions through MGM.) As it turned out, Louis B. Mayer had no interest in "Night Bus." Apparently he objected to the character of the father. So when Columbia came calling at the Hearst offices, the story was not only available, it was cheap at only $5,000.

By the time Capra and Riskin had finished "Lady for a Day," they no longer remembered what had initially appealed to them about "Night Bus," but they decided to proceed anyway. Their boss, Columbia's head honcho Harry Cohn, had other ideas. Capra was being loaned out to MGM. Thus was set in play a series of events that would culminate in an Oscar night that remains legendary even after seventy years.

*

To make *It Happened One Night* happen, three people had to be forced to make the picture against their wills. Oddly enough, one of them was Frank Capra.

The director had been born in Sicily in 1897 and had come to the United States with his family as a child. He had entered the motion picture business in the silent era, cutting his teeth in various jobs for producers Hal Roach and Mack Sennett, learning the nuts and bolts of film comedy. By the time he teamed with the silent comedy star Harry Langdon (often forgotten today in the shadow of Charlie Chaplin, Buster Keaton, and Harold Lloyd), he was beginning to make his mark. He directed Langdon in *The Strong Man* (1926) and *Long Pants* (1927). But Capra had a falling out with the films' writer Arthur Ripley, who resented the acclaim for the director. Langdon sided with Ripley, given that he was nursing his own resentments as to who was responsible for the success of his features. Abruptly, Capra was out. There was sufficient badmouthing around town by the Langdon camp that for some time Capra found himself unemployed. Eventually Langdon's career faded with the coming of sound; Capra moved on and thrived, eventually finding a home at Columbia Pictures.

Columbia chief Harry Cohn was among the first generation of Hollywood moguls. After an apprenticeship at Universal Pictures, he and his brother Jack set up shop with a fellow named Joe Brandt, creating a partnership on what came to be known as Poverty Row. There fly-by-night studios and production companies that didn't have the land or talent of the major studios managed to eke out an existence. Known as C.B.C. (for Cohn, Brandt, and Cohn), Columbia slowly got a toehold in the business. By 1924 they had were tired of hearing their operation referred to as "Corned Beef and Cabbage," so they renamed it Columbia Pictures.

Capra and Cohn found each other at a time when they both needed help, though neither would have been the sort to admit it. After leaving Langdon, Capra was reduced to working for Mack Sennett again at a greatly reduced salary. He was a proud man, though, and he showed it when he was summoned to Columbia where he was interviewed by executive Sam Briskin.

According to Cohn's biographer, Bob Thomas, it was a brief interview. Briskin noted, "Your last picture wasn't very good, was it?"

Capra was having none of it. "What *was* my last picture?"

Briskin, taken aback, replied, "You know—that picture you made."

Capra did not suffer fools gladly. "You son of a bitch, you don't even know what the picture was!" And with that, Capra was out the door, slamming it behind him.

Capra's agent convinced him to go back, but the director decided to take a hard line. Briskin was offering him a picture he could write and direct, and he was told to name his price. He asked for a thousand dollars. Briskin said that was okay with him, but they'd need Cohn's approval. Cohn was in his typical mode, on the phone and browbeating whoever had the misfortune to be on the other end of the line. Without interrupting the call, Cohn asked Briskin what the deal was. Briskin said a thousand dollars. Cohn gave his okay and waved them out of the office.

Capra would end up staying at Columbia for the next twelve years, doing some of the greatest movies of his career. By 1933 he was the studio's star director. He had quickly learned that if he were to control his fate at the studio, Cohn respected only one thing: people who fought back. Those who wilted under his bullying didn't last long. On his first film Capra stormed into Cohn's office and made it clear that he would not accept the studio's penny-pinching ways. He needed fifteen extras for a scene and had been sent seven. Cohn wanted to know what the problem was. Capra said, "Harry, I really need a *hundred* extras on that set. I asked for fifteen because I figured that, by juggling, I could make fifteen *look* like a hundred. But I can't make *seven* look like a hundred. Now what are the rules of the game? How many people do I have to ask for to *get fifteen*?" Capra got his fifteen extras.

Capra didn't win every battle with the man who would greet him as "Dago," but they came to respect each other. Capra turned out films that earned money—and prestige—for the scrappy studio, and in return Cohn gave Capra the leeway to call most of his own shots. Over the next few years Capra turned out adventure films, dramas, and the occasional comedy: *Submarine, Ladies of Leisure, Platinum Blonde, Forbidden, American Madness,* and *The Bitter Tea of General Yen* among them.

By 1933, especially after the success of *Lady for a Day,* which would earn both Capra and star May Robson Oscar nominations, Capra had a growing reputation that other studios noticed. So it was no surprise that he became part of an elaborate swap between Cohn and MGM's *wunderkind* producer Irving Thalberg in which Capra was loaned to MGM for a big production and one of MGM's major stars was to be loaned to Columbia. In the studio era, that was not an unusual deal. A star or director didn't have to be loaned out, but if the studio got something it wanted in return—a star under contract to the other studio, a payment greater than what they were paying the talent being lent out—it made sense. Only the biggest, most important names had a right of refusal. For an operation like Columbia to have an MGM star for one of its features was a big deal, and though Capra was not enthusiastic, he did as he was told and reported to work for Thalberg.

Thalberg, who was married to the actress Norma Shearer and would be the model for F. Scott Fitzgerald's *The Last Tycoon,* had a storied if brief career in the Hollywood firmament. Although he could be as hardnosed as any other Hollywood prince (famously destroying the excised footage from Erich von Stroheim's massively overlong masterpiece *Greed*), he could also take unusual chances, as in hiring the Marx Brothers after their Paramount contract expired and then sending them on the road to test and hone their comedy bits for *A Night at the Opera* and *A Day at the Races*. In an ego-driven business, it's not surprising that some people resented Thalberg. What's unusual is that his greatest rival was his ostensible boss, Louis B. Mayer. Thalberg had been given a free hand in his MGM productions, a fact greatly resented by Mayer. (Both men answered to Loews, Inc., MGM's parent company.)

Capra arrived on the MGM lot ready to work on a project to be called "Soviet," about an American engineer building a massive dam in Russia. It was to have an all-star MGM cast: Clark Gable, Joan Crawford, Wallace Beery, and Marie Dressler. The movie was never made. Thalberg took ill and went on a long ocean cruise to recuperate. (Suffering from a congenital heart condition, he would be dead three years later.) While Thalberg was away, Mayer decided to assert his authority and gleefully set about canceling various Thalberg projects, including "Soviet." Suddenly Capra found himself back at his Columbia offices with nothing to do. Harry Cohn, however, was not about to pay Capra to sit around. Cohn wanted to put him to work immediately. The only project ready to go, however, was "Night Bus." The studio boss had never been keen on the project, but he now decreed that "Night Bus" would be Capra's next picture.

*

Clark Gable was a rising talent at MGM, proving to be a reliable leading man but not yet landing a role that would establish him as a big star. Louis B. Mayer expressed little respect for him, considering him little more than "a gigolo with brass knuckles." In truth, Gable had become an MGM workhorse. In 1932 he appeared in no less than eight films, and he had completed three more in 1933 before asking for a break. He had been particularly fed up with his role as a stage director opposite Joan Crawford in *Dancing Lady*, a forgettable trifle remembered today for showcasing both Fred Astaire's first appearance on film and an early credit for the Three Stooges, then still partnered with the comic actor Ted Healy. It made money, but it was not the sort of film that would advance Gable's career.

Mayer, for his part, had little use for complaining stars. As far he was concerned, they should be happy to be working and glad they were at MGM, the pinnacle of the studio system. Indeed, Mayer felt that Gable's ego (and demands for more money) were exceeding his worth to the studio, so he decided to loan him to Columbia to demonstrate to the actor who was boss.

Mayer and Cohn had worked out a deal whereby Columbia could borrow an MGM star for "Night Bus," and Cohn had asked for Robert Montgomery. Montgomery, though, had just made a "bus picture" entitled *Fugitive Lovers* that had flopped, and he turned it down. It says something about Montgomery's relative clout at MGM that he could refuse the picture while Gable could not. Mayer laid out the deal to Cohn: "Montgomery says there are too many bus pictures. And Herschel, no offense, stars don't like changing their address from MGM to Gower Street [where Columbia was located]. But Herschel, you caught me in a good mood. I got an actor here who's been a bad boy. Wants more money. And I'd like to spank him. You can have Clark Gable."

Cohn was less than thrilled. Gable was not as big a star, but he was in no position to negotiate. Besides, doing a favor for the powerful Mayer could pay off down the road. So Gable was dispatched to Gower Street to meet with Frank Capra and read the script. It was a meeting that could have come out of a Capra movie and, in fact, would end up influencing this one.

When Gable arrived it was obvious that he was unhappy with the prospect of making a movie at Columbia. He was also drunk. "I always wanted to see Siberia," slurred the actor, "but damn me—I never thought it would *smell* like this."

Capra, holding his temper, replied, "Mr. Gable, you and I are supposed to make a picture out of this. Shall I tell you the story, or would you rather read the script yourself?"

Gable sneered back, "Buddy, I don't give a fuck *what* you do with it."

It was not an auspicious beginning. Gable went home, drank some more, and—bowing to the inevitable—read the script. To his surprise, he liked it. Recalled Gable, "I thought, 'It can't be that good. I'd better look at it later.' I had dinner and read it again. It was still good."

The next morning, now sober, he called up Capra and apologized for his theatrics of the day before, having only one question. Why was he being cast in a comedy? It was a good question, because *It Happened One Night* was about to redefine how the romantic comedy would be played. First, though, they needed a leading lady.

The part of Ellie Andrews was not a glamour part. In fact, other than a man's bathrobe and a wedding gown, she wears only one outfit for most of the entire film. In an era of stars like Greta Garbo, Norma Shearer, Joan Crawford, and Marlene Dietrich, this was not the sort of role likely to put an actress in the best light. As a result, it was turned down . . . everywhere. Among those who rejected it were Margaret Sullavan, Constance Bennett, Miriam Hopkins, and Myrna Loy. Mayer clearly played favorites. Just as he had accepted Montgomery's rejection and sent Gable in his place, the paternalistic studio boss defended Loy's refusal, "I never ask one of my little girls to play a part she doesn't want." Bette Davis expressed interest, but Warner Bros. had just loaned her to RKO for *Of Human Bondage* and had no desire to send her to another studio again so soon. Carole Lombard, then dating the film's screenwriter Robert Riskin, was offered the part but couldn't clear her schedule. Columbia, with no roster of big stars of its own, desperately needed a leading lady for the film.

Harry Cohn's solution was to borrow Claudette Colbert from Paramount. Colbert was a star there, but getting her to Columbia posed two problems. First, like Gable, she was overworked and exhausted. She had released four films in 1931, five in 1932, and another four in

1933. In 1934, the year *It Happened One Night* appeared, she could
be seen in three other films, including the starring role in *Cleopatra*
under the direction of Cecil B. DeMille and the classic tearjerker *Imitation of Life*. She was planning on a hard-earned ski vacation in Sun
Valley, Idaho, when the offer from Columbia arrived. This might be
worked around, but the second problem was harder: she hated Frank
Capra.

Capra had directed her debut film in 1928, *For the Love of Mike*,
which had almost ended her career before it could begin. Although
Capra's career had taken off since then, Colbert wasn't impressed.
He was, after all, working on Poverty Row while she was a major star
at Paramount. Still, she had an opening in her schedule—when she
was planning to be on vacation—and her contract with Paramount
allowed her to take one job at an outside studio each year. Capra was
skeptical that Colbert would work with him again, but Cohn told him
to ask anyway. "I hear that French broad likes money."

Capra and Riskin were dispatched to meet with Colbert, who
quickly made it clear that she had no real interest in the project. At
the meeting, in a bad omen, her poodle bit Capra. They wouldn't
give up, figuring it was easier to keep trying than to go back and face
Cohn. Attempting to end it, she made what to her seemed like outrageous financial demands. She asked for $50,000 (much more than
she was receiving per film at Paramount) plus overtime. Amazingly,
Cohn, who now was eager to see the picture in production, agreed to
her demands. Gable later complained, "She made more in overtime
than I made for the picture."

*

So the two stars arrived not especially thrilled with the project. Although Gable was now on board with the script, he still wasn't quite
sure what he was doing there. He had played a number of heavies and
was uncertain about the change of pace, yet he was a lot gamer than
at his first meeting with Capra. "One thing I liked about it," he would

later say, "was that at no time was I called upon to beat up Miss Colbert." Colbert, for her part, was there for the money and because she thought playing opposite Gable might be a plus.

Then something odd happened. The actors started having fun. The story itself follows Peter Warne (Gable), an unemployed reporter who meets the story of the year on a bus: the runaway heiress Ellie Andrews (Colbert). Over the course of the film they begin to realize they're not so different and, in fact, start to learn from each other. Ellie's education is more obvious. A pampered rich girl who has run away because her father objected to her eloping with a pompous aviator, she doesn't have a clue about the real world. At one bus stop she tells the driver she'll be late getting back and please wait. She's stunned when she returns and the bus is gone. She is also exposed to motels, eating on a tight budget, and outdoor plumbing. (When she is shocked that the showers are outside their cabin, Peter assures her that's the way it's done in all the best homes.)

But Peter also has a lot to learn. He's an arrogant sort who has lost his job because he's been drinking and sending trash to his editors. Capra used Gable's initial insolence in the first scene, with Peter playing to a pack of his reporter friends as he tells off his editor in New York over the phone. Capra got even with Gable for their initial meeting by showing Peter having to bluff his way through the performance after the editor hangs up on him. Ellie will teach him some humility, notably in the celebrated scene where the now stranded duo attempt to hitchhike. Peter gives another in a series of pompous lectures, explaining to her the different methods of thumbing a ride. He could write a book on the subject, he declares, before several cars zip by ignoring him.

Ellie decides to take her turn, bringing a car to a screeching halt by showing a good deal of leg (as racy as they could get under the new Production Code which had taken effect that year). They get the ride and Peter sulks, snidely commenting she could have taken off all her clothes and stopped a whole fleet of cars. This time Ellie gets the last word: "I'll remember that the next time we need a fleet of cars."

It's arguably one of the great on-screen moments in the eternal battle of the sexes, yet Colbert didn't want to do it. She had already filmed a scene for DeMille where the purportedly nude Cleopatra bathes in asses' milk, and wasn't interested in that sort of exposure . . . until Capra brought in the stand-in who would provide the leg for the close-up shot. Colbert took one look and changed her mind about doing the scene. "Get her out of here. I'll do it. That's not *my* leg."

If Colbert started out being difficult, Gable quickly began having a ball. He discovered there were other ways to make movies than the MGM method, and he felt a freedom under Capra's direction he had not previously enjoyed. To cite but one example, MGM movies of the time usually kept the characters in three-quarter shots, showing them from their heads to their knees, so we could see them interact. Capra pulled back and gave Gable the freedom to move within the frame. When Peter and Ellie are playing a bickering couple to throw a couple of detectives off the trail, Gable moves back and forth between Ellie's bawling "wife" and trying to intimidate the investigators. Capra would later say he let Gable be Gable: "Really, that's the only picture that Gable ever played himself. He was that character and loved doing those scenes."

Gable got in the spirit of the thing, even pulling off one prank that could never appear on screen, and probably would have gotten him in trouble with the notoriously prudish Mayer. They were filming the "Walls of Jericho" scene, where Peter has set up a blanket on a rope to divide the cabin in half and permit Ellie her privacy (not to mention her chastity). Capra announced there would be a delay in shooting. Colbert wanted to know what was wrong.

"Well, there seems to be a slight problem here," said Capra. "Clark wants to know what can be done about this." Colbert came around the blanket and there was Gable lying under the covers with a huge bulge poking up his covers in the area of his crotch. He had taken one of the props and stuck it there to get a reaction out of Colbert, who laughed, "*You guys!*"

The "Walls of Jericho" permit the unmarried Ellie (Claudette Colbert) and Peter (Clark Gable) to spend the night together, helping invent the screwball comedy in the process.

In this movie Frank Capra seemed to find his full voice as a film-maker, using the film to celebrate the "little people" with whom he identified. Unlike Lubitsch, Capra could never have made a comedy set in a world of polished wealth. Indeed, as in *Lady for a Day* or his success a few years later with *You Can't Take It with You* (1938), he showed that the rich would have to come down to Capra's level, not the other way around. This was noticeable in all the moments where Ellie faces the realities that most people in the audience took for granted, but also in scenes like Peter's car being stopped by a passing train and his waving to the hoboes riding the empty boxcars.

One of the most celebrated moments in the movie is when a bus-load of passengers join together in a rendition of "The Man on the Flying Trapeze." The scene was supposed to be about some "hillbilly" musicians singing and playing their instruments in the back of the bus, but as they rehearsed the scene Capra saw the other "passengers" tapping their toes and joining in. He ordered additional cameras set up so that the whole bus would be covered, then told the actors to cut loose. That they did, boisterously singing the chorus and even making up new verses. Capra directed Gable and Colbert, whose characters were still at odds at this point, to slowly loosen up and join in if they felt like it. It was a great democratic moment, but Colbert had a problem with it. Why would all the people on the bus, strangers to one another, join in a group sing-along? And how would everyone know the words?

"Don't worry about it," Capra told her. "If the scene doesn't work, it can come right out of the picture without interfering with the plot."

So they shot the scene, and as they were shooting Colbert noticed that off-camera her personal maid was smiling with delight.

Capra and Riskin ended the film on a note that exemplified Hollywood's new rules. Movies could still be sexy, but now, instead of the blatant, anything-goes attitude of the early thirties, things would have to be subtle, so subtle in fact that some viewers might not realize what had just happened. After Ellie's father (Walter Connolly) has met Peter, who has shown up not for the reward for helping get Ellie back but merely for the few dollars of his expenses, he realizes Peter's an all-right guy, much better for a son-in-law than the stiff King Wesley she's getting ready to remarry in an official ceremony. On the way down the aisle with his daughter, he tells her to run off with Peter and make her old man happy—and that she does, her bridal train trailing behind her.

We don't see the couple in the final shot. We know they have been awaiting word that the annulment of her marriage to Wesley has gone through so that their marriage is official. They have reset the Walls of Jericho, and the kindly couple running the motel muses over the lovebirds, wondering why Peter wanted a toy horn. We hear the horn blow and see the blanket come tumbling down. The film ends with what is clearly the physical consummation of the marriage. But because nothing is said or even directly implied, the film got away with it, and audiences left theaters satisfied.

*

It didn't happen in one night. At the end of shooting, Columbia still didn't know what it had. Gable may have had fun, but Colbert went on her delayed vacation declaring, "I just finished the worst picture in the world."

The film previewed in January 1934 to favorable though not overwhelming reaction. There was positive buzz on Capra the director coming into his own, but reviews were mixed—many of them complaining about how contrived the story was—and though initial box office was good, it soon dropped off. It was pulled from Radio City Music Hall after only two weeks. Other cities around the country had similar results. Then something odd happened. Theater owners in small towns all over America didn't want to let the film go. It was playing to packed houses, with word of mouth building as people dragged family and friends to see it.

Capra heard from a linotype operator in Seattle who took his family to the pictures once a week. They saw *It Happened One Night* and loved it. The next week he asked what movie they should go see and they all wanted to see *It Happened One Night* again. They ended up seeing it six weeks in a row. The film was soon brought *back* to Radio City Music Hall. In its first year of release it earned more than a million dollars (the equivalent of more than $15 million today).

The capper came with the 1934 Oscars ceremony. The awards had been established only in 1927, and the event was still a banquet rather than the lavish auditorium shows we know today. A year earlier, Capra had been nominated for best director for *Lady for a Day*, and when the emcee Will Rogers had announced the winner was

"Frank," Capra bounded from his table only to learn that the winner was Frank Lloyd for *Cavalcade*. Capra was mortified. This time would be different.

It Happened One Night had been nominated for five Oscars. Capra and Riskin's little "bus picture" had turned into Cinderella's coach. The humorist Irvin S. Cobb was the emcee in 1934, and when he announced the winner for best adapted screenplay was Robert Riskin, the writer was nowhere to be found. He was reportedly on a date with Carole Lombard (who, ironically, would end up marrying *It Happened One Night*'s male lead in one of the great real-life Hollywood love stories).

When Cobb summoned "Frank" to receive the best-director Oscar, Capra hesitated. The people at his table—the same ones as the year before—pointed out that this time there was no other director named Frank. Capra had won. Since the film never would have happened if Capra hadn't found the story and worked with Riskin in turning it into a film, it seemed only fair. But the evening wasn't over. The next winner, a stunner, was Clark Gable for best actor. He had been sent to make the movie as punishment, and for it he now had the top acting prize in the business. Gable could be heard muttering to himself after thanking everyone, "I'm still going to wear the same size hat."

(In a charming footnote to this win, several years later a friend and her young son were visiting with Gable and Lombard. The boy spent the afternoon amusing himself crashing his toy car into a gold statuette he had found lying around. When asked if he could take it home, his mother was horrified to see that it was Gable's Oscar for *It Happened One Night*. Gable gave it to him, saying, "Having it doesn't mean anything. Earning it does.")

Two more categories to go. The winner for best actress was Claudette Colbert, who also was not attending. Figuring that there was no way she would win for that little movie, she was boarding a train in downtown Los Angeles and heading for New York. But Claudette

Colbert was a movie star, not a petulant heiress, and if she needed the train to wait, it waited. A publicist for the Motion Picture Academy pleaded with her to make a quick trip to accept the award in person, answering her demurral with, "But it's the Nobel Prize of motion pictures."

While Colbert was being fetched, the announcement was made for best picture: *It Happened One Night*. It became the first film to sweep all five top awards, and since then has been joined by only two others, *One Flew Over the Cuckoo's Nest* (1975) and *Silence of the Lambs* (1991). Cohn, who was seeing his scrappy Poverty Row studio making movie history, thanked everyone and then modestly added, "I was just an innocent bystander."

At this point Colbert, not dressed for the formal occasion, rushed in. A young Shirley Temple, who was receiving a special honor that evening, was pressed into service to present Colbert with her Oscar. Colbert finally acknowledged she had been wrong about her director: "I want to tell you how grateful I am to Frank Capra. If it hadn't been for him, I wouldn't be here." She then rushed out, having attended the ceremony for all of six minutes.

With the benefit of hindsight it's amusing to see the movie dismissed as one that would be little remembered. It is now certified as an American classic by the American Film Institute, the Library of Congress, and, most important, audiences who continue to laugh and wonder if Ellie will do the right thing at the end. It left a lasting model for the structure of romantic comedies to the present day: the mismatched pair who end up learning from each other and playing together until you can't imagine them *not* being a couple. Movies with fairy-tale couples—with the comic relief left to others—would still be made but not long remembered.

It also had a lasting impact on the career of Clark Gable. When he took off his shirt in the "Walls of Jericho" scene and was revealed to be bare-chested, sales of undershirts reportedly plummeted. Whether true or not, Gable's good humor and natural manliness represented a break from the heavies and stiff leading-men roles he had been play-ing at MGM. All that would be different now.

"Well, Mayer sent us over a good actor and we sent him back a star," Capra would recall years later, adding, "MGM had to triple Gable's salary after that." Capra had gotten the last laugh.

3

MY MAN GODFREY

🐛 OSCAR NIGHT, 1937. All eyes were on what has been described as "one of the most glamorous and unlikely 'double dates' in the history of Hollywood."

First there were William Powell and Carole Lombard, stars of one of the year's comedy hits, *My Man Godfrey*. Both were nominated for their performances, and everyone knew the backstory of their working together. They had been husband and wife and then divorced, but remained good friends. People wondered if their pairing in the movie signaled a reconciliation.

The other two people turned just as many heads: Clark Gable and Jean Harlow. They had appeared together in *Wife vs. Secretary* and would soon appear on-screen together in *Saratoga*. Gable, of course, had won an Oscar three years before for *It Happened One Night* while Harlow was one of the stars of *Libeled Lady*, in which she co-starred with Powell, Myrna Loy, and Spencer Tracy, and which was up for Best Picture.

What made the evening especially interesting was that Gable was Lombard's date and Harlow was Powell's. It was a situation no odder than anything that had appeared in—or occurred during the filming of—*My Man Godfrey*. The movie perfectly captured its time, besides demonstrating there was no limit to the zaniness a film could have and still be a romantic comedy.

*

The movie of a Fifth Avenue socialite and the butler she finds on an ash heap had begun life as *1011 Fifth*, a comic novel that had been serialized in *Liberty* magazine. It had been purchased by Universal Pictures, which brought along author Eric Hatch to adapt his story into a screenplay. Eventually the comic writer Morrie Ryskind—whose credits included collaborating with George S. Kaufman on *The Cocoanuts* and *A Night at the Opera* for the Marx Brothers—was brought in, and Ryskind and Hatch ended up sharing screen credit.

Universal was an odd place for a screwball comedy. The studio was not in Hollywood's first rank (though far from Poverty Row) and was probably best known for its classic horror films like *Frankenstein* and *The Mummy*. But in a regime change, the founding Laemmle family had been forced out. The new administration decided to proceed with what promised to be a relatively inexpensive production (after the studio had spent a small fortune on a film version of the musical *Showboat*) and brought in director Gregory LaCava to make the picture.

LaCava is one of those directors whose career drives film critics and historians to distraction. Unlike a Lubitsch or a Capra, he's not easy to categorize. Although he made a number of memorable films— he was at his peak with *Godfrey* and his next film, *Stage Door*—he didn't wish to be pinned down as a director of film comedies or, indeed, as a director at all. He had come out of the silent era but had worked as an artist and animator, and had even boxed at one point. He maintained his interest and studies in serious painting, which may have had a greater claim on him than the movies. According to his friend and sometime producer Pandro S. Berman, "Greg was most off-the-cuff creative when he was drinking. And his career only stalled when his doctors told him to go on the wagon in the 1940s."

Universal executives had definite ideas about casting for *Godfrey*. For the bum with an upper-crust past there was good interest from various actors, including Ronald Colman. When LaCava came aboard, however, he said he felt that William Powell would be perfect for the part, and the studio agreed to offer him the role.

Powell had just experienced a major Hollywood comeback. Born in 1892, he had taken to the stage in his twenties and arrived in Hollywood in 1924 under contract to Paramount. Although he worked steadily, he was not happy at the studio. He had not done badly there and had easily made the transition to sound, appearing as the detective Philo Vance in *The Canary Murder Case*, his second talkie, in 1929. Nonetheless, two years later he moved to Warner Bros. and continued to work. Along the way he divorced his first wife (whom he had married in 1915) and married an up-and-coming young actress named Carole Lombard. After a year or so of marriage, the two decided to go their separate ways, though they said they would remain friends, and they did.

For Powell, now in his early forties, with Warners cooling to his talents, it was time to move on again. He ended up at MGM and in 1934 appeared in the film that would make him a star all over again, *The Thin Man*. It earned him his first Oscar nomination, spawned five sequels, and paired him again with Myrna Loy, with whom he had already appeared that year in *Manhattan Melodrama*. They would end up playing in no less than fourteen movies together—some members of the public thought they were married in real life. They were really just friends and work colleagues, but the gag was such that when Powell appeared in *The Senator Was Indiscreet* in 1947, a running joke had Powell repeatedly referring to his wife back home. At the end of the film she appeared, played by Loy.

Now Powell had just finished filming the gargantuan *The Great Ziegfeld*. He played the fabled showman while Loy played Ziegfeld's second wife, the actress Billie Burke. The film ran for some three hours. Powell was tired and wanted a break. Unlike Clark Gable, not yet a big star when he was sent to Columbia Pictures to make *It Happened One Night*, Powell had a clause in his contract that permitted him to refuse loanouts to other studios. So he was predisposed to turn down the offer to make a movie at Universal . . . until he read the script. The Ryskind/Hatch screenplay was a gem of comic construction, and the part of Godfrey was a plum role. Powell would have been a fool to pass on it, and he was no fool.

He agreed to do the film on one condition: they should hire his ex-wife Lombard to play the part of the spoiled younger sister Irene. Universal had been thinking about Constance Bennett, but LaCava balked. He had worked with Bennett on two films, *Bed of Roses* (1933) and *The Affairs of Cellini* (1934), and had no desire to tangle with her again. LaCava's sets were about having a good time, not about the care and feeding of pampered movie stars. So when Powell's suggestion arrived, LaCava immediately agreed. LaCava and Lombard had worked together in an early talkie in 1929 called *Big News*, which turned out not to be very big news at all. But LaCava remembered the former Mack Sennett bathing beauty as someone with a good sense of humor and no airs. So with her participation a condition of getting Powell, everyone was on board. The title was changed from *1011 Fifth* to *My Man Godfrey* so that Powell would have the "title role"—more for the benefit of studio advertising than any demand by the actor.

How Lombard had reached this stage in her career was equally improbable. As the film critic Andrew Sarris once put it, "No American novelist of the past half-century has created a woman character one-tenth as fascinating as Carole Lombard." She was feisty, and enjoyed sharing raucous jokes with the guys, but was also undeniably glamorous. She could have cows brought to the set of her movie directed by her friend Alfred Hitchcock because he had once suggested that actors were like cattle, and she could throw parties that violated Hollywood protocol by having stars and filmmakers rub shoulders with crew members and laborers. If she liked you, she wasn't interested in your status in the industry.

Born Jane Peters in Indiana in 1908, she moved to Hollywood at age six with her mother and two brothers. She made her movie debut at twelve when she landed a bit part in *A Perfect Crime* as the sister of the main character. Four years later she was named Queen of May at Fairfax High School, landing a contact at Fox in the process. She appeared in a few films, but her career at Fox was cut short when she was scarred in a car accident and the studio dropped her contract. She went to work for Mack Sennett's comedy factory, appearing as one of his bathing beauties near the close of the silent era. Like Powell, she came to Paramount in the early thirties. The studio wasn't quite sure what to do with her, trying to build her up as a dramatic actress. She was cast opposite Powell in *Man of the World* in 1931, and they were married that same year. Lombard kept losing plum roles to actresses higher in the pecking order, though she worked with Powell again the following year in *Ladies Man*.

In 1932 after less than two years of marriage, Powell and Lombard split. It was an amicable breakup. As Lombard told one interviewer, "I must like the man or I wouldn't have married him in the first place. Now that we're divorced, we're still the best of friends." She would meet the great love of her life that same year when she appeared opposite Clark Gable in their only film together, *No Man of Her Own*, but it would be some time before the sparks of that romance burst into flame. Instead Lombard went from film to film, taking leading roles but not making a lasting impression on the public. It was in 1934 that Hollywood began to see her as a comic leading lady. She appeared in *We're Not Dressing* with Bing Crosby and then, more notably, in Howard Hawks's rambunctious film version of *Twentieth Century*. Lombard played a stage diva whom the impresario John Barrymore is trying to sign for his new production. He needs her, but he can't let her forget that he was the one who discovered her when she was a nobody named Mildred Plotka, before she became the renowned stage star Lily Garland.

Hawks, who would later help Katharine Hepburn make the transition to knockabout farce with *Bringing Up Baby* (1938), urged Lombard to be natural. The director recalled telling Barrymore, "You've just seen a girl that's probably going to be a big star, and if we can just keep her from acting, we'll have a hell of a picture." Barrymore was skeptical but by film's end had been completely won over, inscribing a portrait to Lombard, "To the finest actress I have worked with, bar none." *Twentieth Century* was not a success at the time, though today it is considered along with *It Happened One Night* as the birth of the screwball comedy. Lombard also remembered Barrymore's support, and when he appeared a few years later in a supporting role in her *True Confessions*, she insisted his part be built up.

The casting of Powell and Lombard in *My Man Godfrey* had the town buzzing. Hollywood wags tried to think of when two previously married stars had played a romantic duo on screen. Ironically there was another couple doing just that the same year—Henry Fonda and Margaret Sullavan—but it was in *The Moon's Our Home*, a film that never achieved the profile that *Godfrey* did.

*

My Man Godfrey is a comedy that works only in the context of the depression. It falls into that category of movies in which people who are poor or working stiffs get to show up the wealthy as spoiled, greedy, stupid, or simply in need of commonsense guidance. The relationship between the heiress Ellie Andrews and the unemployed reporter Peter Warne in *It Happened One Night* is a perfect example of a sub-genre that resonated with 1930s moviegoers, who tended to identify with the common man rather than high society. Films like Frank Capra's *Mr. Deeds Goes to Town* and *You Can't Take It with You*, *Holiday* (with working stiff Cary Grant refusing to buy into the values of his fiancée's wealthy family) or *Easy Living* (where Jean Arthur sees what it's like to be rich when a mink coat literally drops into her lap while she's riding on a bus), buoyed depression-era audiences by symbolically placing the blame for the nation's economic problems on the rich. Rather than preach revolution, however, the movies turned the situation into a simple matter of being ready to fall in love while learning how the other half lived.

Godfrey succeeded in part because it pulled out all the stops. The Bullock family is not simply out of touch, it is stark raving mad, or at least the women are. The head of the household is Alexander Bullock (Eugene Pallette), whose business is falling apart even as he lacks any control over his flighty wife (Alice Brady) or his two headstrong daughters, Irene and Cornelia (Lombard and Gail Patrick). In the film's memorable beginning, the Bullock women are engaged in a citywide scavenger hunt, ostensibly for charity, though, as Irene allows, after the expenses are paid there never seems to be any money left over. They are all searching for a "forgotten man," and Godfrey, rather articulate for someone living in tattered clothes inside a crate at the city landfill, tells off the haughty Cornelia, chasing her off.

Irene laughs at this comeuppance of her older sister, and Godfrey asks if perhaps she too ought to be pushed into an ash pile. Irene's response is telling, because it shows the glimmer of the moral awakening that ultimately redeems her character, "You know, I've decided I'm not going to play any more games with human beings as objects. It's kind of sordid when you think of it." Godfrey sees that Irene is, at core, a good person, and agrees to be her "forgotten man" if it will mean beating Cornelia. (In the history of romantic comedy, this may be one of the most subtly complex "meet cutes" ever.) At the hotel where the various teams check in, Cornelia's father delivers the line that could sum up the whole era of screwball romances. Told that the place looks like a madhouse he replies, "Well, all you need to start an asylum is an empty room and the right kind of people."

Godfrey's arrival allows Irene to win—after the judge (the character actor Franklin Pangborn) certifies that Godfrey's stubble is authentic. Now her growing moral sense makes her want to do something for Godfrey in return. When he wonders if she has any jobs lying around, he is offered the position of butler at the Bullock manse. It's a three-ring circus, as Godfrey soon learns, but he's up to the task, and this too ties the film to its era. As the film historian Maria DiBattista notes, "If, as Godfrey later insists, the only difference between a derelict and a man is a job, then Irene has made a man of him by the simple expedient of employing him. That is the first and perhaps most essential standard for manliness for Depression-era America."

As the story progresses, Irene falls in love with her "protégé" Godfrey while he insists on a very proper relationship. One begins

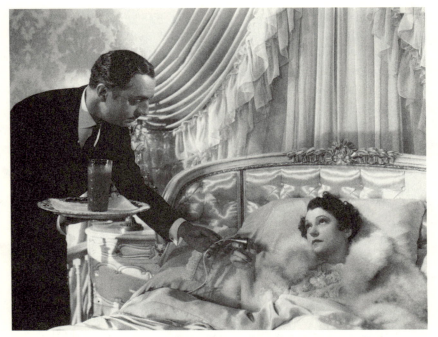

Going from bum to butler, Godfrey (William Powell) helps Mrs. Bullock (Alice Brady) with her morning hangover, though her daughter Irene (Carole Lombard, not pictured) will prove an even greater challenge.

to wonder where a derelict got such polish and sophistication, but it turns out that Godfrey has a past. (Indeed, he's not the only one. We're told one of his neighbors at the landfill was a former bank executive who protected his depositors at the cost of his own wealth.) He was the embittered scion of a Boston family, who chose life as a bum over suicide when he saw the other men at the riverside landfill hanging on and not giving up. Over the course of the film's brisk running time, Godfrey brings the Bullock family the stability it has desperately needed. He helps correct Alexander's finances and gives him the spine to eject Carlo (Mischa Auer), Mrs. Bullock's sponging "protégé." He teaches Cornelia humility. He even rebukes Irene after she fakes a dramatic fainting spell, by throwing her fully clothed into the shower.

The film's ending is quirky even by the era's standards. Godfrey has used his money (and the investment of a wealthy friend who nearly revealed Godfrey's secret to the Bullocks) to open a restaurant on the former landfill, employing the men who once lived there. He has fled the Bullocks not so much in triumph but instead to avoid becoming involved with Irene. Now it's Godfrey who needs help. Irene bustles in, rushing Godfrey into marriage before he's fully aware of what's happening. "Stand still, Godfrey, it'll all be over in a minute," she says in the film's closing line. Will Godfrey and Irene be more successful as husband and wife than Powell and Lombard were? That's for the viewer to decide as the screen fades to black.

That the film is inextricably a part of its times might not seem obvious until you compare it with the 1957 remake, a lavish color version that fails because it has no reason to exist other than the fact that the studio already owned the property. David Niven was cast as Godfrey, which is not a bad choice. Niven and Powell had different screen personas, but Niven was able to project a sense of propriety that fit the role. June Allyson, on the other hand, is too much of the "girl next door" to play the essential zaniness of Irene while projecting Carole Lombard's inner toughness. (One couldn't imagine Allyson responding to a foul-mouthed studio executive like Harry Cohn at Columbia who once told Lombard that her platinum blonde hair made her look like a whore. Lombard replied that if anyone knew what a whore looked like, it would be Cohn. They got along just fine after that.)

Casting aside, the problem with the remake is that the story lacks a context. According to one plot summary, "Godfrey, the butler to an eccentric New York family, wasn't a Harvard-educated hobo but an Austrian refugee enjoying illegal U.S. citizenship." Indeed, the focus was so different that Godfrey was originally set to be played by the German actor O. W. Fischer, who left the production shortly after shooting began and was replaced by Niven. Depression-era audiences had responded to Godfrey's determination to make good when given a chance to redeem himself, especially as so many hardworking people had been beaten down by economic forces beyond their control. Somehow, getting a green card or eluding the immigration authorities didn't resonate in quite the same way, at least not in 1957.

*

Powell and Lombard were not the only ones from *My Man Godfrey* waiting to see the Oscar results at the Biltmore Hotel in Los Angeles in 1937. Also nominated were LaCava for direction, Ryskind and Hatch for screenplay, Alice Brady for supporting actress, and Mischa Auer for supporting actor.

Perhaps the most surprising nomination was that of Auer, who had played the small supporting role of Mrs. Bullock's protégé Carlo. Only thirty-one, he had been kicking around Hollywood for nearly a decade in supporting, often comic, roles. What made his turn stand out was the scene in which Mrs. Bullock beseeches him to cheer up Irene by imitating an ape. Slowly he transforms himself, and before long he is leaping around the room and climbing the curtains, acting like a chimpanzee. Noted one writer, Auer's antics "should be honored as the definitive film performance of man imitating ape." (Auer would lose the Oscar but enjoy a long career as a supporting player in Hollywood and Europe, working until his death in 1967.)

Alice Brady had played a number of comic dowagers but had begun as a serious actress both on stage and in silent movies. She had made her film debut in 1914 at the age of twenty-two. It made the casting a little strange: Mrs. Bullock was played by the forty-four-year-old Brady. Irene, the younger daughter, was played by twenty-eight-year-old Lombard (suggesting that Mrs. Bullock had been a child bride), while the older Cornelia was played by twenty-five-year-old Gail Patrick. This led to some amusement on the set, but not for the expected reasons. Lombard was getting serious with Clark Gable, and she learned that Brady and Gable had appeared on Broadway together seven years earlier and had enjoyed a fling. According to one biographer, "When Lombard asked Brady for pointers on how to handle Gable, Brady couldn't remember many details of that brief affair." Brady lost the Oscar race that night as the *My Man Godfrey* nominees went home empty-handed, but the following year she won for playing Mrs. O'Leary, the owner of the incendiary cow in the movie *In Old Chicago*.

As for the double-dating couples, there were sad times ahead. Powell, who had been divorced twice, and Harlow, who had been divorced three times, had fallen in love despite a twenty-year age difference. Unfortunately Harlow would be dead of kidney failure at twenty-six, just a few months later, falling ill during the shooting of *Saratoga* with Clark Gable. Indeed, the film could only be completed with a stand-in for Harlow for the scenes she had not completed. Powell was heartbroken, and Harlow's family—which had been living off of her earnings—pressed him to pay for the funeral, worsening matters by letting his generosity be known.

Gable and Lombard would enjoy a few years of happiness together. She had some of her best films ahead of her, particularly *Nothing Sacred* (1937), which might be even zanier than *Godfrey*, and her final film, Ernst Lubitsch's *To Be or Not to Be* (1942), released after she died at age thirty-three in a plane crash during a wartime bond drive. No less a person than President Franklin Roosevelt was moved to send condolences to Gable: "She is and always will be a star, one we shall never forget, nor cease to be grateful to."

Gable and Powell mourned, went back to work, and later married again. Gable made movies into the early 1960s—with a break for wartime service—ending his career with *The Misfits* (1961). A day after he finished that film he suffered a heart attack and died a few days later. It was also the final film for his co-star, Marilyn Monroe.

Powell's career and life had its share of troubles, but he worked steadily up until 1955, even winning his third Oscar nomination for *Life with Father* in 1947. Then, after a droll turn as the ship's doctor in *Mister Roberts*, Powell decided to retire. No real explanation was offered. He simply had had enough work. He had married actress Diana Lewis in 1940 (she ended her brief screen career a few years later), and the two lived their remaining years together away from the hustle of Hollywood. It was a long retirement. Powell died in 1984 at the age of ninety-one, having enjoyed his later years in comfort with privacy and dignity. Godfrey undoubtedly would have approved.

4

THE SHOP AROUND
THE CORNER

BY THE END of the 1930s Ernst Lubitsch was on his own, having left Paramount after a decade there with some of the best work of his career behind him. In the remaining years of his life he would work as an independent filmmaker at various studios. While not every film was a gem, some of his finest movies were still ahead. With hindsight it might seem easy to see what projects Lubitsch or, indeed, any director, might have been better off to skip. In the moment, though, filmmakers are not always the best judge of their work.

Take the year 1939, legendary in Hollywood history as the greatest year the film industry has ever known. It was the year of *Gone with the Wind* and *The Wizard of Oz*, of *Mr. Smith Goes to Washington* and *Gunga Din*, of *Stagecoach* and *Wuthering Heights*, and many more. It was also the year Lubitsch would work on two movies at MGM. One was a project he had little interest in but that the studio thought would do well; the other was a movie he had been nurturing but in which Hollywood had shown little interest. The studio and the director made a deal: if he'd make the first film, they'd finance the second.

At the time MGM seemed to have gotten the better of the deal. Lubitsch first directed *Ninotchka*, a sparkling political satire in which Greta Garbo's icy Russian commissar has her heart melted by Melvyn Douglas's highborn playboy. The ad campaign noted what a break this was for the dramatic star of such movies as *Camille*, *Grand Hotel*,

53

and *Anna Karenina* by trumpeting that in this movie "Garbo Laughs!" MGM then dumped the other Lubitsch picture into theaters in January 1940, a downtime when moviegoers were still catching up with the major end-of-the-year releases. But that other film, very different in tone, would prove to be just as enduring. It was *The Shop Around the Corner.* The story would be told many times, but this version was the best.

*

When Lubitsch left Paramount in 1938, hard on the heels of two expensive flops (*Angel* and *Bluebeard's Eighth Wife*), negotiations with other studios led nowhere. He finally set up his own production company, with the first project to be based on an obscure Hungarian play entitled *Parfumerie*, about love between clerks in a perfume store. Lubitsch's frequent collaborator Samson Raphaelson, with whom he had done *Trouble in Paradise*, was brought in to do the screenplay adaptation for a modest fee and a piece of the profits. The German actress Dolly Haas was contacted about playing the female lead while Raphaelson and Lubitsch worked on the script. When it was completed, Lubitsch was pleased with the result and told his business partner, the agent Myron Selznick (brother of producer David), to put together the financing for it.

Hollywood in the late 1930s was a very different world from what it is today, and independent productions were a rarity. Add Lubitsch's recent record at the box office and Myron Selznick's shaky reputation as businessman, and—to paraphrase Samuel Goldwyn—investors stayed away in droves. Lubitsch began having second thoughts about Haas. Recalled Raphaelson, "Lubitsch lost his nerve, that's all. She was a European star, not widely known in the U.S., perfect for the part, heaven sent. But he got nervous. . . . He felt a movie was at best such a gamble he wanted to play safe at every point where he could get established pros." Unfortunately stars were not lining up to work with Lubitsch, and neither were the studios. It looked like *Shop* would never be made.

Around this same time MGM was developing a property that would eventually become *Ninotchka*. From an original story by Melchior Lengyel, the studio went through draft after draft with various writers coming and going but unable to bring the script to life. George Cukor was to direct Garbo and William Powell as the leads. In late 1939, however, Cukor departed to work on *Gone with the Wind* (he'd be one of many directors behind the cameras of the Civil War epic, though final credit would go to Victor Fleming), and the studio asked Garbo what she'd like to do. One of the biggest stars of the era, she had earned the right to approve the directors of her films, and she notified MGM that only two people were acceptable to her, Edmund Goulding (her director on *Grand Hotel*) or Lubitsch, with whom she had always wanted to work. For whatever reason, MGM chief Louis B. Mayer decided that Goulding was too old-fashioned, and the project was offered to Lubitsch.

This was the sort of whimsical touch we might expect from a Lubitsch film. At a moment when his career is at a dead end, a series of decisions are made that end up with the most powerful studio in Hollywood not only requesting his services but offering to buy the rights to—and finance the making of—*The Shop Around the Corner*. Lubitsch was not only well paid, getting $147,500 to make the two movies, but he was also paid $62,500 for the rights to *Shop*, which he had bought for only $16,500. What's more, the studio had been looking for a vehicle to reunite Jimmy Stewart and Margaret Sullavan, who had been paired twice before, most notably in *Shopworn Angel* (1938). As 1938 drew to a close, Lubitsch signed the deal with MGM.

*

Jimmy Stewart hadn't intended to become an actor. At Princeton, where he performed in a number of student theatricals, he was nearing graduation and planned to attend its architectural school that fall. Then the future theater director Joshua Logan, who had graduated Princeton the year before and had worked with Stewart on a number of school productions, invited him to join his summer stock theater on Cape Cod in Massachusetts. Stewart said he had no interest— until Logan said the one thing that could make him change his mind: nineteen-year-old Margaret Sullavan had agreed to be the stock company's leading lady. Stewart had had a crush on her before she went off to Broadway and the start of her professional stage career. Now she had agreed to spend the summer with Logan's University Players, and Stewart just couldn't say no. He was no doubt disillusioned that Sullavan had married another actor, another up-and-comer named Henry Fonda, but heartened when he learned they had divorced after only two months.

It was an interesting group that congregated on the Cape the summer of 1932. Besides Stewart were Mildred Natwick, Arlene Francis, Martin Gabel, and Fonda. Fonda had been one of the first members of the troupe and had left, but now offered to come back. The financially strapped producers offered him five dollars a week and room and board for the season, and he took it. Not among the actors was Sullavan who, as it turned out, would *not* be performing with the troupe that summer. This was a disappointment to both Stewart and Fonda, but it removed a distraction that not only led Stewart to begin honing his craft but would also lead to a lifelong friendship between the two actors.

By 1935 first Fonda and then Stewart had been brought out to Hollywood, as had Sullavan. Stewart's eventual stardom was perhaps the least likely. Signed as a contract player at MGM, it was clear that the casting people at the studio simply didn't know what to do with the lanky, slow-speaking actor from Pennsylvania. He was given a small speaking role in a forgettable Spencer Tracy vehicle, *The Murder Man* (1935), then began popping up in a variety of roles, to the consternation of future movie buffs. It would be a while before anyone thought of a part as a "Jimmy Stewart role" (*It's a Wonderful Life*) or considered casting Stewart dramatically against type (*Vertigo*), so when Stewart appears in a mid-1930s film there's no telling what they intend to do with him. In movies like *Rose Marie* and *After the Thin*

Man he was a killer. He danced opposite Eleanor Powell in *Born to Dance*. He was even given a screen test for the role of a Chinese peasant in *The Good Earth*.

Bit by bit Stewart began gaining notice. He got his biggest break when he was loaned to Columbia Pictures where Frank Capra was adapting the George S. Kaufman / Moss Hart Broadway hit *You Can't Take It with You*. It was a big ensemble comedy, with Stewart and Jean Arthur as the romantic leads but not having the burden of carrying the story—that was left to acting heavyweights Lionel Barrymore and Edward Arnold—and it was the start of an important partnership. Stewart would become the personification of the Capra hero in two subsequent films, *Mr. Smith Goes to Washington* (1939) and *It's a Wonderful Life* (1947). It's *Mr. Smith*, more than any other film, that put Stewart on the map. There (opposite Arthur again) he did carry the weight of the film—and, seemingly, the weight of the world—on his shoulders, and he did so magnificently.

While Lubitsch was struggling to get *The Shop Around the Corner* made, Stewart was becoming a star. He would appear on screen in five films in 1939, including *Destry Rides Again* and *Made for Each Other* (the latter opposite Carole Lombard), but *Mr. Smith* gave him his first Oscar nomination, up against no less than Clark Gable in *Gone with the Wind* and Laurence Olivier in *Wuthering Heights*. (The award went to Robert Donat for *Goodbye, Mr. Chips*.) Thus when MGM offered Lubitsch a team of Stewart and Sullavan, these were stars of the caliber he was used to working with at Paramount but had been unable to attract as an independent producer.

Sullavan's path to the film was a bit different. She had already been a hit on Broadway when she came to Hollywood. In the movies she was getting starring roles but not star-making roles. One of her notable early films was *The Good Fairy* (1935) directed by William Wyler. Off-screen she and Wyler began a relationship that ended in marriage. Clearly believing they had a hot commodity in Sullavan, Universal began prepping what they hoped would be her career-making role in *Next Time We Love*. To their surprise, she told the studio's executives that she would make the picture only if the role of her husband were played by that new actor at MGM, Jimmy Stewart. Universal had no idea whom she was talking about, but reluctantly agreed.

Sullavan had spotted Stewart on the streets of Hollywood while she was being driven to the studio one day. She stopped the car and invited him in. They caught up, and Sullavan decided to use what little clout she had in his behalf. Biographers of the two stars have tried to figure out what made their friendship work. Clearly he was attracted to her, and just as clearly she had feelings for him, but it never seemed to blossom into a romance. Myron McCormick, an actor and mutual friend, observed, "She was protective, loving, maternal toward him. She wasn't usually like this with most men. If she wasn't getting sexually predatory with them she was indifferent, or contemptuous." Whatever her feelings, Sullavan made looking out for Stewart a priority. When the studio began making noises about replacing him after the screening of the initial rushes, she took him under her wing for private rehearsals and coaching. There were rumors of romance—guaranteed to upset her husband, who was off making another film—but whatever feelings were expressed seem to have been sublimated into the movie. It was definitely a turning point for Stewart, who was later quoting as saying, "I'll never marry until I find a girl like Margaret Sullavan."

By 1938 Sullavan was ready for her moment in the spotlight, having shed her second husband (Wyler) and married the agent Leland Hayward. Opposite Stewart and Walter Pidgeon she appeared in *Shopworn Angel*, a tearjerker in which an entertainer (Sullavan) marries a young soldier (Stewart) before he ships out for World War I, hoping to give him a reason to stay alive. She tells the man she's supposedly involved with (Pidgeon) that it's a lark, that they'll get a divorce when he returns home. Naturally, Stewart's character is killed in battle, and everyone in the audience ends up having a good cry. Once again rumors flew about a romance (now to the consternation of Hayward), but from MGM's perspective it was the on-screen chemistry of the two actors that made it imperative to find another vehicle for them.

Before that could happen, Sullavan appeared in *Three Comrades*, earning her only Oscar nomination. There she played the object of the affections of the three title friends, played by Franchot Tone, Robert Young, and Robert Taylor. By the end of the year, when Lubitsch was pitching Louis Mayer about his story about a romance between two luggage store clerks, offering him Sullavan and Stewart seemed like a shrewd move on Mayer's part. Here were two actors who were linked on screen and in the public imagination. That just might attract attention to the trifle MGM was bankrolling in return for getting Lubitsch to direct *Ninotchka*. Meanwhile the studio could look for a more serious vehicle for the actors.

*

The Shop Around the Corner is set in a luggage store in Budapest. It is an early example of what would become a staple of 1970s television sitcoms: the workplace as family. Nearly all the action is set at Matuschek and Company, where paternal Mr. Matuschek (Frank Morgan) presides firmly but fairly over his staff. First and foremost is Kralik (Stewart), clearly the son he never had. There's Pirovitch (Felix Bressart), the comic uncle. There's Vadas (Joseph Schildkraut), always sucking up to Matuschek, often to the disadvantage of the others. New to this world is Klara (Sullavan), who needs a job and wins over Matuschek by selling a corny music box that the owner likes but that Kralik had argued the store shouldn't carry. She wins the job, but in one of those Lubitsch "touches" we see that Kralik was right about the music boxes, which are soon marked down for clearance. The romance comes from the fact that Kralik and Klara are conducting a courtship through letters, without either one realizing the other is the secret pen pal. The comic tension between them at the store, where they seem to rub each other the wrong way, changes when Kralik discovers Klara's identity, which he keeps to himself for the time being.

Klara (Margaret Sullavan) lands a job by admiring a tacky cigarette box ordered by storeowner Matuschek (Frank Morgan), while the skeptical Kralik (James Stewart) is in fact her secret pen pal.

Not until the story's end does Kralik reveal himself. A sub-plot involving Mrs. Matuschek having an affair must also be resolved, since Matuschek unjustly accuses Kralik for the betrayal.

If the story of the romantic pen pals seems familiar, it should be; it has since served as the basis for at least three other vehicles. There's the 1949 MGM musical *In the Good Old Summertime*, which moves the action to nineteenth-century Chicago and casts Van Johnson and Judy Garland as the romantic duo; the 1960 musical *She Loves Me*, done by the Broadway team of Jerry Bock and Sheldon Harnick shortly before they went on to even greater fame with *Fiddler on the Roof*; and *You've Got Mail*, the 1998 Nora Ephron film starring Tom Hanks and Meg Ryan, which updates the correspondence to e-mail. Whatever their virtues, none of these later efforts fully captures the charm of the Lubitsch film, but they do show that he and Raphaelson were clearly on to something when they adapted the plot of *Parfum-erie* for their own purposes.

For Lubitsch this was a most unusual film. It's set in a workaday world, with no millionaires or nobles in sight. Matuschek is the closest to wealth here as the store owner, and it's merely in comparison to his employees. His clerks are caught up with everyday concerns in a way that was extraordinary for Lubitsch, and not at all typical of the romantic comedy. Characters worry about finding or keeping a job, getting a raise or a promotion, and even of their status among the other workers. Pirovitch has a wife and children to support, so keeping the boss happy is his priority. He's well aware of the ironic trade-offs this entails ("The other day he called me an idiot. . . . I said, 'Yes, Mr. Matuschek, I'm an idiot.' I'm no fool"), but he feels it's worth it to enjoy being a family man. Then there's Pepi (William Tracy), proud of his position as a lowly errand boy, though he has ambitions. When Pepi saves Matuschek's life he finds himself in a serious conversation with a doctor who is stunned at the pride and brashness of this glorified gofer. When he says as much, Pepi doesn't miss a beat, asking if the doctor wishes to be thought of as merely a "pill pusher."

Although Lubitsch had become wealthy in Hollywood and was used to making movies in that world, it was in the environment of Matuschek and Company where he could explore his roots. He had worked in just such a store for his father and, later, in his early years as an actor, had played the sorts of comic clerks depicted here. He *knew* these people because he was one of them. Said Lubitsch, "Never did I make a film in which the atmosphere and characters were truer than in this film."

Andrew Sarris places the film in the context of the depression, which by the late thirties was beginning to seem like a past event. "This ode to the modesty of middle-class yearnings came out at a moment in American history when people were turning away from the pathos and resignation of the Great Depression toward the dynamic challenges of a world at war and the economic recovery thereof." Instead of creating a fictional "Paris, Paramount," Lubitsch wanted a realistic Budapest store at MGM. No detail was too small. "To assure authenticity in the setting, research expert Henry Nordlinger worked for weeks before the film went into production, checking on all items such a store would carry," noted one critic. "He obtained an inventory from Budapest as a guide."

One of the most oft-told incidents involved the dress Sullavan would wear upon her entrance in the film as the humble job applicant. She found a dress for the lordly price of $1.98, but Lubitsch declared it was "too smart for a clerk looking for a job." He not only had alterations done so that it *wouldn't* fit so well, he then ordered it hung outside so it would fade in the sun.

But it was the casting where Lubitsch showed his true mastery. Watching it years later one quickly forgets that Frank Morgan's most enduring performance was as *The Wizard of Oz* (1939) and accepts him as the flawed but essentially decent Matuschek. It is Stewart and Sullavan, though, who get to express the affection for each other that they obviously felt in real life but perhaps never really articulated. Stewart's wife Gloria (whom he married in 1949 and remained married to until her death in 1994), spoke of how her husband's and Sullavan's feelings informed the film: "Margaret had recently had a child, and Jim was dating a lot of other women. Lubitsch knew that by casting Jim and Margaret, they would have a chemistry that was always there between them on screen, but their private lives would provide a certain amount of detachment the story required them to have."

The film was shot quickly. The entire production took just twenty-eight days (half the time allotted to *Ninotchka*), but at least part of that was the efficiency that came with most of the story taking place on the set of Matuschek and Company. This allowed Lubitsch to shoot mostly in chronological sequence, permitting the stage-trained Stewart and Sullavan the rare luxury of building a performance over the course of a story.

Both were at the top of their game. As screenwriter Raphaelson observed about Stewart, "Stop and contemplate the lanky, drawling

American playing a Hungarian clerk so flawlessly that no one seems to realize it is one of the great performances in cinema history."

Sullavan still gently coached Stewart. She'd make faces at him off-camera, making him angry—which, as he noted, was precisely the reaction he was supposed to have. Another time, recalled Stewart, she complained he wasn't looking at her properly. "She'd say, 'Stop, right there. What the hell are you doing? You're not making me feel the way I'm supposed to feel.' And I'd say, 'You're not even in the shot, so how's anybody going to know?' And she'd say, 'Well, *I'll* know.' And then I'd just crack up with laughing."

Only one fight between them was reported during the making of the movie—a fairly ridiculous tiff but one that speaks volumes about the relationship between Stewart and Sullavan, on-camera and off. Tellingly, it is the self-effacing Stewart who related the story for posterity to Brooke Hayward, Sullavan's daughter. In the film there's a continuing joke about whether Kralik is bowlegged. When Kralik finally reveals his identity to Klara, she resolves to get the answer to this question before the final clinch. Stewart was not bowlegged, but he did have skinny legs, and he kept stumbling over his lines in take after take since the scene required him to roll up his pants legs for the camera. Stewart claimed it took forty-eight takes, and at one point he was ready to quit. He told Hayward:

"For some reason I couldn't say the line. Your mother was furious. She said, 'This is absolutely ridiculous.' There I was, standing with my trousers rolled up to the knee, very conscious of my skinny legs, and I said, 'I don't want to act today; get a fellow with decent legs and just show them.' Your mother said, 'Then I absolutely refuse to be in the picture.' So we did more takes." They finally got it.

*

The Shop Around the Corner was released in January 1940 to mixed reviews, with some critics recognizing it as a small gem and others dismissing it as old-fashioned. Returns at the box office were modest.

It would be a while until it took its place in the pantheon of the great romantic comedies. Lubitsch, however, was back on top, more due to the success of *Ninotchka* than to *Shop*, and would continue to make films until his death in 1947. Yet a unique style of filmmaking was coming to a close. If it wasn't fully appreciated by the public, it was by the industry where he had worked so long and fruitfully. In March 1947 Lubitsch was the inaugural recipient of what became a sad Oscar tradition: honoring someone before it was too late. By the end of November he was dead.

Coming back from the cemetery service, the directors Billy Wilder and William Wyler lamented his passing.

"Well, no more Lubitsch," said Wilder.

"Worse than that," Wyler replied ruefully. "No more Lubitsch movies."

Sullavan and Stewart finished *Shop* and immediately began work on their final film together (joined by Frank Morgan), *The Mortal Storm*, a wartime drama which may be noticed today primarily for the retrospectively odd casting of Robert Young as a Nazi. Sullavan made only five films after that, working more often on stage. She and Stewart remained friends even as she married and divorced for a fourth time while he found a life partner in his wife Gloria. Sullavan died of an overdose of barbiturates in 1960, a death that was ruled a suicide. Some have speculated that it was a hearing loss, making an acting career increasingly untenable, that may have caused her despondency.

For Stewart, though, the view from 1940 looked bright. His career was finally taking off. He didn't win the Oscar for *Mr. Smith Goes to Washington*, but MGM now considered him one of their stars. After *The Mortal Storm*, Stewart made five more movies before leaving the cameras for war service. Four of the films were quite forgettable. The other became one of the biggest successes of his prewar career, *The Philadelphia Story*.

5

THE PHILADELPHIA STORY

IT'S HARD to see *The Philadelphia Story* today as audiences in 1940 would have seen it. It was a smash hit, running six weeks to sold-out houses at Radio City Music Hall, departing only when the theater was contractually obligated to premiere Alfred Hitchcock's first American film, *Rebecca*. *The Philadelphia Story* cemented Jimmy Stewart's stardom when he won his Oscar for it, which was handy because he was about to leave the screen for several years to go off to war. It won an Oscar, too, for the screenwriter Donald Ogden Stewart, who adapted Philip Barry's hit Broadway comedy as he had earlier adapted Barry's *Holiday*. But for moviegoers in 1940 it also marked the triumphant return to the screen of Katharine Hepburn, whose movie career had seemed all but over just two years earlier.

In 1938 Hepburn had co-starred with Cary Grant in two movies that are now revered comedies, the sophisticated *Holiday*, directed by George Cukor, and the knockabout screwball comedy *Bringing Up Baby*, directed by Howard Hawks. Incredibly, both flopped. This led Harry Brandt, president of the Independent Theater Owners of America, to take out ads in the trade press urging the studios to stop making movies with performers he labeled "box office poison." On his list were Joan Crawford, Mae West, Edward Arnold, Marlene Dietrich . . . and Katharine Hepburn. RKO, where she was under contract, didn't think it was worth fighting to save her career. Yes, she had had a few hits along the way, even winning an Oscar for the 1933 *Morning Glory*. As far as RKO was concerned, Hepburn had had a healthy run. The actress, fed up with the way she was being treated and seeing she had no future at the studio, bought out the remainder of her contract. She had made *Holiday* at Columbia, which wasn't offering her any deals either. She realized that her movie career might have come to a dead end. She left Hollywood and headed back east to her family's home in Connecticut.

By a fortunate coincidence, at the same time two Broadway institutions were also in the doldrums. The playwright Philip Barry, once the toast of Broadway, had had his own series of flops. Alternating between comedy and drama, he had started work on a comedy about a Philadelphia mainline family planning for a wedding while fending off intrusive interest by the press. He saw the central character, Tracy Lord, as being glamorous and willful; in other words, a lot like Hepburn. He began crafting the part for her. Barry knew Hepburn (not only had she been in the 1938 film version of *Holiday*, she had also understudied the part in its original Broadway run) and asked her if she would consider doing his new play. She was interested, but there was one glitch. She was one of many actresses who were under active consideration for the biggest movie role of 1939: Scarlett O'Hara in *Gone with the Wind*.

Hepburn told Barry, "I'd be quite interested in playing Tracy Lord provided I don't play Scarlett O'Hara first."

The part of Scarlett, of course, went to Vivien Leigh and Hepburn found herself starring in a Broadway show. It wasn't quite as easy as all that. Barry's three-act comedy had plenty of laughs, but it also had third-act problems, and it went through several cities of tryouts before he worked them out. In her private life Hepburn had been romantically involved with the industrialist Howard Hughes, but she saw no future with him and they had become "just friends." Still, Hughes was a good friend to have in terms of planning her future. In her memoir, Hepburn relates how she made the shrewdest business decision of her career: "I called Howard and told him that I had a thrilling new project. Howard said, 'Buy the film rights before you open.' And he bought the film rights to *The Philadelphia Story* for me, which insured my success later."

To finance the stage production, Hepburn approached the Theater Guild. She had been cast in their dramatization of *Jane Eyre*, and they had also been gracious enough to let her out of her contract before it got to New York, when she felt the playwright was not making the necessary changes. Feeling she owed them, she brought Barry's play to them, having no idea that the Theater Guild was near bankruptcy. In retrospect it was a perfect marriage of convenience: she didn't realize how desperate they were for a moneymaking hit, and the board of the Guild, paying little attention to Hollywood, had no idea that Hepburn had become virtually unemployable.

The play opened at New York's Shubert Theater on March 28, 1939, and was an immediate success. It took a while before it sank in for the actress. On opening night Hepburn was so nervous to be back in New York that she could be heard pacing her hotel room at the Waldorf-Astoria telling herself, "This is Indianapolis. This is Indianapolis." In addition to Hepburn as Tracy Lord, the cast included Joseph Cotten—a rising star from Orson Welles's Mercury Theater—as C. K. Dexter Haven, Van Heflin as Macaulay Connor, and Shirley Booth as the photographer Liz Imbrie. After a shaky stage career and a troubled one on the big screen, Hepburn was now an unquestioned Broadway star. Noting what a great part it was, Hepburn told her biographer, "An actress doesn't get many of those in a lifetime, and she doesn't need many."

While Hepburn settled in for a long run with the show, it was only a matter of time before Hollywood came calling.

*

The studios wanted not Hepburn but the movie rights to the play. Several saw it as an ideal vehicle for their leading ladies, but they hadn't counted on Hepburn being part of the package. Since she owned the rights, no one would be making a movie of *The Philadelphia Story* except on her terms. And her terms began with the notion that she would repeat her role as Tracy Lord. Also key to the success of this carefully crafted comeback vehicle was that the two male leads had to be big stars. There was talk that if the rights had gone to Paramount the cast would include Gary Cooper, and if it had been bought by Warner Bros. it would have starred Errol Flynn.

As adapted for the screen, *The Philadelphia Story* is ostensibly about the troubles that Tracy Lord (Hepburn) faces on her way to her second marriage, to the labor leader and man of the people George Kittridge (John Howard). The Lords don't like publicity, even though their wealth, position, and occasional antics warrant it. Thus Tracy's ex-husband, C. K. Dexter Haven (Cary Grant)—now working for gossipy *Spy* magazine—must sneak in reporter Macaulay Connor (James Stewart) and photographer Liz Imbrie (Ruth Hussey) as friends of Tracy's brother, conveniently out of the country. Connor is a cynic who thinks the assignment is beneath him, but he discovers that Tracy is not only headstrong but intelligent—she's moved by an out-of-print book of his that she found in the library—and Connor starts to come out of his shell. A night of tipsy revelries leads to real confusion as to who she will end up with—unless, of course, one calculates the relative star power at the time of Grant, Stewart, and Howard. Along the way—and this is why the film was so crucial to Hepburn's career—Tracy gets knocked off her pedestal and finds she must get in touch with and express her real feelings. It's a comedy of grace and class, and Louis Mayer decided MGM had to have it. Mayer was so enamored of Hepburn that he was willing to agree to her demands. He could be a difficult, paternalistic boss, but he respected class (the way Harry Cohn, the boss at low-rent Columbia Pictures, respected someone with the guts to stand up to him), and Hepburn recalled Mayer in only the most glowing terms: "I liked him and he liked me. He gave me a lot of freedom and I gave him a lot of respect. L. B. had a sense of romance about the movie business and the studio system. I must say I did too."

Mayer paid Hepburn $250,000—for both the movie rights and her services as star—and then asked who she wanted for the male leads. Since this was MGM, which the ads claimed had more stars than in the heavens, she named the two biggest box office attractions of the day: Clark Gable and Spencer Tracy. Mayer didn't think they'd do it, and they were now big enough stars to refuse projects; but he agreed to send them both the script. Both turned it down.

So Mayer gave Hepburn a counteroffer on casting. He could guarantee Jimmy Stewart for one of the male leads. Stewart's career was on the rise, MGM wanted him in another romantic comedy, and he hadn't yet earned the right to turn down an assignment. Hepburn readily agreed. In return, said Mayer, he'd budget $150,000 to pay for whichever star she wanted for the other part. Hepburn snapped up the deal and went after Cary Grant, with whom she had already made three movies, offering him his choice of the two roles. Grant, whose own career had not been hurt by appearing in three flops with Hepburn, agreed, providing he got top billing. Hepburn knew that the success of her comeback would not hinge on where her name appeared in the credits, and gave pride of place to Grant. Then, perhaps to demonstrate both his heart and just how successful he had become, Grant donated his salary—after taxes and related expenses—to the American Red Cross and British War Relief.

Grant's performance as C. K. Dexter Haven is one of the delights of the film but is sometimes taken for granted because the movie provided such a boost to Hepburn and Stewart. Born Archibald Leach in Bristol, England, he had arrived in Hollywood in the 1930s and was immediately typecast as the handsome young man. The roles got bigger but not better. He has a supporting role in Marlene Dietrich's *Blonde Venus*; he's the naval officer abandoning Sylvia Sidney in *Madame Butterfly*; and then he pops up in two Mae West films, *She Done Him Wrong* and *I'm No Angel*. It's in the former that Grant becomes the object of West's famous invitation, "Why don't you come up sometime and see me?"

In 1936 he made his first film with Hepburn under the direction of George Cukor, *Sylvia Scarlett*. He's a con man who falls in with a father/daughter team played by Edmund Gwenn and Hepburn. To escape police notice, she's disguised as a boy. The whimsical film baffled 1936 audiences, and while it advanced Grant's career by showing he could do character comedy and not just play well-dressed mannequins, it failed. It fails with viewers today for another reason. Since Grant was not yet a star in 1936, the viewer's expectations that Grant and Hepburn would end up together at the film's end are dashed when she winds up with Brian Aherne. Grant got some of the best notices of his career, but stardom was still down the road. It came in 1937 when, first, he played a supporting role in the farcical fantasy *Topper*, as one of a pair of socialite ghosts who tries to make Roland Young's staid banker come to life. Then he was cast opposite Irene Dunne in Leo McCarey's hilarious comedy about a divorced couple breaking up each other's subsequent romances, *The Awful Truth*.

The next year he did two more films with Hepburn, *Bringing Up Baby* and *Holiday*, which didn't get *him* labeled "box office poison." Then, while she headed back to New York, Grant was scoring hit after hit with movies like *Gunga Din*, *Only Angels Have Wings*, *His Girl Friday*, and *My Favorite Wife*. By the time *The Philadelphia Story* was released in December 1940 he had unquestionably earned star billing.

However much Grant worried about status issues like salary and billing, he had no airs on the set. Although his part was built up (in the play it's Tracy's brother who brings the reporter and photographer from *Spy* magazine to the Lord mansion), Grant played his role without trying to upstage his co-stars. In the famous prologue added for the film—in which we see the final fight as Dexter walks out on his marriage to Tracy with her breaking a golf club and him pushing her into a pratfall—the two actors had a great time. The athletic Grant enjoyed getting physical in his movies. He had done tumbling with Hepburn in *Holiday* and showed her an old trapeze trick—grabbing his wrists instead of his hands—when she's left hanging as the massive dinosaur collapses at the end of *Bringing Up Baby*. In *The Philadelphia Story*, recalled the movie's cameraman Joe Ruttenberg, "She enjoyed Cary Grant's pushing her through the doorway in one scene so much

James Stewart won an Oscar, Cary Grant got top billing, and Katharine Hepburn made a legendary Hollywood comeback (after being named "box office poison") in one of Hollywood's classiest films.

she had him do it over and over again. She also threw Cary so enthusiastically out the door, bag and baggage, at one moment he became quite badly bruised. 'That'll serve you right, Cary, for trying to be your own stuntman,' she quipped."

With Grant signed on for Dexter, the script was now sent to Stewart who would play the cynical reporter Macaulay Connor. Stewart was not yet fully aware of his own change of status. "When I first read the script, I thought I was being considered for the part of the fellow engaged to [Hepburn]. As I read it, I thought to myself, 'Ooh, that reporter part is a good one, but I'll be happy to play the other one.'" Hepburn commented, "How he could have considered anything else is totally beyond me. He was very funny in the picture, in a lot of ways I've never completely understood."

*

Such was Louis B. Mayer's faith in Hepburn, once he made the commitment to do *The Philadelphia Story* she was given a free hand in a way few actresses were. There was no question that George Cukor would direct it, but Mayer didn't even balk when they brought in Donald Ogden Stewart to do the script. Stewart was an obvious choice. He was a friend of the playwright's and had done an excellent job adapting Barry's *Holiday* to the screen. But he was also an outspoken leftist, and Mayer was one of the most prominent conservative Republicans in the movie industry. Still, Hepburn wanted Stewart, and Stewart she got.

Cukor recalled, "Donald Ogden Stewart . . . adapted *The Philadelphia Story* with the greatest modesty and unselfishness. He wrote in a couple of original scenes, but very much in the manner of Barry. He served the thing, he didn't try to star himself. . . ." The writer's work earned one of the film's two Oscars, and he was similarly modest about how he earned it: "*The Philadelphia Story* was the least deserving of praise bit of screenwriting I have ever done, since Philip Barry had written it so beautifully that my task was mainly an editing one. My chief contribution otherwise consisted of a few added scenes for Jimmy Stewart, and the Oscar which I received was probably one of the easiest ever obtained."

As for Hepburn's selection of Cukor, that too was easy. This would be their fifth film together. He had directed two of her successful films in the 1930s, her debut *A Bill of Divorcement* and a much-beloved version of *Little Women*. She had also enjoyed working with him on *Sylvia Scarlett* and *Holiday*, even if they had failed at the box office. They would go on to work on five more films, including three of her team-ups with Spencer Tracy and two of her TV movies, *Love Among the Ruins* and *The Corn Is Green* in the 1970s.

Cukor was an enterprising young stage director in New York when he signed a deal with Paramount Pictures in 1928 to try his hand at the movies. By the time he arrived on *The Philadelphia Story* he was known as the director of such films as *Dinner at Eight, David Copperfield, Little Women, Camille*, and *The Women*. Not surprisingly, he developed a reputation as a "woman's director," but it was a misnomer. He directed Spencer Tracy many times, including some films without Hepburn, and directed Ronald Colman's Oscar-winning performance in *A Double Life*. He also directed the classic 1954 version of *A Star Is Born* (having already done its prototype, *What Price Hollywood?* in 1932), gaining James Mason an Oscar nomination in the process. He introduced Jack Lemmon in *It Should Happen to You* and directed Rex Harrison in his Oscar-winning performance in *My Fair Lady*, finally winning a statuette for himself as best director. But there was no denying that actresses felt a rapport with Cukor, who provided an atmosphere in which they did some of their best work.

Unknown to the public but an open secret in Hollywood, Cukor was gay at a time when such matters simply weren't discussed. He was the first director hired for *Gone with the Wind* but was fired reportedly because Clark Gable felt Cukor was favoring the actresses. According to at least one Cukor biographer, it went deeper than that. Gable was what seventy years later would be called a homophobe. When he finally refused to work with Cukor any longer, the producer David O. Selznick, who needed Gable more than Cukor, fired the director. According to Joseph Mankiewicz, producer of *The Philadelphia Story* (and later a director in his own right), "What was special about George was his serene relationships with actresses. They felt comfortable with him; they knew he would never get them into bed."

Mayer might have had to accept Cukor and Stewart, but the studio boss remained *the boss*, and he had to find some way to exert his authority. He did it by picking a fight with someone on his payroll he could control: the costume designer Adrian. Adrian had been designing gowns at MGM for years, dressing such icons as Greta Garbo, Joan Crawford, Jean Harlow, Norma Shearer, Jeanette MacDonald, and countless others. Mayer now decided that Adrian's outfits were growing too revealing. He complained about a pantsuit that Hepburn was to wear "which struck Mayer as yet another example of 'permissiveness.' It took a personal pitch by Hepburn to convince Mayer that the republic could withstand the sight of an MGM heroine in pants." Hepburn saved the outfit, but Adrian was fed up. He left the studio the following year.

Notwithstanding the tussle over the pants, the filming of the movie went smoothly. Hepburn had developed a reputation in Hollywood as being difficult, whether deserved or not, and she intended to show everyone that a different Katharine Hepburn had returned to Hollywood. Jimmy Stewart recalled, "Cary and I used to talk about how Kate had made the whole experience wonderful for everyone—cast and crew. I have never worked on a picture that went any smoother." Indeed, if anyone was making things difficult, it was Stewart.

It wasn't that stardom wasn't going to his head; it was that old concern about his skinny legs. He had a scene where he and Hepburn were to go swimming, and he didn't want to appear on camera in swim trunks. "If I appear in a bathing suit, I know it's the end of me," he said. "I know that and I'm prepared to end my career, but it will also be the end of the motion picture industry." It was Hepburn who came up with the idea of them coming out of the cabanas in bathrobes, which protected audiences—and the motion picture industry—from the sight of Jimmy Stewart's legs.

Another scene that gave Stewart a problem also required a creative solution: his big romantic moment with Hepburn, when both Tracy and Macaulay have gotten tipsy and are letting out feelings they didn't know they had. Stewart has a florid speech where he describes Tracy ("You've got hearth fires banked in you, Tracy, hearth fires and holocausts"), and it wasn't coming easy. In fact it wasn't coming well at all. Hepburn recalled what saved the day: "Just before he did it, Noel Coward stepped onto the set and Jimmy nearly died. So he did the scene, and Noel in one second could see what was going on, and immediately stepped up to Jimmy and told him how devastating he was. And George [Cukor] said, 'roll 'em,' and took advantage of that obvious moment of flattery and Jimmy got a wonderful take."

For the most part, though, the filming was without incident. Hepburn, of course, knew the part inside and out, but she accepted changes suggested by Cukor. In the play she had a big dramatic scene in which she cried. Cukor suggested she underplay it and do it without tears in the film, and she did so to good effect. Hepburn seems not to have been the best judge of her performances, as she discovered when Walter Catlett taught her how to play madcap comedy in *Bringing Up Baby* by *not* trying to be funny. As Tracy, she so identified with the part that she couldn't always see how the character was seen by others.

Cukor recalled Hepburn describing the play's out-of-town try-outs, when a scene where Tracy is agonizing over what to do was greeted with big laughs. "She herself found the situation in the third act quite moving and tragic, but people began laughing. It got worse and worse, she became furious. She had to make a quick exit, and she muttered to someone in the wings, 'They hate it, they hate it!'" Instead of commiserating with her, the people backstage were beaming, realizing the laughs meant it was a success. As the writer and filmmaker Gavin Lambert observed, in his book-length interview with Cukor, "The comedy of the situation is that only *she* thinks it's tragic."

Stewart also responded well to Cukor's direction, and a bit of the actor's dark side—later to be tapped to great effect by Alfred Hitchcock in his thrillers and Anthony Mann in his westerns—emerged. The reporter Macaulay Connor is a bit of a cynic, and Stewart handles his acid comments on the lifestyles of the rich and privileged to great effect. Cukor also let him improvise, which he did in the latter part of his drunk scene when he wakes up Dexter in the middle of the night. Grant, slightly older and more established than Stewart, may have wondered which of them was the male lead in the film, but in this scene you can watch two actors bouncing off the script and having a great time doing it.

Stewart had decided that Macaulay would develop the hiccups from too much champagne, but he didn't tell Grant how he would play the scene. In the middle of the scene Stewart suddenly hiccuped, and Grant ad-libbed, "Excuse me," as if *he* were the one who had had too much to drink. Said Grant, "Jimmy simply mesmerized me on the screen. When I watched him act, I felt like a triangle player in the orchestra who keeps watching the conductor and then, when he finally gets the baton signal, he misses his triangle."

The movie was released at the end of 1940 to great critical and popular acclaim. It succeeded precisely as Hepburn had hoped, restoring her to the good graces of movie audiences. She had finished filming and immediately returned to the national touring company of the show, which finally closed, appropriately, in Philadelphia in February 1941. On her final night she came out for her bows and asked that the stage remained exposed so that the "final curtain" would never fall on the show.

For moviegoers, *The Philadelphia Story* was nothing less than a morality tale in which a beautiful, privileged, and arrogant woman—who may have been called Tracy Lord but everyone assumed was Hepburn herself—is chastised, humiliated, and finally gets her comeuppance. When, at the end, she seems more human and vulnerable, it is as if Hepburn is being forgiven vicariously for the image she had projected in the 1930s. As one writer observed, "It doesn't take much imagination to see here an allegory of Hepburn's own career up to this point: her alleged arrogance, her unpopularity with middle-American audiences, her refusal to play the publicity game, her threatening status as an 'independent woman.'"

At Oscar time the film was nominated for Best Picture, Best Actress (Hepburn), Best Actor (Stewart), Best Supporting Actress (Ruth Hussey, who had played Liz the photographer), Best Director, and Best (Adapted) Screenplay. Only the two Stewarts—who were not related—would win. When Jimmy Stewart won for Best Actor, he told the audience, "I want to assure you that this is a very, very important moment in my life." As one of the local Los Angeles papers observed, "As he has done in many a wild motion-picture scene, he stumbled dazedly back to his table amid shouts and applause." If Stewart had any inclination to let this success go to his head, plenty of people were ready to cut *him* down to size. His roommate, the actor Burgess

Meredith, took a look at Stewart and his Oscar when they finally arrived home together after a night of parties and greeted him with, "Where'd you get that thing—Ocean Pier Park?"

Then Stewart called his father, still running his hardware store back in Indiana, Pennsylvania, and still somewhat skeptical of the career path his son had chosen. Stewart told his father he had won the Oscar for *The Philadelphia Story*.

"What'd they give you, a plaque?" asked his father.

"No, a statue," Stewart replied.

His father suggested he send it home for safekeeping, which he dutifully did. It was displayed in a glass case at the hardware store for the next two decades.

Meanwhile Grant had been overlooked by the Oscars, as he would be his whole career. Not until 1970 did he receive an honorary Oscar, four years after he had retired from the screen with *Walk, Don't Run*. For what it was worth, *The Philadelphia Story*'s producer Joseph Mankiewicz sent Grant a message to let him know that at least one person had noticed what outstanding work he had done. "Whatever success the picture is having, and it is a simply enormous smash, is due, in my opinion, to you in far greater proportions than anyone has seen fit to shout about," he wrote. "Your presence as Dexter, and particularly your sensitive and brilliant playing of the role, contribute what I consider the backbone and basis of practically every emotional value in the piece." Mankiewicz added that he felt Grant had been "unjustly slighted in the general hysteria at Kate's comeback."

For whatever reason, Grant—who would go on to appear in numerous hit films over the next quarter century—never worked with Hepburn or Cukor again. Neither did Stewart, nor did Grant and Stewart ever appear together again. *The Philadelphia Story* remained a unique confluence of talent.

As for Hepburn, she claimed not to be miffed at losing the Oscar to her *Stage Door* co-star Ginger Rogers for *Kitty Foyle*, though she couldn't help noting that she had been offered the part and turned it down. Stewart, for his part, felt he was being paid back for having lost the Oscar for *Mr. Smith Goes to Washington* and had been rooting for his friend Henry Fonda to win for *The Grapes of Wrath*. He had voted for Fonda himself. A few days after winning the Oscar, Stewart left Hollywood and went to war. He did not make another movie until *It's a Wonderful Life*.

Hepburn, however, was now ready to get back to work. She was about to meet the man who would change her life . . . on screen and off.

6

ADAM'S RIB

SPENCER TRACY and Katharine Hepburn made nine films together, of which *Adam's Rib* was their sixth. It is also their best and a movie many feel best captures one of the great Hollywood romances on screen. Yet behind the scenes was a story completely under the radar of moviegoers and the entertainment industry, and it wasn't the then-secret relationship between the two stars. But that's as good a place as any to start.

*

After the triumph of *The Philadelphia Story*, despite not winning an Oscar herself, Hepburn was eager to move ahead with her newly revitalized Hollywood career. She was sent a treatment for *Woman of the Year*—about the relationship between a top sportswriter and a political columnist (loosely based on Ring Lardner and Dorothy Thompson)—and wanted to do it with Tracy, who was still a stranger to her. Louis B. Mayer was interested in acquiring the script but wasn't quick to close the deal because Hepburn was demanding top dollar for novice writers she declined to identify (Ring Lardner, Jr., and Garson Kanin's brother Michael). Unknown to Hepburn, Tracy was involved in an MGM production of *The Yearling* that was plagued with so many problems the studio was about to pull the plug. They *needed* something for Tracy. Mayer bought the script—actually just a treatment—and with Tracy on board the project was a go.

Sometime later the two stars met for the first time. It was a chance meeting on the lot. Tracy was heading for lunch with Joe Mankiewicz when Hepburn saw them. The story would be embellished over the years, but it didn't need any help. Hepburn in heels was roughly the same height as Tracy—he may have had a half-inch on her—and she remarked, "Mr. Tracy, you're not as tall as I expected."

The acerbic Mankiewicz replied, "Don't worry, Kate, he'll cut you down to size." (Over the years the story would be revised to put the cutting remark in Tracy's mouth, but Hepburn finally set the record straight.)

When they went to work it took a few days for them to get used to each other, but then magic happened. As the writer Michael Kanin later recalled, "Kate and Spence fell into a wonderful, natural working relationship. . . . It was easier for Kate. She had known men like Spence before. Like all the rest of us, Spence had never known anyone like Kate."

Off-screen both stars had married, but Hepburn's sole marriage had been a brief one, to the Philadelphia socialite Ludlow Ogden Smith, with whom she remained friends. She had a series of romances but no one with whom she wanted to go the distance. Tracy, on the other hand, was married with children. His wife, Louise, had been an actress on stage whom he had met early in his career. By the time Tracy and Hepburn met, Tracy was living apart from his family, though in constant contact with them. One of the problems that he and his wife had to deal with was that their first child, John, was born deaf. Louise eventually helped establish a clinic to help the hearing-impaired, and John learned to lip-read and to speak. As far the public knew, Tracy was devoted to his family, which, in his way, he was.

During the course of filming *Woman of the Year*, Tracy and Hepburn fell in love and started quietly seeing each other. It was known by friends and co-workers but kept out of the press. As one of Tracy's biographers put it in 1969, "In a town where nothing was sacred, this story seemed to be in a special category." The two would meet privately, Hepburn would respect Tracy's family ties, and the years passed. Occasionally reports appeared, but it wasn't until Garson Kanin's memoir *Tracy and Hepburn* was published in 1971 that the whole story was spelled out in public, four years after Tracy's death. Hepburn was furious at this invasion of their privacy, not to mention a breach of trust by a friend, and would not talk to Kanin for two decades. Late in life, with so many of their contemporaries gone, they finally reconciled. Said Hepburn, "Oh, I'm too old to be carrying grudges."

Following *Woman of the Year* she and Tracy appeared in several films, none of which quite hit the mark:

Keeper of the Flame (1942) reunited Hepburn and George Cukor, directing Tracy for the first time. It was a political melodrama with Hepburn playing the widow of a supposed great man and Tracy appearing as the snooping reporter uncovering the truth. Whatever the film's merits as a statement, it didn't do much for either star.

Without Love (1945) looked like a successful project on paper. Like *The Philadelphia Story*, it was based on a Philip Barry play that Hepburn had played on stage. Donald Ogden Stewart, Hollywood's best adapter of Barry plays, was called in to do the screenplay. The story, though, worked against the two stars. Tracy played a scientist who enters into a marriage of convenience with his assistant. Hepburn had some good lines, but the movie was stolen by Lucille Ball and Keenan Wynn in supporting roles.

Sea of Grass (1947) had Elia Kazan directing and a cast that included Melvyn Douglas and Robert Walker, but it was an overlong drama about farmers and ranchers fighting over grasslands in New Mexico. It was not what the public was clamoring to see.

Finally MGM realized that what they needed to do in order to capitalize on the success of *Woman of the Year* was to put these two stars together in a comedy where the sparks would fly. When Claudette Colbert opted out of Frank Capra's 1948 *State of the Union*, the part of Tracy's wife was offered to Hepburn. It was an odd part given their real-life situation. The story is about a Republican presidential candidate (Tracy) who ends up declining the nomination—and his mistress (played by the young Angela Lansbury)—in order to return to home and hearth. As Capra's follow-up to his career-capping masterpiece *It's a Wonderful Life* (1947), it showed a director who had pretty much said all he had to say. Unlike Jimmy Stewart's Mr. Smith, Tracy's Grant Matthews withdraws from the arena and gives up the fight. Worse, argues Capra biographer Joseph McBride, "The superficially outspoken but fundamentally submissive nature of Hepburn's character shows how much Capra's work was losing by his capitulation to postwar sexist ideology." Given the distorted echo of their real-life situation, one can only imagine how this made Tracy and Hepburn feel.

Clearly what the two stars needed was a movie in which they played characters not unlike themselves, where the love and bantering and joy at being with the other person could be fully expressed. Such a project was heading their way, in fact written with them specifically in mind. And it might never have happened if actor Raymond Massey and his wife Adrianne Allen hadn't gotten divorced.

*

Winter 1947.

The writer-director Garson Kanin and his wife, the actress Ruth Gordon, were driving to their home in Connecticut. The weather was miserable, and Gordon was getting carsick. Kanin tried to distract her by singing, but it didn't work. Perhaps he could get her mind off the weather and her nerves by having her talk. She started talking about car accidents. Just then, as Kanin told the story, they passed a sign that said, "Entering Connecticut."

"Tell me something interesting about Connecticut," he suggested.

Gordon tried to come up with something. At last she had it. "Well, the story of the Whitneys and the Masseys. That's pretty interesting."

It was quite a story. Raymond Massey and Adrianne Allen were both successful performers. Massey is probably best remembered today for such movies as *Abe Lincoln in Illinois* (1940) and *East of Eden* (1955), and, of course, for his playing of Dr. Gillespie on the 1960s TV series *Dr. Kildare*. Allen did some work on screen but was better known on stage. In any event, they had divorced several years earlier. When their marriage was faltering, they spoke to two friends of theirs, William Dwight Whitney and his wife Dorothy Whitney, both of whom were lawyers. The conversation between lawyers and clients must have been something, because when the dust settled, both the Masseys *and* the Whitneys ended up divorced. But the story didn't end there. Raymond Massey and Dorothy Whitney later married (and remained husband and wife until his death in 1983). Even that wasn't the punchline to the story. Adrianne Allen and William Dwight Whitney had *also* gotten married, and they too stayed together until parted by death.

There's probably an interesting movie to be made of such a complicated roundelay, but what intrigued Kanin was the initial notion of married lawyers who ended up on opposite sides of a case. He and Gordon continued to discuss the idea after they got home and began thinking in terms of a screenplay. They had already successfully collaborated in writing *A Double Life* (1947), for which they would receive an Oscar nomination. It earned an Oscar for its star, Ronald Colman, and a nomination for its director, George Cukor. It marked the start of a long collaboration between Kanin and Cukor, and he thought this lawyer idea might be just the ticket to a new project for them.

The next morning he and Gordon began fleshing out the story. Almost immediately they referred to the couple as "Spence" and "Kate," having already cast their friends Tracy and Hepburn in the lead roles of this script they were writing on spec. There was no guarantee any studio would buy it because they were doing it on their own, not on assignment. The finished script was called "Man and Wife," not only because of the married status of the lawyers but because they realized that the best kind of comedy would come out of a conflict that had them playing out the battle of the sexes in the courtroom.

They submitted the script to MGM, which snapped it up. Recalled the producer Lawrence Weingarten, "It was the first time in thirty years that the studio had seen a screenplay that was ready to shoot immediately, without changes." He was exaggerating, of course. The published version of the script indicates that there were a number of changes and additions made along the way, but nothing substantial. One change, however, the studio insisted upon up front: the title "Man and Wife" would have to go. For any other movie couple it might have worked, but given their real-life situation it was asking for trouble.

While the studio was satisfied, and Tracy and Hepburn signed on to play Adam and Amanda Bonner, the Production Code office was making demands. From the imposition of the Code in 1934, which had been successful in staving off government censorship, all movies released by the studios had to be approved by the industry censors. They examined not only the finished film but the scripts, the advertising, and the still photographs used to promote the movie. Studios routinely sent projects in the early stages of development, even novels they were considered purchasing for big-screen adaptation, in order to flag problem areas. While *Adam's Rib* may seem refreshingly innocent and wholesome today, MGM received a number of warnings before they went into production.

Since the case the two lawyers are arguing is about a woman who takes a potshot at her husband when she discovers he's having an affair, the censors saw a situation fraught with problems. "Adultery is not a proper subject for a comedy," they ruled, making it clear that the film should not make light of the institution of marriage. While they were at it, there was to be nothing mocking of our court system as well. Then there was David Wayne's character, Kip, who needles Adam much of the film. At one point he says he's so convinced by Amanda's case that "I may even go out and become a woman."

Adam's rejoinder is, "And he wouldn't have far to go, either."

Spencer Tracy and Katharine Hepburn square off as husband-and-wife attorneys on opposite sides of a case, but behind the scenes they were conspiring with director George Cukor to build up supporting player Judy Holliday (seen between them in the background).

This might have been a bit subtle for Peoria, but in the Production Code office they knew exactly what they were playing with. Cukor biographer Emanuel Levy points out that this is one of the few gay characters in a Cukor film (though Cukor was not above casting some of his gay actor friends in his films), and the censors put their foot down: "There shouldn't be even the slightest indication that Kip is a pansy."

Of course Kip, the songwriter, had not only Cukor as a model but the well-known songwriter Cole Porter, who found himself contributing Kip's song, "Farewell, Amanda," to the film. Originally Hepburn's character was to be named Madeline, and Kanin had composed a little ditty along those lines. One day he played it for Cukor and his stars. Tracy, perhaps in an impish mood, declared, "It's lousy. I like it." As Kanin recalled, Cukor and Hepburn only agreed with the first part of Tracy's review. Miffed, Kanin suggested they come up with something better.

It was Hepburn who suggested asking Cole Porter, then one of the most successful composers on Broadway. Even at MGM there was no way their modest comedy could budget what Porter would get for an original song. Kanin replied that they might as well ask Dwight D. Eisenhower to police the locations while they were shooting. But Hepburn wouldn't be put off.

That evening, as they gathered for dinner, Hepburn was late, which was unusual for her. When she showed up she announced that Porter would not be able to provide a song called "Madeline" for the film. This thoroughly confused everyone, but Hepburn would say no more. Toward the end of the meal the phone rang. It was Cole Porter. He'd provide a song, but they'd have to rename the character Amanda.

Hepburn had given him a copy of the script, and after reading it he had dug through his trunk pieces—songs written but never used—and found one he had done a few years before called "So Long, Samoa," which he had composed during a South Seas trip. He had rewritten the lyrics and now had "Farewell, Amanda," which is the number Kip sings in the film. They trooped over to Porter's New York residence where they met in his "glass room"—the walls, the ceiling, and all the fixtures and furniture were made of glass—and he performed it for them, to their delight. There remained the problem of his fee, which the *Adam's Rib* budget could not afford, but Porter was doing this as a favor for Hepburn and said he'd waive his fee if MGM would make an appropriate donation to the Damon Runyon Cancer Fund. Although the studio was thrilled to have it, it was considered one of Porter's lesser efforts. A *Time* magazine review said of the song that it sounded like something Porter might have written while waiting for a bus.

Porter didn't care. It cemented a friendship he treasured. He wrote his wife, "I think the nicest thing that has happened to me this summer has been getting to know Kate much better. She has a great quality and I am devoted to her."

*

Tracy and Hepburn had very different ways of preparing for a movie. According to Hepburn, they never, ever rehearsed their scenes together. The idea of working out their dialogue while they were together simply wouldn't have occurred to him. It's not the way he worked. As one Hepburn biographer noted, "By now, it was customary of a Kate-Spencer film that he would sit complacently on the sidelines until the cameras were ready to roll, then step forward casually and steal the scene. In contrast, Hepburn . . . would rehearse and worry a scene until she knew it inside out."

Tracy felt acting was a foolish profession—being paid to pretend you were someone you're not—and was often insecure about his career. It may well have been deeper insecurities at play, since Tracy was one of the greatest instinctual actors ever to grace the screen. Actors who worked with him would talk about watching him on the set to try to see how he did it, and coming away baffled because he had done nothing more than, as he famously advised young talent, learned his lines and not tripped over the furniture. Yet what seemed so ordinary on the set became magical on the screen.

Even Cukor, who directed Tracy in five movies—two without Hepburn—was amazed. Cukor once put it to Tracy, "You know, Spencer, I think of a lot of things to say to you, and I don't say them. But then I see the rushes, and it's all there, but I never see you do it."

So it was Cukor and Hepburn who went off researching while preparing for the film, including several days watching a Los Angeles murder trial. They were fascinated by how the defendant, a woman, came in dressed very gaudily on the first day of the trial but then toned herself down over the ensuing days. They would adapt that for the film. What most impressed Cukor, who had spent his life in theater and film, was the role of the judge. His experience with judges was primarily with movie judges; seeing the real deal in action was a revelation, albeit one that he had to put in his own terms: "I gradually understood what a judge does—he can listen to the law and interpret, and make sure the jury makes the right decision. He *directs* the jury—I hadn't known that."

Working with Tracy and Hepburn on the set, once everyone was ready to go, couldn't have been easier, whether on locations in the East or on soundstages in Hollywood. Both were well prepared, in their differing ways, and neither let their egos get in the way. Quite the opposite. During one scene the two stars used every trick in the book . . . to divert attention to the *other*. Each of them had moved so far back to give the scene to the other that Cukor shouted, "I can't see either of you. I really can't!"

Only once was there a dispute between the two, and it was really between Tracy and the producers. This came when it was time to plan the billing for the film, and Tracy insisted that he get top billing, over Hepburn. Kanin couldn't quite believe it. "Didn't you ever hear of 'ladies first'?" he asked.

"This is a movie, not a lifeboat," replied Tracy, whose name would be listed first in the credits.

If Tracy was growing more insecure, it may have been because his years of binge drinking were catching up with him. He was completely professional on the set but was known to take off occasionally for a bender, ending up at a cottage he rented on Cukor's estate to recover, often under Hepburn's care. The general public knew little of this. Tracy was only forty-nine but looked much older. Publicly he brushed it off with a joke: "Chocolates broadened me into a character actor." The following year a nationwide poll named him the actor who "most strongly influences women emotionally." The organization that had sponsored the poll sent Tracy a certificate for this "honor," which he had reframed and sent on to his old co-star Clark Gable with the notation, "Lest you forget."

Tracy and Hepburn continued to be together until his death in 1967, shortly after they filmed their ninth and final film together, *Guess Who's Coming to Dinner*. They also reunited with Cukor, Kanin, and Gordon in 1952 for *Pat and Mike* as well as appearing together in *Desk Set* (1957). Both had some of their greatest roles still to come.

*

Cukor secured a wonderful supporting cast for *Adam's Rib*, including four Broadway actors who were on their way to major acting careers. David Wayne was tapped for the role of Kip, the fey songwriter who professes his love for Amanda because of the convenience of her living across the hall. Tom Ewell was the pathetic excuse for a husband who was the "victim" of the shooting. Jean Hagen was the floozy whom Ewell was seeing at the time. All would go on to notable work on stage, screen, and/or television, with Ewell getting his signature role in the stage and film versions of *The Seven Year Itch* and Hagen achieving immortality as Lina Lamont in *Singin' in the Rain*. Wayne worked steadily in film and TV, but his greatest successes were on Broadway. Before *Adam's Rib* he had won a Tony Award (in that prize's first year) for playing the leprechaun Og in *Finian's Rainbow*. He would also appear in the original stage productions of many other shows, including *Mister Roberts* and *Teahouse of the August Moon*, for which he won his second Tony.

However good they all are in *Adam's Rib*, it was the fourth supporting player who won most of the attention, largely because Hepburn, Cukor, and Kanin conspired to see that it would be so. Judy Holliday was a minor actress and cabaret performer when she got her big break replacing Jean Arthur in the out-of-town tryouts of Garson Kanin's play *Born Yesterday*. Arthur was unhappy with the part and left the show. Holliday was brought in to play Billie Dawn, the kept woman of a vulgar junk-dealer-turned-tycoon who gets her private lessons so she can move in his new high-class social circles. When the show was a smash hit, Holliday became a star. Columbia Pictures obtained the movie rights for the show, and studio head Harry Cohn, a vulgar tycoon in his own right, decided he had no interest whatsoever in casting Holliday as Billie in the movie. He called her a "fat, Jewish broad" and noted that you could get away with that on stage but not on a movie screen.

So even though they were making a movie at MGM, the conspirators decided to offer Holliday the part of Doris—the betrayed housewife who takes a shot at her wayward spouse—in order to land her the *Born Yesterday* role at Columbia. It was a small part that Holliday ought not to have been interested in, but they promised to build it up for her. When the script was sent to Holliday, to their amazement she turned it down.

Shortly thereafter Holliday answered a knock at the door of her home to find Tracy and Hepburn there, urging her to change her mind. They told her how much they had liked her on stage. They explained how this featured role in *Adam's Rib* would do more than any screen test Columbia could offer in helping her get the *Born Yesterday* movie—and Columbia wasn't even offering to test her. According to Holliday's biographer, she had to step out of the room a moment, so overwhelmed was she that two stars she had long admired were coming to ask *her* to be in their movie. "She was not simply flattered," he wrote, "she was floored." Holliday was ready to be persuaded, but she had a problem with the script. Sensitive about her weight, she objected to a line referring to her character as "Fatso."

"Is that all?" replied Hepburn. "One word? It happens *once*."

Holliday made it clear it was a deal breaker, and Hepburn said, fine, it could be changed. When Holliday expressed surprise, Hepburn reassured her, "They're writers. They know lots of words."

Holliday then agreed to take on the role. Later, during filming, now more secure as an actress or with how she looked, or both, she insisted they restore the offending word.

During her first few scenes Holliday was so nervous she kept missing cues and blowing her lines. During breaks she would give the crew passes to the stage play of *Born Yesterday*, which she was still appearing in each night, so they could see she really did know how to act. (Already enjoying an extended run of the show, the producers graciously agreed to let her leave on short notice so she could continue filming

Adam's Rib in Hollywood. In turn, she offered to continue to work while the filming took place in New York, even though it meant she was putting in an almost twenty-hour day.)

Holliday's big scene comes when Amanda interviews her at the jail to prepare her defense. It is a long single take, with the camera favoring Holliday and Hepburn seen largely from the side and back. When it was suggested that perhaps they get some reaction shots of Hepburn, she refused, replying that "that's the way it's supposed to be."

Soon rumors began appearing in the gossip columns about how Tracy and Hepburn were annoyed that this upstart Judy Holliday was stealing the movie from them. She was getting a lot of publicity at the expense of the stars, and Hepburn was in fact delighted. She had been instrumental in getting Howard Strickling, MGM's publicity director, to put the word out about Holliday. At Columbia, Cohn had no reason to suspect he was being played and asked if MGM would mind sending over some footage of Holliday so he could have a look. It was the sort of courtesy the studio executives routinely extended, but thanks to Cukor and Hepburn, MGM sent not the raw takes of Holliday's scenes but the polished and edited versions. And they included a bonus not seen in the final movie version: close-ups of Holliday that weren't needed for the film but would show her to best effect. These shots were edited into the scene that Cohn saw.

In the end, Cohn may have had his doubts. But his glamour star Rita Hayworth had run off with Aly Khan and thus was unavailable, his other stars weren't quite right, and this "fat, Jewish broad" was apparently the hottest ticket in Hollywood. He signed her for the role. When *Born Yesterday* became a hit, and Holliday won the Oscar for Best Actress for it, he was presumably satisfied. The fact that she drove a hard bargain and wasn't fazed by him probably helped.

*

If *Adam's Rib* endures and seems modern to us today, it's because, in the end, no one really "wins" the battle of the sexes. Kanin and

Gordon's script—and Tracy and Hepburn's performances—ensures that each side gets a victory and a comeuppance. Unlike the stars' first pairing in *Woman of the Year*, the movie isn't about taking the successful career woman down a peg.

From the end of the trial to the end of the film there's one reversal after another, with the bravura moment coming when Adam pulls a gun on Amanda and Kip (who has been coming on strong to her but has been largely ignored) and she has to admit that such use of violence is wrong, even though it was precisely what she had been defending in court. Tracy's gleeful look as he bites off part of the gun, made of licorice, is priceless.

Some critics make too much of the final scene, in which Adam announces he's being put up for a "safe" Republican judgeship and Amanda casually asks if the Democratic candidate has been selected. It's a tease, not a threat. Having found their bearings again, this is a couple deeply in love, and part of their fun comes from their playful contention. Those who knew them well suggested that in this film, more than any other, we get a sense of what the two of them were really like together off-screen.

Certainly there's no denying the chemistry they had together. As Cukor put it years later in talking of *Adam's Rib*, "I think doing it without them would have been incomprehensible. They did something special with it."

Adam's Rib continues to play well today because it seems so modern. Amanda's insistence that there should be no double standard for men and women is born of not only Hepburn's (and Ruth Gordon's) independence and feistiness but the dawning of a new attitude about women's roles after they had contributed so greatly to the recent war effort. It would be more than a decade before Betty Friedan's *The Feminine Mystique* was published, but Amanda's case that women should be subjected to the same expectations as men anticipates the debates that would take place in the 1960s and 1970s.

Equally important, Tracy's Adam is no "male chauvinist" (as the type would come to be known) asserting manly prerogatives. He's arguing from principle, not piggishness, which is why his pulling the licorice gun on Amanda and Kip is so satisfying. He wins the argument with Amanda precisely because he's not saying, "Because I'm the man." He accepts her dismissal of double standards and shows she's wrong as a matter of plain justice.

In retrospect *Adam's Rib* seems years ahead of its time. That it is may be in no small part because Tracy and Hepburn's love for each other was years ahead of its time as well.

7

SABRINA

MAKING MOVIES is hard work. Stars may lead glamorous lives, but when they're on the set they're working, not playing. There are lines to learn, costumes and makeup to try, remote locations away from Hollywood, and difficult blocking to choreograph. It may beat digging ditches, but at work stars don't sit around sipping champagne and nibbling at caviar, regardless of what they may do between films.

Nonetheless some movies are a joy to make, when everyone enjoys the pleasure of one another's company, when off-screen romances provide motivation for the passion on screen, or when the work is simply so much fun that the people involved are sorry to see the production come to an end. What remains a mystery is why that feeling doesn't necessarily translate to the finished film. A great time is had during production, but the results are sometimes disappointing. Then there are movies like *Sabrina*, where audiences enjoy the airy, delightful romance and don't have a clue that for the people involved it was one of the most unpleasant experiences of their lives.

Watching *Sabrina* you don't realize that the director and co-stars despised Humphrey Bogart—and that the feeling was mutual. Nor will you notice that the movie's credited (and Oscar-winning) costume designer didn't do the work for which she receives the accolades while the real designer remains unacknowledged. You'll have no sense that one writer left the project in disgust while the other suffered a nervous breakdown. Likewise the physical pain that the director suffered throughout the filming is nowhere to be seen.

This is all as it should be. Hollywood is the dream factory, and we don't go to romantic comedies to experience someone else's nightmares. The only backstory that will be readily available to viewers is that *Sabrina* did what it was supposed to do: it cemented the reputation of Audrey Hepburn as one of the leading stars of Hollywood. That you can't see anything else in the finished film not only shows the professionalism of the people involved, it demonstrates that it is a mistake to make assumptions about the lives of the people who are part of the process, based solely on the movie itself.

*

For audiences in 1954, *Sabrina* was Hepburn's anticipated follow-up to *Roman Holiday* (1953), the movie that made her a star. Hepburn was born in May 1929. Her father walked out on the family when she was only six. One might make much of this trauma in describing Hepburn's formative years but for an even more important fact. In 1939, while she was staying at her grandfather's house in Arnhem, Holland, Germany invaded. Hepburn spent the entire war as a Dutch-speaking child and young teen in Nazi-occupied Holland, warned against speaking English or acknowledging her British father. One of the lasting impacts of this period—most noticeable to her fans—was that her spoken English sounded like no one else's. She had an accent and a tone that was unique.

After the war Hepburn continued her studies in hopes of a career in ballet, but in spite of a lithe figure that would soon become well known, she didn't have the build for ballet. Instead she performed on stage in musicals and began appearing in films. Her most notable early role, in retrospect, may have been her brief appearance in the classic Alec Guinness comedy *The Lavender Hill Mob* (1951), in which a young Hepburn may be seen briefly at the beginning as a cigarette girl in the restaurant where Guinness begins recounting his story.

Her big break came when a stage production of Colette's novella *Gigi* was planned. Colette herself, bedridden or wheelchair bound but still alert at seventy-eight, had seen Hepburn and thought she would be ideal for the part, though it would be her first substantial acting role. This led her to the starring role in *Roman Holiday*.

In a story that would become part of the Hepburn legend, the director William Wyler refused to do screen tests but, at studio insistence, allowed a screen test of Hepburn to be conducted by someone else. At the end of her scene—by prearrangement but unknown to her—the camera continued to roll while Hepburn was encouraged to talk about herself. When Wyler saw the footage, he was enchanted, and he agreed to cast her in *Roman Holiday*. Paramount was more reticent but was ready to approve this charming young unknown if a guaranteed star would play the reporter who escorted the princess on her "holiday." Wyler cajoled Gregory Peck into taking the part, even though Peck realized he would just be along for the ride. At his insistence, Hepburn was given star billing with him, even though he was entitled to have it all to himself.

The finished film was a critical success, if not quite the box office smash that Paramount had hoped for. Later film historians would note that except for immigrants and ex-GIs, most Americans in 1953 had not been to Europe and could not relate to the story and locale—but it succeeded in launching Hepburn's career. She made the cover of *Time*, no small feat in 1953 for an unknown actress in her first starring role. Then she won the Oscar for *Roman Holiday*, proof that she had indeed taken Hollywood by storm. The question became, what would she do next?

*

Samuel Taylor had a play called *Sabrina Fair* set to open on Broadway with Margaret Sullavan and Joseph Cotten. It concerned a chauffeur's daughter who is in love with one of the sons of the family her father works for, but finally ends up with the other. Hepburn read the play and told executives at Paramount that this seemed an ideal project for her next film. The studio acquired the film rights and tapped Billy

Wilder to direct. Wilder was not a readily obvious choice. True, he and Wyler were often confused with each other because of their similar names (and perhaps because they were both European Jews who had ended up in Hollywood), but Wilder's track record as a director, while impressive, didn't suggest that he was a master of light romantic comedy. At the time he was best known as the writer-director behind *Double Indemnity*, *The Lost Weekend*, *Sunset Boulevard*, and *Stalag 17*. All exhibited his sardonic humor, but none were love stories. Earlier in his Hollywood career, however, Wilder had apprenticed under Ernst Lubitsch, working on the scripts of such films as *Bluebeard's Eighth Wife* and *Ninotchka*, as well as other screwball classics for other directors, like *Midnight* and *Ball of Fire*. *Sabrina* would prove to be as important a film for him as it was for Hepburn.

For his part, Wilder was eager to work with the young star. As he told *Time* for their cover story, obliquely noting the kind of star—like Marilyn Monroe—then on the rise, "This girl single-handedly may make bosoms a thing of the past." This was Wilder at his most acerbic, which is the way he presented himself to the world and often expressed himself on film. In another comment on Hepburn, he speaks volumes about Hollywood in the 1950s in a single line: "She gives the distinct impression she can spell schizophrenia."

Wilder set out to work with Samuel Taylor, adapting his play, and an ideal cast was put in place: Hepburn, William Holden (whom Wilder had directed in *Sunset Boulevard* and *Stalag 17*, which earned the actor an Oscar), and Cary Grant. Wilder had long wanted to work with Grant, but it was not to be. Before shooting began, Grant dropped out of the project, as he would later put off Wilder for another Hepburn film, *Love in the Afternoon* (1957). In this later film the Grant part would go to Gary Cooper, with mixed results. Wilder could never understand Grant's refusal, telling one interviewer, "I very much wanted Cary Grant. Although he and I were friends, he never wanted to work with me. I don't know why. Maybe it was my accent." Wilder never gave up. Years later, after Grant had announced he was finished with the movies, Wilder still tried to lure him back.

Said Wilder, "When Cary retired, I started concocting stories for a man with gray hair in his early seventies, but he told me, 'No, I'm not going to do it anymore.'"

Grant's departure created major problems, but in fact headaches had appeared from the very day that Taylor showed up to begin adapting his play to the big screen. Wilder, who had learned his English from listening to radio shows and thus spoke a decidedly colloquial version, preferred to work with a collaborator even after he became a director. His most successful collaborations were with Charles Brackett and I. A. L. Diamond. He and Brackett had parted ways after *Sunset Boulevard* (Brackett launched his own career as a director), and he would not team with Diamond until *Love in the Afternoon* in 1957, a partnership that would continue to the end of Wilder's career even as Diamond took occasional forays on his own. It took a special kind of writer to work with Wilder, who could skewer his collaborator during the process and yet would insist on having his partner on the set during shooting in case changes needed to be made. This was highly unusual, but Wilder privileged the script over anything else and wanted his writing partner there for the duration. For writers who were used to the stage, where the playwright is king, it could be grueling. A typical story is the one about George Axelrod arriving to work with Wilder on adapting his hit play *The Seven Year Itch*. Axelrod brought along a copy of his play for them to use as a guide. Wilder dropped it to the floor and said, "Fine, we'll use it as a doorstop."

Taylor knew his way around Hollywood and knew that changes in his play, which had not yet opened, were inevitable, but he was not prepared for Wilder's wholesale reconstruction. When, after completion of an early draft, he could no longer stomach it, he departed. His play had opened on Broadway to good notices and ran for nine months. Meanwhile Wilder, who hated writing alone, now needed a collaborator, and the screenwriter Ernest Lehman was drafted. Lehman had just adapted the novel *Executive Suite*, and while the film had yet to be released, it helped secure his reputation. He would go on to write or adapt numerous screen classics: *The King and I, The*

Sweet Smell of Success, North by Northwest, West Side Story, The Sound of Music, Who's Afraid of Virginia Woolf? But in 1953, at age thirty-seven—a decade Wilder's junior—he was very much the employee, not the star writer.

Problems occurred throughout the scriptwriting process, not the least of which was caused by Grant's departure. In a romantic triangle with Hepburn and Holden, where his character of Linus was destined to win, it could have been a sophisticated romantic comedy of the sort that Grant had proven himself an acclaimed master. Now he was replaced by the biggest star they could find on short notice, Humphrey Bogart. Bogart was fifty-four and Hepburn only twenty-four, and however much Bogart had proven himself the romantic star opposite Ingrid Bergman in *Casablanca* and with his future wife Lauren Bacall in *To Have and Have Not* back in the 1940s, his casting created problems that would plague the production throughout shooting.

*

Bogart had arrived in Hollywood in the mid-1930s for the film version of *The Petrified Forest*. Born into a comfortable New York family, he had launched a stage career by often playing the sort of upper-class lad who might say, "Tennis, anyone?" His big break came with the stage production of *Petrified Forest* where, as gangster Duke Mantee, he held a group of people hostage in a roadside café. The play's star was the matinee idol Leslie Howard, but Bogart won his share of the notices, with scalpers getting top dollar for seats near the stage for those who wanted to see Mantee's stubble, since Bogart would shave only intermittently during the run of the play. When Warner Bros. acquired the movie rights, Howard said he'd agree to star in the film only if Bogart were permitted to play Mantee. Bogart was brought out to Hollywood and had his first big role, but this was Warner Bros. After *Petrified Forest*, when there was casting to be done for gangster roles, Bogart was at the bottom of a list headed by

Edward G. Robinson, Paul Muni, James Cagney, and George Raft. Bogart would get the occasional good role, like "Baby Face" Martin in *Dead End*, but more often he was the guy that Cagney or Robinson rubbed out in the final reel before facing his own fate.

By 1939 Bogart had had it. While he would have a notable role in *The Roaring Twenties*, he played in *Dark Victory* as an Irish stable hand and in *The Oklahoma Kid* as a cowboy (opposite an equally miscast Cagney). He reached the nadir of his career with *The Return of Dr. X*, in which he was cast as a mad scientist's assistant who is turned into a vampire. Bogart could see the handwriting on the wall when he was put into *Invisible Stripes*, a George Raft vehicle about ex-cons trying to make a go of it, where he was billed *beneath* newcomer William Holden. Holden had come to Hollywood as the young lead of *Golden Boy* and was nearly twenty years younger than Bogart. In one scene in *Invisible Stripes*, Holden was to drive a motorcycle with Bogart in the sidecar, and Bogart wasn't reassured by Holden's claim he knew what he was doing. He was even less assured when Holden crashed the bike. Injuries were minor, but it was the start of ill feelings between the two actors that would resurface fourteen years later.

Ready to quit Hollywood and return to New York, Bogart saw his chance with *High Sierra*, a 1941 film in which he got the lead role by default. The classic gangster cycle was over, and Muni had left Warner Bros. Raft, Cagney, and Robinson all turned down the part of "Mad Dog" Earle, the newly paroled gangster looking for one last score but finding that time had passed him by. It was the role that would launch Bogart to film stardom and, typically, Warners didn't know what they had. The young actress Ida Lupino was billed over Bogart in the film. After its release, however, Warners saw that they had a new star on their hands and began giving Bogart roles in the kinds of movies that filmgoers still revere today: *The Maltese Falcon, Casablanca, To Have and Have Not, Key Largo, The Big Sleep*. By the time he won the Oscar for *The African Queen* (1951), he was amazed by his own success and the respect of his peers.

Certainly *Sabrina* offered a great deal of star power. By the time the film was released in the fall of 1954, all three of its stars were Oscar winners: Bogart for *African Queen*, Hepburn for *Roman Holiday*, and Holden for *Stalag 17*. Besides having directed Holden to his award, Wilder had already won the first of his two directing Oscars for *The Lost Weekend*. (He would later win several Oscars for *The Apartment*.) The problem on *Sabrina* was not prestige but social ties. Holden was a Paramount star, and Wilder had spent his entire Hollywood career at the studio. (This would in fact be his final film there.) Hepburn was a Paramount star as well, by dint of *Roman Holiday*. Bogart, however, was a product of Warner Bros. and was used to working with directors like John Huston and Howard Hawks, macho types with whom Bogart felt comfortable. Wilder was a European Jew who collected art and was known for his sardonic humor. Wilder already had a good friendship with Holden (this was their third of four films together) and, like everyone in Hollywood at the time, he fell in love with Hepburn on sight. Already happily on his second marriage, Wilder kept his relationship warm but professional. (He quipped about the fact that his wife was also named Audrey: "It was good in case I talked in my sleep.")

Bogart was the outsider here. Already feeling resentful because he knew he had been the second choice for the role, he arrived for the production insecure and ready to take offense. It probably didn't help that he had just finished shooting *The Caine Mutiny*, where he played the suspicious and paranoid Captain Queeg. Some thought he carried the part with him into this next project.

When he and Wilder had met to discuss the part, they were joined by Samuel Taylor and Bogart's agent, Phil Gersh, who had suggested him for the role. They drank and kibitzed, and eventually ran out of time as each needed to be elsewhere. Bogart said, "Look, Billy, don't tell me the story. I just want to shake hands with you, that you'll take care of me. I don't have to read the script if I have your handshake." They shook hands. Everything was friendly. It would be a long time before things would be friendly between them again.

*

When shooting began on location in September 1953, the film might have seemed charmed in spite of casting and writer changes. They needed a large Long Island estate, and it just so happened that Barney Balaban owned one. It was no problem convincing him to allow the Paramount production to shoot in his backyard: Balaban was head of the studio. Even the inevitable problems on location weren't insurmountable. Scenes at the train station—where Sabrina the chauffeur's daughter returns in a glamorous Paris original—would have to be reshot back at the studio, but these things happen. The big problem was that Wilder and Lehman hadn't finished the script.

On some days actors would get their new lines shortly before shooting the scene. And on other days Wilder had nothing to shoot at all. They might do retakes of earlier scenes that needed to be re-done, but they would quickly run out of them. Once, Wilder asked Hepburn to feign a headache and retire to her dressing room until the scene was written. She accommodated him, even though it made her seem like a prima donna. But the script problems were no secret. One day Wilder told his assistant, Doane Harrison (billed as "editorial advisor" in the credits), "Please get the electricians to invent some complicated lighting effect for the next scene. Get them to do something that will take time."

Harrison agreed to do so but had to ask, "What for?"

"We haven't got the dialogue written yet."

Then there were the stories that Wilder planned to change the ending of the play, and that Sabrina would choose the younger brother after all. This played right into Bogart's growing insecurities, and Wilder didn't help matters when he told an interviewer why Sabrina had to end up with Linus: "But it is so logically and easily explained. Bogart was making $300,000 while Holden was getting only $125,000."

Bogart hated the talk that he was too old for Hepburn, even though he obviously was. After the film's release he answered reviewers who made that point by saying, "That talk I shouldn't get the girl is insulting. One of the things that Hollywood does is bury you after you reach the age of Tony Curtis [then a rising star]. The tombstone's already up."

Bogart took out his frustrations on the most convenient targets. He began snarling at Wilder about the quality of the script he *was* getting. One day as he read over the pages, he turned to Wilder and asked the director if he had any children. Wilder replied that he had a young daughter. "Did *she* write this?" asked Bogart, and it wasn't just in good fun. He was feeling increasingly like the outsider at a party to which he hadn't really been invited. This became literally true when Wilder, Lehman, Holden, and Hepburn would meet for a drink after work and Bogart was not asked along. Later they would claim they assumed Bogart wanted to get home to his wife, Lauren Bacall, and it's possible that was the case. But Bogart was insulted that he hadn't been asked even if he intended to turn them down.

"Those Paramount bastards didn't invite me?" he'd say, "Well, fuck them." The hard-drinking actor would have his own party. Every day toward the end of shooting he'd have his assistant bring a glass of scotch to the set, which he'd quickly down. His contract stipulated that he didn't have to work beyond 6 p.m. for day shoots, and he stuck to the terms to the letter. If an elaborate scene had been set up that would require just a few more minutes, Bogart wasn't interested. Come six o'clock he was out the door, to everyone else's exasperation. Holden, who did not return Bogart's enmity, could take only so much. After one such exit he turned to Wilder and asked, "You want me to kill him now or later?"

Considering all the animosity between them, initially caused by Bogart but eventually drawing in Holden as well, their big "fight scene" near the end of the film is actually one of the movie's lightest moments. David is trying to get Linus to admit he has feelings for Sabrina, and he does this by insulting her, leading Linus to take a swing at him. Wilder explained to Holden what he wanted: "It's very simple. You just take the blow, do a back flip, then roll down the length of the table."

Holden wasn't fazed. "I know, Billy. It's just the usual roll-down-the-board-table shot."

In the finished film Bogart takes his (fake) swing at Holden, who reels back, does a reverse somersault on the table, and ends up in the seat at the other side, completing his dialogue. It's not a trick shot. There's no cut and no stunt man. It's the still athletic Holden doing it all himself. If only the rest of the film had been that easy.

For Lehman, the constant pressure to write and rewrite, with an entire film production at a halt because he and Wilder hadn't finished a scene, grew to be too much. Wilder had chronic back pain that was acting up during the shooting of *Sabrina*, which didn't put him in a mood for coddling his collaborators, particularly in the crisis atmosphere on the set. As the production was on its final leg, Lehman suffered a nervous breakdown, exhausted and in tears. He later described it as "the scariest experience I've ever had in my life." Wilder instantly shifted gears. He might have an acidic sense of humor, but now was the time to take care of the man who had, after all, helped Wilder get through the script. The director sent Lehman home where his doctor ordered two weeks of bed rest.

Being away from the set worked wonders for Lehman, who made a full recovery. As his doctor left one day—in a scene that might have come from a Billy Wilder movie—he turned to Lehman and said, "You can tell Mr. Wilder to come out now." The director had come over for consultation on just a few details, and when he heard the doctor's arrival he had hidden in the closet. It says something about Wilder's regard for the written word that he would not make changes in a script without the approval of his collaborator.

*

Sabrina is the story of a romantic triangle in which Sabrina (Hepburn) loves David (Holden) but has to end up with Linus (Bogart). It didn't help that Bogart mocked Hepburn's clipped way of speaking and the fact that she was still learning the skills of moviemaking. This was her

Audrey Hepburn's character gets over a crush on William Holden and falls instead for the older brother played by Humphrey Bogart—while off-camera the situation was quite different.

first big Hollywood studio film—*Roman Holiday*, after all, had been shot on location—and she was picking up the basics that had long become second nature to Bogart, now in his third decade in the industry.

Nor was Bogart private about his complaints. When he ran into the actor Clifton Webb, Webb asked him, "How do you like working with that dream girl?"

Bogart replied, "She's okay if you like to do thirty-six takes."

Part of the problem was that Wilder was clearly favoring Hepburn during the shooting of her scenes with Bogart, and the actor knew it. Bogart told his agent, "I don't even need my hairpiece; the guy's shooting me from behind."

That you can see none of this in the finished film speaks volumes about Bogart's professionalism when the cameras were on. He had learned the skills of acting on film, and he would know his lines, hit his marks, and do whatever was required. Wilder called him "a strange mixture of the laziest and most conscientious actor." Bogart would learn everything he needed for the shot about to be filmed, but he would not learn the whole scene. His awkwardness in the part fits his character, and he received mostly good reviews for his performance. Perhaps the one line of dialogue that Wilder or Lehman slipped in as a nod to Bogart's past as a screen gangster came in a scene where David is recovering, having sat on two champagne glasses. He's now lying on his stomach in a hammock of Linus's devising, permitting his buttocks to heal. Bogart's exit line is priceless: "So long, Scarface."

Such moments were rare during the production. As hostilities grew, Bogart would try to rile Wilder with insults, calling the Jewish director who had lost his mother and other family members in the Holocaust a "Nazi" and recounting a conversation about the great Hollywood directors with John Huston where Wilder's name pointedly *didn't* come up. Wilder refused to rise to the bait. "Bogart had a peculiar sense of humor," said Wilder. "It was both uncouth and sadistic. But I learned from the master, Erich von Stroheim. Compared to him, Bogart was a kindergarten pupil. You have to be much wittier to be good and mean."

While all this was going on, with Hepburn having to act out Sabrina's transfer of affections from David to Linus, something quite different was taking place off-camera. It was Ernest Lehman who discovered it. He had gone to Holden's dressing room to drop off the latest pages and discovered him there with Hepburn. "They were standing a foot apart, facing each other, their eyes meeting. Something profound was happening between them."

Holden was married to the actress Brenda Marshall and tended to be conservative, but not when it came to his private romances. He fell for Hepburn hard, and she was not immune to his obvious charms. Depending on whom you believe, they began either an affair or one of the most intense chaste relationships on record. (For his part, Wilder played the agnostic: "People on the set told me later that Bill and Audrey were having an affair, and everybody knew. Well not *everybody*! *I* didn't know. I still don't know.") Certainly the feelings were strong, and there was some talk that Holden would seek a divorce to marry Hepburn. But things took a turn for the worse when Holden revealed he had had a vasectomy, an operation which in 1953 was deemed irreversible. Hepburn wanted a large family. Already involved with the actor Mel Ferrer, who was in the midst of his own divorce, she broke off with Holden.

Holden's reaction says much about the intensity of his feelings. He later went on a round-the-world trip, determined to have a fling in every country he visited. That would show her. When he returned he sought out Hepburn and told her what he had done, perhaps intending that she become jealous. Instead she looked at him with disappointment and said, "Oh, Bill."

Recalled Holden, "That's all. 'Oh, Bill.' Just as though I were some naughty boy. What a waste."

They remained friends and were even reunited on-screen a decade later in *Paris—When It Sizzles*.

*

After shooting the film, everyone went their own ways. Hepburn and Holden were reunited with Wilder in separate films many years apart; Bogart would be dead in three years from the cancer that may already have played a role in his behavior during shooting. He and Wilder smoothed over whatever bad feelings they may have had. Three years later, as Bogart was dying, many members of Hollywood royalty came to pay their respects, including Wilder. He later recalled, "He was very brave and, in the end, I forgave him everything and held him in the highest esteem."

But to end the story of *Sabrina* here would overlook one of the farthest-reaching uproars over the film, though it occurred far from the set. When Hepburn had signed for *Roman Holiday*, she had been turned over to Edith Head, the famed costume designer, who would plan her outfits for the film. Head and Hepburn hit it off immediately. Head recalled about that first meeting, "Her figure and flair told me, at once, here was a girl born to make designers happy. . . . Audrey knows more about fashion than any actress since [Marlene] Dietrich."

Now here she was in California making plans for *Sabrina* and Head was once again assigned the costuming chores. She and Hepburn went on a shopping spree, looking over current fashions. Head had paper dolls made up with Hepburn's face that they could use to sketch ideas for designs. Given that the movie would show the transformation of Sabrina from a gangly servant's daughter to a chic, Paris-educated woman, Head was relishing designing the gowns and dresses for Hepburn.

But someone—perhaps Hepburn, or Wilder, or even Wilder's wife, Audrey—had the idea that instead of Hollywood imitations of Paris designs, why not send Hepburn to Paris and get the real thing? Hepburn, every bit as knowledgeable about clothes as Head believed, relished the idea. According to David Chierichetti, an expert on Hollywood design and a confidante of Head's, "Hepburn said that 'Edith was very good about it,' but if Hepburn truly believed that, then Edith was a better actress than most, for she was seething, even thirty years later."

While Head fumed, Hepburn went off to Paris where, at Audrey Wilder's suggestion, she approached the famous designer Balenciaga to see if he would make her clothes for the film. Instead he sent her to his protégé, Hubert de Givenchy, then just twenty-six and in the process of establishing his own house of design. In an oft-repeated story, Givenchy was told that the famous actress "Miss Hepburn" was coming to see him about some outfits for a film, and he eagerly anticipated meeting the famous Katharine Hepburn. Instead, in walked the lovely but largely unknown Audrey.

"My first impression was of some extremely delicate animal," he recalled. "She had beautiful eyes, and she was so extraordinarily slender, so thin."

The designer may have been taken by her beauty, but he was in the midst of designing the next season's line and had no time to give her his attention. They agreed that she would look over his current fashions, and if she saw something she liked, she would be able to buy it. "She knew exactly what she wanted," said Givenchy.

It would be the start of a great friendship between the two. "I depend on Givenchy in the same way American women depend on their psychiatrists," Hepburn would later say, not entirely joking. But first they had to contend with Edith Head.

Like Sabrina, Hepburn returned to the United States with a designer wardrobe. Unlike Sabrina, Hepburn had to deal with the powers at Paramount. The legal department advised her to declare the outfits as her personal clothing upon her return, thus avoiding the heavy taxes that might apply if she declared them to be costumes being imported into the country for a Hollywood film. The legal ramifications of that action became clear in the finished film, where the sole costume credit went to Head. Givenchy's name was nowhere to be found. Hepburn discovered this at an early screening of the film where the designer was her guest. She was supremely embarrassed.

Upon the film's release, Givenchy's cocktail dress with the angular neckline created a sensation and would soon be copied as the "Sabrina neckline." As far as the public knew, however, this was all the work of Head, who said nothing even as she won her sixth Oscar—the sole win for *Sabrina*—for costuming in a black-and-white film. Years later she was called on her continued omission, even in failing to correct the mistake in books when she had the opportunity to do so. Head, who won two more Oscars in a career that continued up to her death in the early 1980s, was unrepentant. "I lied. So what? If I bought a sweater at Bullock's Wilshire, do I have to give them credit too?"

If Givenchy was miffed, he could afford to move on. He was a Paris designer, after all, whose fortunes didn't rise or fall with the Hollywood box office. In just a few years his name would appear on Hepburn's films, even when the rest of the costumes were designed by Head, and it would make him a well-known name in the United

States. "Audrey Hepburn . . . made my house so well known that many prominent Americans decided to 'wear Givenchy,'" said the designer. "Thanks to Audrey, my clientele became essentially Anglo-Saxon."

Givenchy dressed Hepburn off-screen for years, and for many of her best-known films, including *Charade, Love in the Afternoon* (directed by Wilder again), and *Breakfast at Tiffany's*. Although he didn't win, he had the honor of an Oscar nomination for Hepburn's musical with Fred Astaire, the 1957 film *Funny Face*. In it Hepburn is a fashion model and Astaire is a photographer (inspired by real-life fashion photographer Richard Avedon). In one of life's ironies, Givenchy had to share the nomination . . . with Edith Head.

*

For all the turmoil in its making, *Sabrina* on screen is a light, airy, and delightful romantic comedy, with none of the stars giving the slightest indication of their off-camera conflicts or liaisons. It was a success for all concerned. Yet the stars were to be denied the happily-ever-after endings of their characters.

Years later, looking back, director Billy Wilder (who died three months short of his ninety-sixth birthday in 2002) was saddened to have outlived his stars in *Sabrina*. Bogart had succumbed to cancer in 1957; he was only fifty-seven. Holden died in 1981 at the age of sixty-three, from injuries sustained in a fall in his home. Hepburn was also only sixty-three when she died in 1993 of colon cancer.

In spite of his sardonic humor, Wilder found something especially bitter about this. "I miss them very much," he said of Holden and Hepburn. "I never expected to be missing *them*. They should have been missing *me*. It was all out of turn."

8

PILLOW TALK

OF THE on-screen romantic duos who would win the hearts of moviegoers, none was more unlikely than Doris Day and Rock Hudson. She was a singer/actress in a troubled marriage whose career was on the skids. Her previous few films had opened with a thud, and she was no longer a happy member of the Warner Bros. stable. She faced a possible slow fade to obscurity. Meanwhile Hudson was one of the new generation of stars, who had risen in the fifties, who seemed to be cast for their youth and looks rather than any immediately apparent acting talent. Hudson would prove the naysayers wrong, but in 1959 he had a mostly middling career behind him and no experience at all in romantic comedy. He was recently divorced and, as was known to only a few people at the time, had a secret that could have destroyed his career if it were made public. He was gay.

Surprisingly, their match-up in *Pillow Talk* in 1959 was one of the biggest hits of the year. Audiences positively adored their on-screen chemistry. This may be surprising to readers too young to have seen the film upon its release. Of all the films in this book, it is the one least able to transcend its time. Its creaky, misogynistic plot—which seemed like a breath of fresh air and incredibly daring in 1959—makes this more of a period piece today than a timeless comedy. Yet its influence persists, both in the myths that have grown up around the film and in the fact that so many viewers who never saw it or saw it years ago have strong feelings about it. A sign that the mythology around the film survives was the terribly unfunny 2003 send-up of *Pillow Talk* and its genre, *Down with Love*. It was released to a generation that not only wouldn't recognize what was being spoofed, but most likely missed the in-joke casting of Tony Randall as a tip of the hat to his roles in the Day/Hudson films.

Going back to the original *Pillow Talk* tells us much about where we were and where we would be going.

*

Doris Kappelhoff was born in Cincinnati, Ohio, in 1924. As a girl she won a talent contest dancing with another child, and their mothers made plans to launch them on a professional career. But at age fifteen Doris was injured in a car accident, severely damaging her leg. During her recuperation she took a fall and suffered another break. Any chance of a dancing career was over before it even started. Yet the spunky characters she would later play found their basis in the real woman and how she coped with these crushing setbacks. Recovering from her injuries, she began singing with various vocalists on the radio. Her mother arranged for her to having singing lessons. At an early age she developed a style that would stand her in good stead as an actress. Her teacher, a woman named Grace Raine, told her, "Sing each song as if you are singing directly to one person, not a large audience. You're acting."

From a local restaurant to an Ohio radio show with a national audience was just a few short steps. It was the bandleader Barney Rapp who persuaded her to change her name. While she was working at his club, he told her that Kappelhoff was a bit too much of a name for advertising. He suggested Day, and it was Doris Day she became—even though she didn't care for it. As she recounted in her memoirs, "I never did like it. Still don't. I think it's a phony name." It was a feeling she would later share with Hudson. On the sets of their films, and forever after, he would call her Eunice and she would call him Ernie. Their joke was that these unsexy nicknames better described who they were than the names they performed under.

Newly rechristened, Doris Day was soon singing with some of the leading bands of the day. Off-stage, though, things were not as pleasant. By the time she was eighteen she had been married to and divorced from musician Al Jorden. Incidents of abuse were alleged. Not only was she was a young divorcee, she was also a mother. She returned to singing on local radio, where she attracted the attention of the bandleader Les Brown (with whom she had previously performed), and suddenly she was on the road singing again, her little boy left in the care of her mother. Before the end of World War II, Day had recorded several hit songs, especially "Sentimental Journey," which put her on the map. A country weary of war embraced the song and its singer, giving her a measure of fame that soon translated into a movie career.

Her break came with the 1948 musical *Romance on the High Seas*. Judy Garland had been the first choice for the lead, but the deal had fallen through. Betty Hutton was the next choice, but she got pregnant. Warner Bros. did not have a stable of musical comedy stars to draw on, and when Day's name came up the director Michael Curtiz (whose career included *Yankee Doodle Dandy* and *Casablanca*) agreed to meet with her. She won the part, and if it wasn't quite a star being born, it was certainly a career launched.

Over the next few years Day made a number of films, many of them forgettable but a few of them standouts. By the mid-1950s she was indeed a star, appearing in movies like *The Pajama Game* and *The Man Who Knew Too Much*, a remake by Alfred Hitchcock of one of his British films from the 1930s. It allowed Day to introduce what became one of her signature songs, "Que Sera Sera." While she was developing as an actress, she was still not sure of herself. During the Hitchcock shoot she became convinced that the director hated her and might even have her replaced. When she asked for a meeting with him, he was surprised to hear that she thought she was not meeting his expectations. She had taken his lack of direction for disdain when, as he explained, it meant she was performing perfectly.

By the late 1950s, though, Day's career was running out of steam. No longer at Warners, she was free to pick and choose her projects.

Tunnel of Love paired her with Richard Widmark in a Gene Kelly–directed comedy about a couple trying to adopt a child. *It Happened to Jane* had her running a Maine lobster operation with Jack Lemmon as her attorney and Ernie Kovacs as the comic villain. Both pictures fizzled. Doris Day had tried to reinvent herself as a serious actress, and while the Hitchcock film had done well, her fans were miffed at her starring as singer Ruth Etting in *Love Me or Leave Me*, used and abused by a gangster played by James Cagney. Clearly she needed some new way to attract audience favor. It was the producer Ross Hunter who would be her savior.

*

Ross Hunter was one of the last of the old-fashioned Hollywood producers. He rejected the notion that audiences wanted more realism on screen. In his mind they wanted the same thing they had always wanted: glamour. Early in his career, in 1952, he was asked where he was headed. "I would like to do a movie about the beautiful people," he said. A former actor, he had scored big in 1954 with *Magnificent Obsession*, a remake of a 1934 tearjerker about a playboy who becomes a surgeon so that he can restore the sight of a woman he has injured in a car accident. It was the sort of movie that had little interest for studio executives and critics, but which the public loved. Directed by Douglas Sirk (whose own career would be discovered and reevaluated by a later generation of critics), it was a solid hit for Jane Wyman and Rock Hudson, who finally had a breakthrough role after a number of forgettable movies. Even before *Magnificent Obsession* was released, it was screened by Hunter and Hudson's agent for the director George Stevens, then on the verge of casting William Holden as the male lead in his epic *Giant*. As a result, Hudson got the role, achieving new consideration as a real actor.

Hudson had been born Roy Fitzgerald in 1925 and had his first encounter with Doris Day—or at least her voice—while in the navy at the end of World War II. As his ship was departing San Francisco, the ship's speakers began playing "Sentimental Journey." The sailors had no idea that one of their number would be linked on-screen with the singer fourteen years later. (The song apparently brought up quite different feelings for Day. When Hudson recounted the incident to her years later, he recalled, "She just looked at me and said, 'Oh,' and walked off. For some reason, she wasn't impressed.")

By the late fifties Hudson's career had struck a rut. He had starred in the remake of *A Farewell to Arms*, based on the Ernest Hemingway novel. The producer David O. Selznick, making his final film, had cast his wife Jennifer Jones opposite Hudson. Some viewers found them both miscast, and the results were mixed. Hunter, however, was sold on Hudson as a star and had used him several times, scoring another hit with *All That Heaven Allows*. Now, though, Hudson was in much the same boat as Day. His career was going nowhere, and it had been a few years since his biggest hits and best films. Hunter's lifeline was greeted with gratitude by the two stars, but also with skepticism. He wanted to team them up for a sex comedy.

Day cultivated a wholesome and clean-cut image, and for her this would be a very different role. Although her success in *Pillow Talk* would lead to Oscar Levant's famous crack, "I knew Doris Day before she was a virgin," the character she played—as we shall soon see—was anything but a virgin. As for Hudson, his concern was not that he was a closeted gay but that the film was a comedy. He had done dramas and westerns and war movies but had no experience at all in this kind of role. He wasn't sure he was up for the part.

Hunter told Day that he understood the sort of role she could do well better than she did herself. "Doris hadn't a clue to her potential as a sex image," Hunter said, "and no one had realized that under all those dirndls lurked one of the wildest asses in Hollywood. I came right out and told her: 'You are sexy, Doris, and it's about time you dealt with it.'" Day allowed herself to be convinced. Looking back, she saw what a break it was from her earlier films: "The plot, for 1959, was quite sexy, and even involved a climactic scene in which the leading man grabbed me from bed and carried me, in my pajamas, down an elevator, through the lobby, and out onto the street. Clearly, not the kind of part I had ever played before."

Indeed, one of the enduring myths about this film—taken as gospel by film historians, critics, academics, and the general public—is that in *Pillow Talk* and in subsequent comedies of the same ilk she was playing a virginal character who attempted to protect her chastity until marriage. But that view completely misses the point of the film. Day's character, Jan, in *Pillow Talk* is almost (but not quite) as daring as Katharine Hepburn's in *Adam's Rib*. She's an independent woman with a successful career as an interior decorator. She has no husband and no children, not that that seems to bother her, and she doesn't worry about taking care of her own home since she has a maid (played by the great character actress Thelma Ritter) to take care of the cooking and cleaning. Instead Jan gets to go around in fashionable, sexy outfits by Jean Louis and feels free to accept or reject the attentions of the men around her. Ultimately Jan and Brad (Hudson) do not bed before marriage, but that's his fault, not hers. When Jonathan (Tony Randall) sends Brad away for the weekend to finish the songs for a show Jonathan has invested in, Brad—as Tex, the alter ego he has adopted to woo Jan—invites her to come along. She willingly agrees. She doesn't ask who else will be there or what the sleeping accommodations are. They're two grown-ups, and they know exactly what is implied by his invitation. So what goes wrong?

It's the plot, not Day's character, that intervenes. Brad is the obnoxious person with whom she shares a party line and whom she detests. They've never met before, so when they do finally cross paths and Brad is smitten, he pretends he's someone else. Worse, he continues the charade, even having Brad insult Tex so as to make his Tex persona more appealing to Jan. If it's confusing to read about, one can imagine how humiliating it was to be the butt of this charade. When Jan discovers Brad's duplicity, she walks out on him, and not because she's standing up for eternal female purity. As the perceptive Tom Santopietro puts it in his book-length examination of Day's career, "All of the jokes about Doris Day's perpetual virginity made people

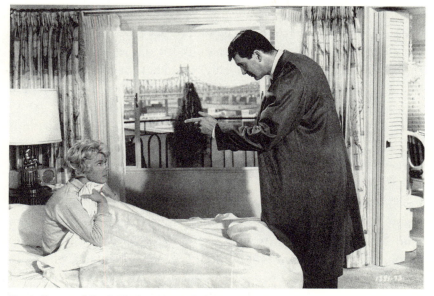

Doris Day and Rock Hudson rescued their careers with a sex comedy in which moviegoers assumed her character was a virgin and nearly everyone assumed the actor was straight in real life. Neither was true.

forget what these films were really all about. It certainly wasn't about her refusal to have sex: It was about demanding truth and respect from the men in her life."

Molly Haskell, the groundbreaking feminist film critic, writing in the early 1970s, saw in Day not a repressed figure but an Everywoman, someone a lot closer to American reality than the European film actresses her colleagues swooned over. Wrote Haskell, "Actually it is the comical obstacle course of Doris Day's life, her lack of instinctive knowledge about 'being a woman,' and the concomitant drive, ambition, and energy that are closer to the American reality than the libidinous concentration of Jeanne Moreau or the metaphysical purity, uncomplicated by the little details of life, of Ingmar Bergman's women."

Most telling of all was Sara Davidson's experience when she was working on what would become Hudson's posthumous memoir and went to see Day. "I was astonished, when I interviewed Doris Day twenty-six years later, to learn she did not feel she was playing a virgin." Day told Davidson, "I don't think I was a virgin. I went off to the country with him and I probably would have succumbed, except I found out he was a phony and ran away. The audience—*you* thought I was a virgin."

When *Pillow Talk* became one of the biggest hits of the year, it revived Day's movie career. She would be the nation's top box office attraction for four years running. Ross Hunter understood best what he was doing for her image. It may be hard to imagine today, but *Pillow Talk* was positioning Day as a sex idol. If American women had trouble seeing themselves as Marilyn Monroe or Audrey Hepburn (and American men had trouble seeing themselves with Monroe or Hepburn except in their fantasies), Doris Day presented a wholly attainable vision of what a modern American woman could be circa 1959. When Day balked at the notion of doing a sex comedy, he told her, "If you allow me to get Jean Louis to do your clothes, I mean a really sensational wardrobe that will show off that wild fanny of yours, and get some wonderful makeup on you, and chic you up and get a great hairdo that *lifts* you, why, every secretary and every housewife will say, 'Look at that—look what Doris has done to herself. Maybe I can do the same thing.'"

Hunter had to do a similar job convincing Hudson. At least they had a track record together, since he had produced a number of Hudson's previous movies. Hudson reluctantly agreed to take the plunge.

Although they had not previously met, it helped that Day and Hudson had an easy rapport working together and an undeniable chemistry on-screen. Neither of them took themselves too seriously. Moreover Hudson appreciated that Day knew a lot more about playing comedy than he did, since he had never done it before. "Doris gave the best acting lessons I ever had; her sense of timing and instincts were terrific. I just kept my eyes open and copied her."

Hudson recalled going to the director Michael Gordon for advice: he was nervous about trying to get laughs. Gordon's advice was not to notice it was a comedy. "Just treat it like the most tragic story you've ever portrayed. . . . If you think you're funny, nobody else will."

Nonetheless, making the film turned out to be fun. Day and Hudson got to the point where they could make each other start laughing in the middle of a scene. Off-camera the antics continued with a silly game in which they tried to top each other with reports of excruciatingly boring—and wholly imaginary—vacation plans. Though they had a good working relationship, Day remained in the dark about Hudson's private life.

It wasn't only sex that had to be carefully suppressed and packaged in the 1950s. Politics was also on Hollywood's agenda. Since November 1947 the studios had blacklisted those who were charged with being Communists or who had supported causes deemed to be "pink," and many actors, writers, and directors suddenly found themselves unemployable. By 1959 the blacklist had begun to unravel, but for some people it was still a time where a single wrong move could end a career. Tony Randall discovered this not through any accusation directed against himself, but because he objected to a joke. Randall had come to prominence on television in the 1950s, particularly as part of the cast of *Mr. Peepers*. He had made his big-screen debut with *Oh, Men! Oh, Women!* (1957), with Nunnally Johnson directing and co-writing this adaptation of his Broadway hit. His greatest success lay ahead with his five seasons as Felix Unger in the TV version of Neil Simon's *The Odd Couple*, but he was also part and parcel of the Day/Hudson films, appearing in all three of them as Hudson's friend and in *Pillow Talk* as his putative romantic rival.

When Randall showed up for his first scene, he asked the director for the new pages. Michael Gordon knew nothing about any new pages and said so. Randall said he had objected to the stupid jokes about psychiatry and had been promised they would be rewritten. If they were not, he would not play the scene. This was presumably less about ego than principle, but either way Randall was adamant. At a loss, Gordon called an early lunch. Randall wandered over to the studio commissary, where Ross Hunter found him.

"What are you trying to do?" Hunter demanded.

Randall was stunned. "What do you mean?"

"Are you trying to destroy the man?"

Thinking this was about the psychiatry jokes, Randall repeated that he had been promised the lines would be rewritten. But Hunter brushed that aside. "This is the first day Mike has worked in five years. He's been blacklisted. And you practically destroyed him in front of the entire crew. If you destroy him now he'll probably never work again for the rest of his life."

If objecting to stupid jokes about psychiatry had been a matter of principle, this was a far more important principle. It had not been Randall's intention to embarrass Gordon, and he decided he must apologize. Since he had seemingly attacked Gordon in public, to Randall the only way to properly make up for that was to apologize to him publicly. He returned to the set and did just that in front of the entire crew. This may have been a sex comedy, but the highly political tensions that had led to the blacklist were still in place.

The only other problem during the making of the film was the climactic scene in which Jan has exacted her revenge on Brad by redecorating his bachelor pad to look like a bordello. Brad correctly sees that such intense feelings must mean she really loves him, if only she will forgive him. So he goes to her apartment, finds her in bed, and then bodily picks her up and carries her down to the street, over to his building, and then up to his apartment. The strapping Hudson was clearly up to the task . . . once. But movie scenes are shot over and over, sometimes to get different angles, sometimes because there's a mistake. It didn't help that in the sequence they pass a police officer, and when Jan asks to be rescued, the cop says, "How are you doing, Brad?" That's what he was supposed to say, but he kept blowing his line by calling him "Rock."

In any case, either Hudson was about to strain something or Day was going to be unceremoniously dumped on the "fanny" Ross Hunter wanted everyone to see, so they had to rig a platform and wires to carry Day and create the illusion that it was Hudson doing the carrying all by himself. According to Hudson, it was a "shelf" with two hooks attached to wires, with Day sitting on it. All he had to do was hold her legs and shoulders as they went through some twenty takes. Through the magic of the movies, though, it's all he-man Rock Hudson, without any help at all. The scene ensured that he would be a sex symbol—a heterosexual one—for some time to come.

*

Of all the films in this book, *Pillow Talk* probably has the least to say to us today. Where *My Man Godfrey* is a period piece and yet is still immensely entertaining seventy years later, *Pillow Talk* seems less the throwback to screwball comedies it seemed to 1959 audiences than an odd time capsule of a culture on the verge of the sexual revolution. Even Michael Gordon, looking back years later, admitted, "I have certain misgivings about it. It stemmed out of a certain male-chauvinist view. An amusing picture, though, no question."

The critic Marjorie Rosen writes of Day's character as being on the cusp of two very different views of woman's place in the world: ". . . Doris managed to combine a quite modern ability to express her anger at men and a certain élan in taking care of herself with a comfortingly old-fashioned attitude toward love and marriage. Those older audiences who disapproved of the disturbing changes in morality found her a pleasant ally in their bewilderment. . . ."

One can only imagine how bewildered those 1959 audiences would have been had they known that Rock Hudson was gay. Before we get too smug in declaring that actors are playing roles and therefore should be able to take on any part, let's note that even today there are few openly gay and lesbian performers, and those who are inevitably end up in character parts. Ellen DeGeneres's most notable movie role in recent years was as a cartoon fish in *Finding Nemo*. Nathan Lane is deservedly the toast of Broadway, but his movie roles have included being the voice of a cat (*Stuart Little*) and a meerkat (*The Lion King*), and playing the flamboyant showman Max Bialystock in the film of his Broadway smash musical of *The Producers*. Some stars are rumored to be gay, but if they are they have remained deliberately closeted in public so that their choice of roles is not limited. Yet straight actors can take gay roles. They can even win Oscars for them, as William Hurt did for *Kiss of the Spider Woman* and Tom Hanks did for *Philadelphia*. That's different, says the public, they're *acting*. A double standard persists. It may not be as harsh as it was for Hudson, but it's there nonetheless.

Even in Hollywood, it was okay for a director like George Cukor to be "out" about being gay, because it meant only that it wasn't a secret from his friends and associates in the industry. He was discreet, and the general public wasn't much interested in the private lives of the people *behind* the camera. Those on-camera were another story. Although the Production Code forbade any depiction of homosexuality on screen, there were certain characters or actors who audiences knew were "different." One of the most famous examples is Clifton Webb, who in one of his films played the acid-tongued newspaper columnist Waldo Lydecker in the 1944 mystery *Laura*. When Webb was first suggested for the part, studio executives balked. If Webb played the part, they argued, people would think the character was homosexual. But that was precisely the point. Webb was cast and proved to be brilliant in the part.

For a leading man like Rock Hudson, however, such a reputation would be the kiss of death. Vito Russo, perhaps the foremost historian of how Hollywood has depicted gays, succinctly explained the studio mind-set: "If someone said that, for instance, Rock Hudson was gay, then the reaction was, 'Why do you hate Rock Hudson so?' People didn't think about outing in terms of truth, they thought about it as a way of harming someone's reputation. . . ."

So Hudson remained closeted for most of his life. Only when he was diagnosed with AIDS in the 1980s did it became known. To their credit, former co-stars like Doris Day and Elizabeth Taylor (who had appeared with him in *Giant*) rallied to his side. Yet if secrecy was the price to be paid for success in the movies and still have a satisfying private life, there were times when it must have hurt. At the very least, Hudson must have wondered about these romantic comedies that inserted jokes about gays while having a gay man portraying what was being sold as the heterosexual ideal.

In *Pillow Talk* there's a scene where Brad is mocking his alter ego Tex to Jan, presumably so that she'll want to spite Brad by becoming more interested in Tex. He tells her, "Some men are very devoted to their mothers. They like to exchange cooking recipes." Viewers sophisticated enough to read between the lines knew exactly what Brad was implying, and the spin on the joke was that Brad could get away with implying his alter ego was gay because he himself was so manly and virile that the question couldn't possibly come up.

Indeed, it didn't. While all three of the Hudson/Day comedies have their moments of such innuendo—*Send Me No Flowers* even contrives a scene where Hudson and Randall share a bed—it seems not to have occurred to anyone outside his intimate circle that Hudson wasn't anything but what Hollywood sold him as, the embodiment of all-American manliness. Randall said he may have heard hints about Hudson's private life but found it hard to believe, since in public he always seemed to be involved with one starlet or another. Randall noted that if the truth had come out, it would have been the end of Hudson's career as a leading man. "All the women in America were crazy about him. He was the idealized all-American boy. He really looked like a truck driver who'd gotten some class." Day, who went on from *Pillow Talk* to co-star not only with Hudson again but with Cary Grant, Rod Taylor, and James Garner, said that at the time she didn't have a clue. "I really didn't know. He seems very straight to me. He doesn't seem any different than James Garner."

Perhaps that's the real story here. However dated *Pillow Talk* may be, there's no question that Day and Hudson are perfectly convincing and entertaining as the romantic comedy couple. If off-screen he was more interested in men and she was suffering an unhappy third marriage, did it really make any difference to the viewer watching the movie?

*

When *Pillow Talk* had finished filming, Ross Hunter found the studio and the theaters less than excited about showing a romantic comedy starring Hudson and Day. It was considered to be an old-fashioned film at a time when people were demanding wide-screen epics, westerns, and war movies. Hunter managed to get a two-week booking in New York, and once everyone got a look at the reviews and, more important, the box office, there was no holding it back. Said Hunter, "The public found it was starved for romantic comedy, and all those theater owners who had turned me down now had to close their deals on my terms. It was a bonanza for Doris and me—critically, and in the bank, where bonanzas count the most."

When the Oscar nominations were announced in early 1960, to Doris Day's shock and amazement she had been nominated for Best Actress. It was a tough field. The other nominees were Audrey Hepburn for *The Nun's Story*, Katharine Hepburn and Elizabeth Taylor, both for *Suddenly, Last Summer*, and Simone Signoret for *Room at the Top*.

Day's was one of five nominations for *Pillow Talk*. It was also up for musical score, art direction, screenplay, and supporting actress honors. Thelma Ritter had received her fifth nomination, but she had already lost four times and didn't see this as a sign of changing fortunes. She invited friends to a "Come and Watch Me Lose Again" party at her home on the night of the awards. She was right. The Oscar went to Shelley Winters for *The Diary of Anne Frank*. In selecting the presenters, the Academy officials have no idea who the winner will be; they can only hope. Presenting the Best Actress Oscar was Rock Hudson, and what a dramatic moment it would have been had Day won. Instead the winner was Signoret.

Pillow Talk did not go home empty-handed, however. The Oscar for best story and screenplay written directly for the screen went to the two writing teams who had worked on the film but had never met.

Russell Rouse and Clarence Greene were credited with the original story while Stanley Shapiro and Maurice Richlin received credit for the finished script. All shared in the prize, but they still didn't get to meet. Richlin read a note from his writing partner Shapiro: "I am trapped downstairs in the gentlemen's lounge. It seems I rented a faulty tuxedo. I'd like to thank you upstairs for this great honor."

*

Years later there was talk of reuniting Hudson, Day, and Randall in a fourth movie. How far it got depends on whose version you believe. According to Tom Clark, a Hollywood publicist and close friend of Hudson's, Tony Randall had an idea for a movie and arranged for a lunch with Hudson and Day. The story supposedly had Day and Hudson married, but Day decided to have an affair with Randall. According to Clark, Hudson and Day found the notion ludicrous.

"Forget it, Sonny Boy," Clark quoted Hudson as quoting Day. "It could never happen."

A different version—and a different plot—has Hudson meeting with Jimmy Hawkins, an actor turned producer, who had an idea for "Pillow Talk II." A writer was engaged and a synopsis put together. In this movie Day and Hudson are divorced, but their daughter is marrying Randall's son. Hudson arrives a week early and Randall, still carrying a torch for Day, thinks Hudson's going to try to win her back. They make a bet over whether he can do it. In a plot contrivance quite faithful to their earlier films, Hudson has an accident with a golf cart and gets amnesia. The doctors say he needs to revisit the people and places of his past to try to jog his memory back. Day agrees, and they go to all the places they went to when they were younger, and fall in love all over again. Then it turns out that Hudson was faking, but Day knew it all along. She was trying to figure out a way to effect a reconciliation, and this silly scheme was as good as any.

It was fluff, but Hudson loved it and offered suggestions. They rushed the material to Day to see if it appealed to her. It did, and she had her own suggestions as well. Suddenly this was a project on a fast track, with executives at Universal expressing interest and everyone waiting to see the final script, but events intervened.

A week or two later Hudson received the diagnosis that he had contracted AIDS. It would be more than a year before that news became public, and it was a bombshell when it did. The AIDS epidemic was still far from most people in 1985, and the announcement that a prominent and popular movie star had been stricken by it was a shock. Hudson was dying and would be gone before year's end. Elizabeth Taylor helped spearhead a star-studded charity benefit that would raise a million dollars for AIDS research, with actress Morgan Fairchild noting, "Rock's illness helped give AIDS a face."

Ironically, Hudson's final public appearance was as a guest on Doris Day's television show, "Doris Day's Best Friends." He was already very sick, but he didn't want to disappoint Day, with whom he had made some of his most popular and successful films. She had told him not to appear, to rest, not yet realizing that he was dying of AIDS. Hudson said, "Forget it. I came here to do your show and that's exactly what I'm going to do." The segment was taped and aired after Hudson's death, with an introductory tribute by Day who said, "I feel that without my deep faith I would be a lot sadder than I am today. I know that life is eternal and that something good is going to come from this experience."

Then the interview segment was run, during which the two stars discussed their favorite film together. It was, of course, *Pillow Talk*.

9

SOME LIKE IT HOT

THE FIRST PREVIEW for Billy Wilder's new comedy, *Some Like It Hot*, was a disaster. The eight-hundred-seat theater in Pacific Palisades was packed, and no one was laughing. Actually, exactly one person was laughing. When the houselights came up and the audience exited, Wilder saw who it was: the comedian Steve Allen. Allen loved it, but it was going to be hard to sell the film as a surefire laugh riot based on his reaction alone.

The Mirisch Brothers, who had financed the film, were nervous. Their independent production company had just started up, and their first few releases had not been successful. They needed a big hit to stay afloat. Wilder was nervous too, as the distributor, United Artists, was now making "suggestions" for massive edits of the film.

What had gone wrong?

It wasn't fully clear until the *next* preview audience got a look at the film, started laughing from the beginning, and howled all the way through. What was the difference? The second audience hadn't just sat through a preview of *Suddenly, Last Summer*, Joseph Mankiewicz's adaptation of Tennessee Williams's grim potboiler about murder, madness, and cannibalism. It turned out that that wasn't exactly the best pairing of a double feature in the history of motion picture exhibition. For *Some Like It Hot* it was just one more bump along the way in the eventual release of what the American Film Institute, in 2000, would name as the funniest American movie of all time.

*

The process began with Wilder and his new writing partner, I. A. L. Diamond, deciding what to do as a follow-up to *Love in the Afternoon* (1957). With Diamond, Wilder had found a kindred spirit with a similar sense of humor. It said something about Diamond's view of the world that the man who had been born in Romania as Itek Domenici, and would become Isadore Diamond when his family brought him to the United States, didn't think that was an impressive enough name on screen. So Iz, as he was known to Wilder and his other friends and colleagues, added the initials A and L. They didn't stand for anything, but they certainly looked important up there on the big screen. The mind that could see the humor in such empty pomposity attracted Wilder to Diamond. Although Diamond would have some success writing *Cactus Flower* (1969) as a solo project, they were otherwise a writing team from 1957 through their last collaboration, the regrettable *Buddy, Buddy* in 1981.

As a rule the two partners refused to parse out their contributions after the fact. When they won Oscars for their script for *The Apartment* (1960), their acceptance speeches were terse and to the point. Said Wilder, "Thank you, I. A. L. Diamond." Replied Diamond, "Thank you, Billy Wilder." But on *Some Like It Hot*, it's possible to accredit a few of the choices. It was Wilder who discovered the source for their inspiration. Even if he finally threw out the original material, Wilder liked to have a jumping-off place, and in this case it was a 1951 German film entitled *Fanfares of Love*, itself a remake of a 1935 French film of the same name. The premise of the movie is that two struggling musicians don a series of disguises in order to get work: they put on blackface to perform in a Dixieland band, wear earrings to join a gypsy music act, and put on wigs to join an all-girls band. Wilder found it clumsy, but it gave him the spark of inspiration.

"It was quite poor, a rather heavy-handed Bavarian *Charley's Aunt*, replete with dirndls and lederhosen. And yet there was that platinum nugget: two male musicians latching on to an all-girl's band," Wilder recalled.

So now they had their premise, but it immediately raised two questions. First, it was the late 1950s. How could they get away with a movie in which the two male leads were in drag much of the time? Second, assuming they could solve that problem, why would the men *remain* in drag when they weren't performing? Where would the plot complications be when they merely had to remove their wigs and reveal who they were?

Diamond pointed out that the then-classic man-in-drag comedy, *Charley's Aunt*, was inevitably staged in period costume. Reasoned Diamond, "When everybody's dress looks eccentric, somebody in drag looks no more peculiar than anyone else." It was Wilder who came up with the notion of setting it in the Roaring Twenties. This allowed them to play with all sorts of Jazz Age notions, from Prohibition and speakeasies to gangsters and the stock market boom. All would be a part of what became *Some Like It Hot*, with the gangster element solving the problem of why the men *had* to be in drag. When Joe (Tony Curtis) and Jerry (Jack Lemmon) witness the St. Valentine's Day massacre in Chicago, they have a very good reason to remain in disguise: if they're discovered, they'll be killed.

So Wilder and Diamond set to work on their script, going through several titles in the process (including "Fanfares of Love" and "Not Tonight, Josephine") before settling on *Some Like It Hot*. There had been a 1939 Bob Hope movie with that title, but the pre-1948 Paramount films were now owned by the entertainment conglomerate MCA, which was selling the films to television. This was convenient since MCA was also a powerful talent agency whose clients included writer-director Billy Wilder. Whatever issues were involved with the use of the title were quickly resolved.

Casting, on the other hand, was not as easy. Wilder knew right off that he wanted Jack Lemmon. They had never worked together, but Lemmon was a young actor on the rise who had already won an Oscar for best supporting actor for *Mister Roberts* (1955). In 1958 Lemmon was not a box office attraction, however, and United Artists, which had some say in casting since they'd be distributing the film, insisted on a big star. They suggested that Danny Kaye and Bob Hope might be a good pair for the musicians, but stars at the time were not falling over themselves to play parts in drag, unless it was with Milton Berle on television. Lemmon explained the mind-set: "They thought that Wilder had lost his marbles. . . . Because how could you take two men . . . and dress them in women's clothes for eighty-five percent of the film? I mean, it's a five-minute sketch. It certainly can't be a film. Everybody's in drag."

Needing a star, Wilder approached Tony Curtis, who agreed, even though Wilder didn't know which part he would play. Curtis was, essentially, insurance. He could play the "straight" role *or* the comic role. With Curtis on board, UA still was not placated. Curtis was good, but they wanted someone who, in today's parlance, could "open a picture." In other words, they wanted a star with such a large following that there would be immediate interest in the film. One name that came up, for the part of Sugar, was that of Mitzi Gaynor, who had recently starred in the movie version of Rodgers and Hammerstein's *South Pacific* (1958). The more intriguing idea was for the other male lead. They suggested that Wilder meet with Frank Sinatra.

There's no question that Sinatra would have been a big enough star, and it would be easy to assume he'd take the role of Joe, leaving Jerry for Curtis. Wilder agreed to a lunch meeting with the singer, then for reasons that were never made clear, Sinatra didn't show. At the same time Wilder was being approached by the star of one of his past films about working with him again.

*

As with Doris Day and Audrey Hepburn, Marilyn Monroe was one of the iconic actresses of the era. A complex and troubled woman who exuded sex appeal and yet was tired of playing characters who were primarily targets of male lust, she had taken time off from making movies after filming one of the oddest entries in her career, *The Prince and the Showgirl* (1957), which had her playing opposite Laurence Olivier. She was now on her third marriage—to the playwright Arthur Miller—and had suffered a miscarriage. Miller thought going back to work might pick up her spirits, and Wilder—who had directed her in the smash hit *The Seven Year Itch* (1955)—was on her short list of directors with whom she automatically agreed to work.

It was fortuitous timing, for the casting of Monroe not only satisfied United Artists' desire for a big star, it also freed Wilder to offer the other musician role to Lemmon. He made his initial pitch when he noticed Lemmon at a restaurant. Wilder stopped by his table and said he wanted Lemmon for a movie but didn't have time to explain it. He'd be chased by gangsters and would be in drag. Lemmon didn't know what to make of it but this was Billy Wilder. He told the director that he'd have to see if he was free for their shooting schedule.

The rest of the casting was easier, if not necessarily without problems. Since the story was set during Prohibition, Wilder decided they needed some of the classic actors of gangster films to appear. George Raft, whose most recent screen appearance had been a cameo in the all-star *Around the World in Eighty Days* (1956), agreed to take the part of "Spats" Columbo. Pat O'Brien, so memorable as the priest who was buddies with James Cagney in *Angels with Dirty Faces* (1938), was now working mostly in television and took the part of the police detective chasing after Spats. Perhaps the luckiest casting was that of the comic actor Joe E. Brown as the millionaire Osgood Fielding III. Like O'Brien, Brown still worked in television, and like Raft, he had had a cameo in *Eighty Days*, but by 1958 Brown was more of a businessman than an actor, his last really notable role being as Cap'n Andy in the 1951 film of *Showboat*.

As Wilder recalled, "Joe E. Brown had been out of sight for quite a while. When I saw him at a Dodgers game, I thought he would be perfect as Osgood. That was one time where 'somebody's perfect.' He was also a part owner of the Pittsburgh Pirates, so I got a lot of inside information about trades while we were making *Hot*."

The one who got away was Edward G. Robinson, whom Wilder had wanted to play Little Bonaparte, the mob kingpin who presided over the "Friends of Italian Opera" convention at the end of the film. Wilder even cast the actor's son, Edward G. Robinson, Jr., in a small role as a way of enticing him, but there was apparently bad blood between Raft and Robinson going back several years, and he refused to do the film. The part was eventually played by Nehemiah Persoff.

So the cast was in place. Now the aggravation could begin.

*

Marilyn Monroe had it in her contract with Twentieth Century-Fox that all her films had to be in color. She looked better in color, she felt, and her fans preferred it that way. That contract was not binding on Wilder, however, since Twentieth was not involved in the production of *Some Like It Hot*. But that didn't mean Monroe wasn't upset anyway when Wilder announced plans to shoot the movie in black and white. Monroe, who had entered into psychoanalysis and was also studying acting with Lee and Paula Strasberg, would no longer accept "Because I said so" as an explanation for why things were not being done her way.

Wilder and Monroe argued back and forth for a couple of days, with Wilder insisting the film had to be in black and white. His reasoning was that it would maintain the illusion of a period piece since it would look like a 1930s gangster film. There was a further problem: utilizing the makeup and lighting effects available at that time rendered Lemmon and Curtis perfectly hideous in color when they were made up in drag. Indeed, the heavy makeup gave the actors a greenish tinge more suitable for the Frankenstein monster than for a jazz band. Finally Wilder showed Monroe the color film tests, and she had to agree that Wilder was right. It would not be the last time they had a difference of opinion on how things should be done, but it was the last time she gave in so easily.

Transforming Joe and Jerry into Josephine and Daphne was nowhere near as easy as it appears in the movie. Wilder was proud of the way they handled the transition in the movie. Curtis is shown on the phone, with the feminine voice he's adopting, taking the job with the all-girls band. Wilder then immediately cuts to the two of them dressed as women sashaying their way down the train platform to join the band and escape from the mobsters. It's a moment that gets a huge reaction because it leapfrogs over dull questions like where they got the wigs and outfits and propels us right into the story. Their awkwardness in high heels and women's undergarments got such big laughs that Wilder found he had another problem: People were laughing so much they were missing the dialogue. The set had only three train cars on it, so there was a limited amount of footage they had of the two men walking. Wilder ended up using all of it, artfully editing it so you don't realize they keep walking by the same cars.

Off-camera this sexual transformation was a much more complex problem. Decisions had to be made not only about wigs, costumes, and makeup but about how the characters would comport themselves. They had to be believable enough that audiences would buy them onscreen as women, but not so realistic that moviegoers lost the comedy aspect of these two guys trying to pass themselves off as "girl musicians." Wilder brought in a famous European female impersonator by the name of Babette to show Curtis and Lemmon how to act like women. They had to learn how to sit down, how to walk, even how to hold their arms. As Curtis remembered, "If we held them up, our muscles showed. If we held them palms down our muscles disappeared." Curtis practiced diligently, but the lessons rubbed Lemmon the wrong way. He decided that Jerry/Daphne would not be comfortable as a demure woman and tried to find his own way to play the part. Babette had suggested that when they walked they cross one foot in front of the other with each step, which would cause their hips to sway. After a few days, though, Babette was through with Lemmon's awkwardness. Recalled Lemmon, "He told Wilder that Curtis was fine but Lemmon was totally impossible."

Tony Curtis and Jack Lemmon smile even though they're in drag hiding from mobsters. But behind the scenes there were fewer smiles as they waited and waited for co-star Marilyn Monroe (not pictured) to show up.

When they were finally made up, they still weren't sure they could pull it off. At someone's suggestion (it's variously attributed, depending on who was telling the story), Curtis and Lemmon went to the studio commissary ladies' room and sat in the outer lounge at the makeup mirror, doing whatever they imagined ladies do when they "freshen up." Women walked in and out, and not one of them said a word. That's when they realized they had what they needed as far as the look. How they would *play* Josephine and Daphne was another hurdle. Curtis was extremely nervous and didn't know what direction to go in. "I didn't want to come out first," he later recalled. "I wanted him out first to see what Jack would be like, what kind of woman he would be, what he would enjoy doing. Then I see Jack come dancing out of his dressing room, and he looked like a three-dollar trollop. You know, skipping along, talking in a high voice." Curtis decided to play Josephine as very proper and demure.

During the production Lemmon's mother came to visit the set, and a picture was taken of him as Daphne with his mom. When he saw it, he was flabbergasted. They looked almost like sisters. He had unconsciously been modeling Daphne, at least in some ways, on his mother. Ultimately he decided just to dive into the part and see where it took him. "The only way to play it was to let it all hang out and just go, trusting that Wilder would say 'Cut' if it got out of bounds."

So they were all set—until Monroe got a look at Josephine's and Daphne's dresses and decided that she'd look better in one of their flapper outfits, so she simply took it. Since she was the star of the film (she was billed first, over Curtis and Lemmon), no one said boo. Designer Orry-Kelly simply whipped up another outfit to replace it. He later got back at Monroe during fittings for her memorable outfits by telling her, "You know, Tony's ass is better looking than yours."

"Oh yeah?" she replied. "Well, he doesn't have tits like these!"

She then opened her blouse for him in case there was any doubt.

*

In many ways *Some Like It Hot* represents Wilder at the peak of his powers, where he would stay at least through his next film, *The Apartment*. Sometimes direction could be as simple as handing an actor a pair of maracas, which is what Wilder did to Lemmon before they were about to shoot one of the scenes. Lemmon would go on to make seven films with Wilder and they would become close friends, but this was their first movie together. For Lemmon, at least, the relationship was still on a trial basis.

Lemmon recalls his then girlfriend (later his wife), the actress Felicia Farr, asking him during shooting how things were going with Wilder. "I told her, 'I guess he's okay.' She's never let me forget that one." For Wilder's part, it was already love at first sight, at least of the director/actor variety. "Within three to four weeks after the start of production, Diamond and I decided that this was not to be a one-shot thing with Jack. We wanted to work with him again."

The morning Wilder handed him the maracas, Lemmon had his doubts. He'd rehearsed his lines, he knew how he wanted to play the scene, and suddenly Wilder was throwing him a curveball. "I was upset with the crazy maracas when we started the first take," said Lemmon. "It wasn't until I saw it with an audience that I realized how wise Billy was."

Wilder had realized that he needed to slow down the scene or the audience would be laughing so much they'd miss most of what was going on. This was the scene after Jerry/Daphne has spent the night dancing with Osgood and has come back with a marriage proposal. Jerry has gone so deep into the role-playing that he's forgotten it's only a disguise. When Joe asks why a man would want to marry another man, "Daphne" doesn't miss a beat, "Security!" Wilder had Lemmon shake the maracas every line or so to give them breathing spaces between the jokes, and also because it was a comic echo of the big tango scene preceding this one. As for the tango scene itself, Wilder was lucky in having cast George Raft, who had started out as a professional dancer. The teacher who had been brought to show Brown and Lemmon the steps didn't know what he was doing, and Raft stepped in—even though he wasn't in the scene—to show them how it was done. As Lemmon later recalled, "It was the most outrageous, funniest real scene on the set. Just visualize George Raft, Joe E. Brown, and Jack Lemmon seriously engaged in doing the tango together. Somehow Billy should've worked the three of us dancing into the film."

A different scene that actually involved Raft should have been simple but wasn't. After the shootout in the garage—this film's version of the St. Valentine's Day Massacre—Spats was supposed to kick away the trademark toothpick from the body of the rival gangster who had betrayed him, one Toothpick Charlie. Charlie was played by the character actor George E. Stone, whom Raft had known for many years. He was afraid of hurting Stone if he misjudged he kick, and they kept doing take after take without getting what Wilder wanted. Finally Wilder showed him how to do it. He went over to kick the toothpick out of Stone's mouth, and ended up kicking Stone in the face. The actor was rushed to the hospital but lived to tell the tale.

The gangster trappings of *Some Like It Hot* have some of the film's slyest gags, which depend on the viewer's familiarity with classic 1930s gangster movies, particularly *Little Caesar* (1930), *Public Enemy* (1931), and *Scarface* (1932). Besides Wilder having wanted Edward G. Robinson to send up his *Little Caesar* role by playing Little Bonaparte, there is also the priceless moment when Spats is checking into the Florida resort for the mob meeting, and there's a dapper young punk (played by Robinson's son) flipping a coin. Raft seizes the coin and snarls, "Where'd you learn that cheap trick?" Knowledgeable audiences knew the answer: from seeing Raft himself do the same shtick in the original *Scarface*. Later at the banquet, one of Spats's henchmen says something stupid and Spats picks up the half-grapefruit on his plate as if to slap him with it. Unlike James Cagney, who shocked depression-era audiences by doing just that to Mae Clarke in *Public Enemy*, Spats is restrained.

Raft, Brown, and O'Brien enjoyed being in a major movie again, reminiscing about the old days, but they served another purpose on the film besides nostalgia. They were the old reliables who could be counted on to be ready quickly if needed whenever the film's female lead was staying in her dressing room or had not even arrived at the studio. If Wilder thought working with Humphrey Bogart on *Sabrina* had been difficult, nothing—not even his work with her on *The Seven Year Itch*—prepared him for working with Marilyn Monroe.

*

Once Joe and Jerry disguise themselves as Josephine and Daphne, the story is really quite simple, in spite of the disguises. They join the all-girls orchestra and head to Florida while they try to earn enough money to figure out what to do next. Both are attracted to the band's singer, Sugar Kowalczyk, played by Monroe. Jerry gets a hilarious scene where he's trying to put the moves on Sugar in his upper berth while still dressed as Daphne, and suddenly finds he's hosting the entire band for a late-night pajama party. What had started out as a dream (he likens it to childhood fantasies of being locked in a bakery) turns into a nightmare. Meanwhile Joe also has designs on Sugar, and this will necessitate yet another disguise, that of "Shell Jr.," the impotent oil millionaire who sets up a situation where Sugar must seduce *him*.

A later generation of academic film critics, filled with feminist and Freudian theories among others, would have a field day following the gender confusion in the movie. Between Joe and Jerry, Joe is clearly the "masculine" one of the pair, calling the shots and even getting Jerry to pawn his overcoat in the middle of winter. As Josephine and Daphne, on the other hand, Josephine is the more demure and classically "feminine" character, while becoming Daphne seems to liberate Jerry into asserting himself. Things get so confusing that at one point Jerry has to remind himself, "I'm a girl, I'm a girl, I'm a girl." Yet later, when he plays the part too well by accepting Osgood's proposal of marriage, he now has to remind himself, "I'm a boy, I'm a boy." As Shell Jr., Joe becomes the sort of man he never is: refined, passive, empathetic. Of course it's only a character he's created based on what Sugar has told Josephine she's looking for in a man. And Sugar has her own level of changing identities, adopting some of Josephine's and Daphne's made-up background for herself, thinking it will impress Shell Jr.

Add one more twist. Even though Jerry mocks Shell Jr.'s accent ("Nobody talks like that!"), audiences were expected to recognize the voice, which was yet another joke layered onto the film. Wilder gave the credit for this bit of invention to Curtis. He went to the actor and explained that he would need to use a different voice for Shell Jr. than he used for Joe or Josephine.

"What can you do?" the director asked.

"I can do Cary Grant," replied Curtis. Wilder told him to go ahead, and that was the voice he used in the film. As the director put it, "It was a huge wonderful plus for the picture. I didn't know he could do such a perfect imitation." When the movie came out, Grant, who remained friends with Wilder even after having twice turned down the chance to be in a Wilder film, thought it was a great joke. Wilder had only hoped Curtis could do a Boston accent, or something else that sounded "rich."

Wilder was always open to suggestions from his actors, even the difficult ones like Monroe. When it came time to shoot her entrance into the story—walking down the platform to the train "like Jell-O on springs"—she felt it was nothing. She needed an *entrance*. Wilder saw her point and agreed. They came up with the moment when she gets a blast of steam from the train, allowing her an extra wiggle. Sugar now didn't merely board the train, she arrived. If only everything else with Monroe had been that simple.

When she was offered the part and was preparing for it, she consulted with Lee and Paula Strasberg, the husband-and-wife team who helped change the way American actors operated by adopting what was popularly called "the Method." Essentially it was a way for actors to build a performance from the inside out, exploring their own feelings as a way to figure out how to play the character. Monroe might not seem a likely contemporary of, say, Marlon Brando and Montgomery Clift, but her performance in *Bus Stop* (1956) showed her to be capable of serious work. She seems to have been concerned that Sugar represented a step back to the dumb-blonde parts earlier in her career. After all, she must be really stupid if she couldn't tell that Josephine and Daphne were men in drag.

Lee Strasberg suggested that she see Sugar's situation as an extension of her own. "A lot of men have wanted to be your friends, but you haven't ever had friends who were girls," he told her. "Now suddenly here are two women, and they want to be your friend! They like you. For the first time in your life you have two friends who are girls."

Wonderful, insightful advice. If only Monroe had run with it instead of continuing to agonize over the role. In many ways her involvement with the film became a battle of wills with Wilder as to how Sugar would be played, and since the stakes were often so small, it turned into a frustrating grudge match where Wilder just had to bite his tongue, regardless of the provocation, because he needed her performance. As he would say in many later interviews, when asked why anyone would want to work with Monroe, "I have an old aunt in Vienna. She would be on the set every morning at six and would know her lines backwards. But who would go see her?"

Monroe became so wrapped up in her own problems—her fame, her marriage, her desire for motherhood, her grappling with the part—that she treated everyone from Wilder on down without the least bit of consideration. This was apparent from the beginning, when Harold Mirisch, one of the brothers who were financing the film, threw a party to welcome Monroe. Cocktails were set for 7 p.m., dinner for 9. Monroe and her playwright husband strolled in at 11. This was par for the course for her, and it would only get worse. Wilder tried to assert control, but short of using a two-by-four nothing seemed to get through.

Early on there were tests to shoot. Curtis and Lemmon reported on schedule and were ready to go at 11 a.m. Knowing that Monroe would be late, it was arranged that she was not expected until 1 p.m. She showed up at 3:30, then withdrew to her dressing room and did not emerge until after 6:00 when she was at last ready. She found a deserted set. The normal daytime work schedule was 9 a.m. to 6 p.m., and after that the crew got overtime. Wilder dismissed the crew at 6:00 and left shortly thereafter. Not only were people put out waiting for her, it started costing the production money. The film would end up a half-million dollars over budget.

"Late? Look, if we had a 9 a.m. call she'd make it by 11," said Curtis. "That was on her good days. On her bad days she didn't show up until after we came back from lunch." This would aggravate the actors, particularly Curtis who had numerous scenes with her. If it was a day when Curtis and Lemmon were in drag, it meant they were in uncomfortable clothes and shoes waiting around for no reason. "Tony and I suffered the tortures of the damned in those high heels," said Lemmon.

To make sure there were no masculine bulges where there shouldn't be, both of them were bound up in foundation garments that were not easily removed. This created problems if, say, they had to go to the bathroom. Without telling anyone, Curtis rigged a device involving a funnel and some tubing that allowed him to relieve himself without getting out of costume. Everyone remarked on the actor's supposed stamina. Curtis offered to make one for Lemmon, but he declined.

Besides Monroe's chronic lateness, she also refused to cede to Wilder final authority over the shooting of her scenes. As demonstrated by Lemmon balking at the addition of maracas to a scene, the actor is usually not in the best position to judge how a particular scene or bit of business fits into the overall picture. There's no reason he should; it's not his job. It is, however, the job of the director, whose word is law on the set. Wilder was always open to suggestions, but in the end it was his call, no one else's. Monroe didn't see it that way. She arrived on the set with Paula Strasberg in tow, and she could be seen huddling with her coach before and after takes while Wilder waited for his star to return to the set. Early on, the director put Strasberg in her place when, at the end of a take, Monroe looked not to Wilder but to Strasberg to see if her acting had been acceptable. Wilder turned to Strasberg and asked, "How was that for you, Paula?" The accusation in the innocent question was enough. Strasberg did her best to blend into the background after that.

Still the problems came. If Monroe didn't like the direction she was getting from Wilder she'd keep making mistakes, knowing that sooner or later he'd get a take that was acceptable and go with it. This didn't endear her to Curtis and Lemmon, who had a running bet on how many times they'd have to do a particular scene. The most notorious example was late in the film, after Shell Jr. has dumped Sugar when Joe and Jerry have been discovered at the hotel by Spats and his gang and must flee. While they're in their Josephine and Daphne drag, Sugar comes in the room absolutely crestfallen and ready to drown her sorrows in drink. Her line was simply, "Where's the bourbon?"

It took eighty-three takes and two days to get her to say that simple line. She would say, "Where's the bottle?" and "Where's the bonbon?" Wilder tried to help her through whatever mysterious difficulty she was having. "I took her aside—we're on the second day already—and I said to her, 'Don't worry about it, Marilyn. We'll get it.' She just looks at me like she doesn't know what I'm talking about and says, 'Worry? About what?'"

When at another point Wilder tried to talk to her, she snapped at him, "Don't talk to me now. I'm thinking about how I'm going to play this scene." Everyone, including Wilder, was stunned. She was off in a world of her own.

Her defenders—and she has them among the shelves of books about her life and career that have appeared since her death by overdose in 1962—argue that she was fighting for her own vision of the character. If that was so it was a selfish, childish fight that assumed her view of the character trumped everything else in the movie. Wilder lamented that in editing he was forced to go with the shots where she finally had it together, even if the other actors on camera—who had been on time and doing great work from the start—were now tired out. It's no wonder that one of the most infamous quips ever made about Monroe came out of the shooting of *Some Like It Hot.*

Several people were in the screening room watching the rushes (the raw footage from the previous day's shooting) of Curtis and Monroe's love scene aboard the yacht. When someone said it looked like Curtis was having a good time, a clearly aggravated Curtis replied, "It's like kissing Hitler."

When the lights came on, it turned out that Strasberg was in the room, and she was in tears. "How could you say a terrible thing like that, Tony?" she said.

"You try acting with her, Paula, and see how you feel."

That was Marilyn Monroe at her worst. At her best—and there's no question she did some of the best work of her career in *Some Like It Hot*—she could be funny and sexy and vulnerable all at the same time. The scene in Daphne's berth with all the other women piling in was shot in one take. Her scene on the beach where she meets Shell Jr. for the first time was scheduled for three days of shooting. She was letter perfect, and they had the scene in only two takes. There was just no telling whether good Marilyn or bad Marilyn would show up. As Wilder lamented, "We were in mid-flight, and there was a nut on the plane."

Late in the production Monroe had big news: she was pregnant again. Arthur Miller approached Wilder and asked if she could be free by 4:30 each day so she could get extra rest since she had already suffered one miscarriage. Wilder's reply shows he was ready to be helpful, if Monroe would only take some responsibility herself: "Look, Arthur. It's now four o'clock. I still don't have a take. She doesn't come to work until eleven-thirty and wasn't ready to work until after one. I tell you this, Arthur. You get her here at nine o'clock, ready to work, and I'll let her go not at four-thirty but at noon."

Her pregnancy explains the curious final shots of the movie, when Osgood rescues Joe, Jerry, and Sugar, and they head off together in his motorboat. Joe confesses he's exactly the sort of lying heel she's dealt with before, and she forgives him. They meet in a clinch and then drop out of sight of the camera. In reality this meant that Monroe was no longer needed, and that the final scene between Osgood and Jerry could play out with just Brown and Lemmon.

Unfortunately Monroe's was a doomed pregnancy—the egg had implanted in her fallopian tube—that ended in another miscarriage. This led to an ugly and public exchange of telegrams between Wilder and Miller. Having finished the shoot, and before they knew what a phenomenal success the film would be, Wilder sounded off against Monroe in a series of interviews. He let loose with a torrent of barbed comments that had apparently been building while he was dealing with her unprofessional behavior. One of the most famous cracks was his answer to the question whether he would ever work with her again, having now made two movies with her. Wilder replied, "I have discussed this project with my doctor and my psychiatrist, and they tell me I'm too old and too rich to go through this again."

Monroe was insulted, and Miller fired off a telegram berating Wilder for his treatment of her. It implied that Wilder was somehow to blame for the miscarriage too, which occurred just twelve hours after her final scenes for the movie. Wilder expressed sympathy for their loss but also made it clear who was the real problem. "Had you, dear Arthur, been not her husband but her writer and director, and been subjected to all the indignities that I was, you would have thrown her out on her can. . . . I did the braver thing. I had a nervous breakdown."

Only one other director dealt with Monroe twice, and that was John Huston, whose *The Misfits* (1961) would prove to be the final film for both Monroe and Clark Gable. But Huston's other film with her, *The Asphalt Jungle* (1951), hardly counts, as she was still an unknown in a small part. So give Wilder the final word on Monroe's career, in a 1968 interview six years after her death: "I have never met anyone as utterly mean as Marilyn Monroe, nor as utterly fabulous on the screen, and that includes Garbo."

*

In spite of its shaky first preview, *Some Like It Hot* opened to mostly good reviews and increasing box office. As word of mouth spread, the film turned into a big hit, ending up as the third biggest grosser of 1959, trailing only *Auntie Mame* and *The Shaggy Dog*. As an independent producer, Wilder now enjoyed his share of the box office receipts, as did Monroe, which may explain why their feud eventually waned. Sometime later an interviewer was surprised when Wilder named *Some Like It Hot* as his favorite picture. Surely he meant to name one of his more serious films, like *Double Indemnity* or *Sunset*

Boulevard? "Nice little pictures," Wilder replied, "but in those days I wasn't getting a percentage of the gross."

At the Oscars the film received several nominations, but only Orry-Kelly won a statuette. Nominations had also been bestowed on Jack Lemmon, Billy Wilder (for directing), Wilder and I. A. L. Diamond (for the script), Charles Lang, Jr. (for the black-and-white cinematography), and Ted Haworth and Edward G. Boyle (for art direction/set decoration). Wilder and Diamond would have to wait until the following year and their next film with Lemmon, *The Apartment*, to clean up at the Oscars.

Meanwhile audiences loved the film, even if in some circles it was still considered too "hot" to handle. State censors in Kansas insisted on trims since they deemed that the film "contains material regarded as too disturbing for Kansans." The Legion of Decency, the censorship arm of the Catholic church, still had clout in 1959 and rated the movie only a B. In a letter to the Production Code Authority, the industry censorship board, the Legion explained its objections: "The subject matter of 'transvestism' naturally leads to complications; in this film there seem to us to be clear references of homosexuality and lesbianism. The dialogue was not only 'double entendre' but outright smut. The offense in costuming was obvious."

Such objections carried little weight. The film was a boost not only to Wilder but to Jack Lemmon, and their collaboration the next year would cement their personal and professional friendship as well as make Lemmon a star. Lest he get too full of himself, however, there was always someone to take him down a peg. After *Some Like It Hot* opened, the Wilders, the Diamonds, Harold Mirisch and his wife, and Lemmon went to Europe to promote the film aboard the ocean liner *United States*. On board with them were the Duke and Duchess of Windsor. They had a print of the movie with them and showed it to the passengers on the trip over. At dinner following the screening, Wilder and Lemmon and their party were at a table near the Windsors, where one of the Duke's dinner companions pointed out that one of the stars of the film they had just seen was aboard ship with them.

"The one I liked?" asked the Duke.

Lemmon and Wilder's party couldn't help but hear the Duchess's reply, "No dear, the other one."

*

And finally there is the famous closing line of the film.

Closing lines can be memorable, but often they rely on the buildup of what has come before. One of the most famous conclusions in the American theater is the curtain line for *The Front Page*, in which the newspaper editor Walter Burns tells an unseen police officer over the phone, "The son of a bitch stole my watch." By itself it's not funny, but coming at the end of Ben Hecht and Charles MacArthur's rollicking tribute to journalism, it invariably brings down the house. (Of four film versions based on the play, only one preserves the line—the 1974 film with Jack Lemmon and Walter Matthau, directed by none other than Billy Wilder.)

Likewise the final line of *Some Like It Hot*: "Nobody's perfect."

Even though Wilder and Diamond did not claim personal credit for the various jokes in their films, Wilder always made a point of giving Diamond full credit for what would prove to be one of the funniest lines in American cinema. "We were set to film that last scene on a Monday and weren't satisfied how to close it," Wilder recalled. Only Osgood and Daphne are on screen, and Daphne is trying to break the news gently to Osgood why their marriage can never take place. He smokes, he says. He's lived with another man. He can never have children. Osgood brushes aside all objections. Finally Daphne rips off the wig and reveals himself to be Jerry: "I'm a man."

To which Osgood, still not thrown, replies, "Nobody's perfect."

Wilder recalled, "That was Diamond's suggestion, and I said, 'That's good, but maybe we can do better, let's think about it over the weekend.' On Monday we didn't have a better line. Who knew it would become so famous?"

INTERMISSION

HAVING SELECTED three representative films from the 1930s, the 1940s, and the 1950s, we now leap over most of the next two decades to pick up the trail with *Annie Hall*, released in 1977. What happened to the romantic comedy in between? Film genres go in and out of fashion, of course. But one of the arguments here is that romantic comedies reflect the times in which they were made, and that helps explain what happened during this gap.

In a nutshell, the problem was that the filmmakers and performers who were adept at romantic comedy were dying, retiring, or moving on to other things, while a new generation had little interest in an "old-fashioned" form. Remember, *Pillow Talk* in 1959 was thought to revive a supposedly dead kind of movie. Consider just a few of the performers.

Following *Some Like It Hot*, Marilyn Monroe worked on only three more films. *Let's Make Love* (1960) was a mild success with Monroe as an entertainer in a show spoofing the wealthy character played by Yves Montand. Monroe continued being difficult on the set, and even the veteran director George Cukor couldn't control her. She went on to do the dramatic *The Misfits* with Clark Gable and the director John Huston, and then worked with Cukor again on *Something's Got to Give*. This last film was never finished, and Monroe was dead—a suicide—in August 1962.

Cary Grant appeared in numerous romantic comedies, and audiences loved him no matter how old he grew. But he made only five films in the 1960s, and you could tell that *he* was getting tired of romantic comedy. *The Grass Is Greener* (1960) and *That Touch of Mink* (1962) were pale shadows of his glory days, even though he was paired with Deborah Kerr in the former and Doris Day in the latter. *Charade* (1962) is easily the best of the bunch, but though there's a bit of romantic comedy there with Grant and Audrey Hepburn, it takes a back seat to the main story, a Hitchcock-like thriller. It says something about Grant's attitude that he insisted the script indicate that Reggie, the young widow played by Hepburn who was many years Grant's junior, should be seen as pursuing him, rather than the other way around. Romance similarly took a back seat in the plot of *Father Goose* (1964), and in his final film, *Walk Don't Run* (1966), Grant isn't even the romantic lead. He's the man playing Cupid to bring Samantha Eggar and Jim Hutton together.

Audrey Hepburn also was headed toward retirement. She made nine films in the 1960s, then left the screen to focus on her family, not returning until Richard Lester's touching *Robin and Marian* (1976), about the latter days of Robin Hood, with Sean Connery as Robin and Hepburn as Maid Marian. Of her sixties films, the romantic comedies are inevitably about something else, or else turn into comedy-dramas. Her iconic performance in *Breakfast at Tiffany's* (1961) has its comic moments but is really a bittersweet story about two broken people who need to grow up. *My Fair Lady* (1964) comes closest to a romantic comedy in George Cukor's film of the hit Broadway show. Of course the notion that Eliza Doolittle and Henry Higgins (Rex Harrison) end up together at the end is wishful thinking, but then even George Bernard Shaw allowed that change from his play in the original film adaptation of his *Pygmalion*. *Paris—When It Sizzles* (1964) reunited Hepburn with William Holden for an over-the-top satire of moviemaking, with their romantic involvement simply a by-product of the plot. Hepburn and Peter O'Toole both looked beautiful in *How to Steal a Million* (1966), but their romance was secondary to the elaborate art heist that drives the story.

As for Doris Day, she did continue to churn out romantic comedies that were mostly attempts to clone the success of *Pillow Talk*. In addition to two more films with Rock Hudson and one with Cary Grant, she also did two with James Garner and two with Rod Taylor. By 1968, though, her career on the big screen was over with the family sitcom *With Six You Get Eggroll*, though she would follow it with a five-year run on her own television sitcom.

The directors who could handle romantic comedy were also growing old. Cukor won his long overdue Oscar for *My Fair Lady* in 1964, and though he continued to work (his last film was *Rich and Famous* in 1981), the closest he came to romantic comedy again was a film made for television with the one-of-a-kind pairing of Katharine Hepburn and Laurence Olivier called *Love Among the Ruins* (1975).

Billy Wilder's take on romance, meanwhile, grew more and more acidic. *The Apartment* (1960), which he considered a "dirty fairy tale," is about a pencil-pushing executive (Jack Lemmon) trying to advance his career by loaning out his apartment to his bosses for their affairs. Shirley MacLaine is the elevator operator who tries to kill herself after feeling rejected by Lemmon's boss, played by Fred MacMurray. It's a marvelous film, but it's hardly a celebration of romance, even though Lemmon and MacLaine end up together at the end. Wilder reunited Lemmon and MacLaine for *Irma La Douce*, with Lemmon as a Parisian cop and MacLaine as a prostitute. Wilder then made *Kiss Me, Stupid* (1964), a troubled production that is almost an anti-romantic comedy. A songwriter (Ray Walston, in a part originally intended for Peter Sellers) wants to convince a singing star (Dean Martin) to use one of his songs by having his wife seduce the singer. Except that he doesn't really plan to use his wife (Felicia Farr). He sends her away and hires a local good-time gal, "Polly the Pistol" (Kim Novak), to pretend to be his wife, and have *her* do the seducing. There's an ugliness about the film that most viewers find off-putting.

Wilder's remaining films have little interest in romance. Three of them co-star Lemmon and Walter Matthau (who won his Oscar for Wilder's 1966 film *The Fortune Cookie*), and another is about

Sherlock Holmes. Only *Avanti!* (1972) is interested in love and, again, it's a skewed look. Lemmon plays a businessman going to collect his father's body in an Italian resort town, where he discovers the daughter (Juliet Mills) of his father's mistress, whom he had been seeing for years, and who has died in the same car accident with him. Lemmon's character is shocked at the revelation, but as we learn how unhappy *his* marriage is, the story's "happy ending" is that he and the daughter will continue the affair. It's not incestuous, but it's not *Sabrina* either.

So where were the next generation of filmmakers and their romantic comedies? For the most part the younger directors had little interest in the form. If you look at the films of Francis Ford Coppola, George Lucas, Martin Scorsese, Brian DePalma, and Steven Spielberg, the closest you get to romantic comedy is Coppola's *You're a Big Boy Now* (1966), more of a coming-of-age story than a true romance, and Scorsese's *Alice Doesn't Live Here Anymore* (1974), more a drama about a woman finding herself, with comic overtones. Of the directors who came of age in this era, the ones who might have reinvented the romantic comedy were Peter Bogdanovich, Mike Nichols, and Paul Mazursky, but though they turned out some great films, they are essentially footnotes in the genre.

Bogdanovich came closest to something new with *What's Up, Doc?* (1972), a rollicking hit in the spirit of the thirties comedies, headed by Ryan O'Neal and Barbra Streisand. While undeniably entertaining, at times the film seems more an *homage* to the screwball comedy than a work in its own right. Among Nichols's offerings during the sixties and seventies were *The Graduate* (1967) and *Carnal Knowledge* (1971). Buck Henry was one of the writers on *The Graduate*, a devastating late-sixties portrait of suburbia, which made "plastics" the catchword that summed up the emptiness and artificiality of the American dream. As a romance, however, it has Benjamin (Dustin Hoffman) seduced by his parents' friend Mrs. Robinson (Anne Bancroft), after which he runs off with her daughter Elaine (Katharine Ross), even though he has to interrupt her wedding to someone else to do so.

The final shot of the film—Benjamin and Elaine sitting together at the back of a bus—suggests this is not a happily-ever-after ending. As for *Carnal Knowledge*, with a script by Jules Feiffer, it is a brilliant portrait of two friends (Jack Nicholson and Art Garfunkel) pursuing their dream girls decade after decade and discovering how miserable they are when they realize their dreams. What romance exists dies, and this comedy draws blood.

Three of Paul Mazursky's six features of this era are of interest as romances, but in the end each is about something else. *Bob & Carol & Ted & Alice* (1969) was notorious at the time for the scene in which the two married couples end up in bed together, but this comedy is really a satiric take on sixties marriage and pop psychology. *Blume in Love* (1973) is about love, but it's not really a romance. Blume (George Segal) is caught having an affair, so his wife (Susan Anspach) divorces him and takes up with a musician (Kris Kristofferson). The problem is that Blume is still desperately in love with his now ex-wife and may not be able to win her back. It's a bittersweet film about renewing ties after they've been broken. But, unlike a traditional romantic comedy like *The Philadelphia Story*, the break here is caused by real betrayal and pain. That makes the film more of a drama than a comedy.

Mazursky's other film primarily about romantic relationships was his 1978 *An Unmarried Woman*, with Jill Clayburgh impressive as a wife and mother who learns that her husband is leaving her for a younger woman. In this important movie of its era, her rebound romance (with Alan Bates) gives way to political correctness. This is a story of female empowerment. If she ends up with another man—the traditional ending of romantic comedy—she will have betrayed her growth and her raised consciousness in learning she can do it herself. A decade later she could have done both, but in the late seventies, it was more important to show her surviving on her own.

Were there, then, no great romantic comedies in this period? The one that stands out is *A Touch of Class* (1973). George Segal again plays a married man having an affair, this time with a British divorcee, Glenda Jackson. They have a great fling in Spain, but when they return to

London problems arise. They have fallen in love, but he is also in love with his wife and doesn't care to leave her. In the end there's only one way the story can go, and since we're invested in the Segal/Jackson relationship, it's not a happy ending. While it bubbles along, though, there are delightful echoes of past romantic comedies, which isn't surprising since the film came from Brut Productions, which had been set up by the cosmetics company Fabergé to produce movies. As was noted at the time, the retired Cary Grant sat on the board of Fabergé.

Clearly what was needed was a new generation of filmmakers who could reinvigorate the romantic comedy. Some of them would come out of television. Some of the films would take the genre in directions that would have shocked earlier generations. No one could have guessed that the man who not only brought back the romantic comedy but set the rules for a generation to come would be a writer/actor/director primarily known in the movies as a clown. Even more surprising, the movie he set out to make wasn't really a romantic comedy at all.

LOVE IS A
BATTLEFIELD

"A relationship, I think, is like a shark, you
know? It has to constantly move forward
or it dies. And I think what we got on
our hands is a dead shark."—Alvy Singer
(Woody Allen) in *Annie Hall* (1977)

10

ANNIE HALL

IN THE MID-1970S there were two great comic filmmakers. Both were Jewish New Yorkers who had done comedy stand-up and writing, had worked on Sid Caesar's legendary 1950s television show, and had gone into the movies in the 1960s. To have a preference between Mel Brooks and Woody Allen was strictly a matter of taste. Brooks was a product of the Borscht Belt (the resort nightclubs of the Catskill Mountains) while Allen favored more cerebral references. Both engaged in what the film historian Gerald Mast called "the clown tradition . . . [a] film built around the physical, facial, and verbal assets of the central comic performer."

Where they differed was in appearing on-screen. Brooks did cameo appearances, at least until his later, less interesting films, like *Silent Movie* (1976) and *High Anxiety* (1978). The stars were people like Zero Mostel and Gene Wilder. Allen, though, was the focus of his own films. When much later in his career other actors took over the "Woody Allen role," it was often a poor imitation. And though both men engaged in parody in their films, for Brooks parody was the great reason for being, as in his western spoof *Blazing Saddles* and his horror send-up *Young Frankenstein* (both 1974). For Allen, parody was a means to a larger end. In *Bananas* he shows his character having a dream of being carried on a cross by hooded monks, who then get into a fight with a similar group over a parking space. If you got the allusion to Allen's idol, the Swedish filmmaker Ingmar Bergman, that was great, but with Allen there was often more to the joke.

Still, for critics and moviegoers alike, the similarities were more important than the differences. Thus audiences were not fully prepared when, in 1977, Allen released the movie that would not only launch a new chapter of his career but relaunch the romantic comedy for a new generation, except that Alvy (Allen) and Annie (Diane Keaton) *don't* end up together at the end. Indeed, Allen hadn't even intended to make a romantic comedy called *Annie Hall*.

*

In the 1970s Woody Allen had found a home at United Artists. There he was given a unique deal because the studio liked being in business with him. He presented the company with a script and a budget. If they approved the script and the (by Hollywood standards) modest budget, they would then leave him alone. There were no "notes," no special screenings of footage for the "suits." Allen had a free hand because the executives knew that (a) he'd come in under budget, and (b) given that economy, the film was guaranteed to turn a profit from his small but loyal group of fans. So movies like *Bananas*, *Everything You Always Wanted to Know About Sex*, *Sleeper*, and *Love and Death* were not blockbusters, but they played well in the cities and in the college towns, and everyone was happy.

After taking a break to appear as an actor in director Martin Ritt and writer Walter Bernstein's comedy-drama about the Hollywood blacklist, *The Front* (1976), Allen got approval for his new film. United Artists was somewhat nervous about the title. The name of the movie was "Anhedonia," a medical condition described as an inability to experience pleasure. In the film Alvy Singer, the character to be played by Allen, would engage in a free-form review of his life, explaining his problems, including his failed relationships with various women. The script was a collaboration with Marshall Brickman, a writer (and later director) with whom Allen had previously collaborated on *Sleeper*.

It was an interesting process. Brickman described it as "walking up and down Lexington Avenue and across to Madison and talking and talking and talking." The result was a stream-of-consciousness script that veered in multiple directions. This was Allen's apparent design since he was calling the shots. After these long conversations, Allen wrote and then sent the pages to Brickman, who revised and rewrote and sent them back to Allen. "We'd shovel it back and forth before we felt reasonably confident to go to United Artists and ask for $4 million."

Given a free hand in casting, as always, Allen chose for the part of Alvy's current girlfriend, Annie, the actress who had, until recently, been *his* girlfriend and now remained a close friend, Diane Keaton. They didn't meet cute on the tennis court, as in the movie, but during auditions for Allen's second Broadway play, *Play It Again, Sam*. She was eventually cast as the married friend with whom his character has a brief affair. They connected in real life as well, and if any actress could be said to be his muse in the 1970s it would have been Keaton. She appeared in the movie version of *Play It Again, Sam* (directed by Herbert Ross, though Allen adapted his play and starred), *Sleeper*, and *Love and Death*. After *Annie Hall* she continued to work with him, on *Interiors* and *Manhattan*, and then disappeared from his film world when he took up with Mia Farrow. She would later have a stellar cameo in *Radio Days* (1987). After his public and ugly breakup with Farrow, Allen turned to Keaton to appear in the trifling *Manhattan Murder Mystery* (1993) as he attempted to run for cover. At the start of filming "Anhedonia," however, all this was beside the point. The movie was about Alvy, not Annie.

Hints of the original film may be seen in the final version. Alvy's flashbacks to his growing up in Brooklyn and visiting his elementary school classroom were, in fact, the starting points for much larger sequences. A science-fiction parody called "Invasion of the Element" was set off by his mother complaining about the "wrong element" moving into their neighborhood. The children revealing what they became when they grew up led to scenes with the actual adults and their messed-up lives. Allen had set out to make a comedy where the humor came from the characters and not simply from setups for comic situations, but he had reverted to the film version of his stand-up routine where there were hilarious observations but no narrative thread. Even the scene in which he sneaks out of a literary party, where his second wife (Janet Margolin) has taken him, in order to catch a basketball game on television was different. In the original version it segued into a game where Alvy joined a fantasy version of a game between the New York Knicks and a team comprised of famous philosophers. There was some very funny material here, but it was not only not a romantic comedy, it was narratively incoherent and hence unreleasable. The first rough cut was nearly two and a half hours. Something would have to be done.

*

Critics and Allen fans may debate whether film editor Ralph Rosenblum oversold his role on Allen's early films when he wrote his 1979 book *When the Shooting Stops*, but there's no doubt he had a major impact on Allen's development as a filmmaker. When he was brought in on *Take the Money and Run*, it may have ensured that Allen *had* a film career.

Take the Money and Run was Allen's first film as director, after having written *What's New, Pussycat* in 1965 and watched as the director and actors did what they wanted with his script. The following year he reedited a Japanese spy movie with a gag soundtrack for *What's Up, Tiger Lily?* The 1968 *Money* would be his first time directing actors, controlling the pacing and feel of the story, and putting the finished film together. Allen spent months in postproduction editing, and when they tested the film it just lay there. As Allen recalled, the film's production manager suggested bringing in Rosenblum: "Maybe you need a fresh mind. You've been working on this for months."

If Allen was a novice, Rosenblum was someone who had come into his own as a film editor, working on movies like *The Pawnbroker*, *A Thousand Clowns*, and, around this same time, Mel Brooks's first film, *The Producers*. Rosenblum saw that Allen had a very funny movie but didn't know how to put it together properly. So he taught him about pacing and about using music, and started putting back into the film material Allen had cut out. It was a revelation. In one scene Rosenblum replaced some funereal music Allen had used with a bouncy ragtime number.

"The whole thing just came to life," Allen recalled. "I was suddenly just bouncing along. It made all the difference in the world. And there are a million little things I just didn't know. Probably seventy-five percent of the movie that was released is from my first edit, but what Ralph did was the difference between living and dying."

Learning how to use music would be important for Allen and would influence not only the director but anyone else working in romantic comedy for years to come. For his first two films Allen hired Marvin Hamlisch, then a young composer on the rise, to score them. But he took to heart Rosenblum's advice on music. Rosenblum told him, "When you edit, take a couple of records, put them on tape and—it doesn't have to be the final music for the film—throw them in behind the scenes." Many Hollywood filmmakers will use what is called a "temp" (for temporary) track to figure out the pacing for a scene. Is it upbeat? Is it sad? Is it exciting or scary? Allen had never done this. When he tried it, he realized he liked his musical choices better than anything else, and his music sound tracks soon distinguished his movies. He used Dixieland for his futuristic *Sleeper* and Russian classical music for *Love and Death*. For *Annie Hall* he would use some old standards that Diane Keaton could sing in the film, "Seems Like Old Times" and "It Had to Be You." That was the beginning of the process of linking modern romantic comedies to what has been called the Great American Songbook, with *Manhattan*—utilizing an all-Gershwin score—becoming the oft-imitated model.

Rosenblum had worked on a few other Allen films when he was presented with "Anhedonia." He put his finger on the problem right away. If he couldn't find the focus of the movie, neither would anyone in the theater seats. He suggested that the focus be not on Alvy's overall anxieties but on his romances, and that the relationship defining the film should be the one with Annie. "Anhedonia" began turning into *Annie Hall*.

*

When the film came out, it was widely assumed to be autobiographical. The evidence was obvious to even the casual Allen fan. Like Allen, Alvy is a stand-up comedian and writer. When Alvy performs on stage, he uses jokes from Allen's old nightclub routines. Alvy prefers Manhattan to Los Angeles, just as Allen did (though this would be his first film shot primarily in New York). Allen and Keaton had been romantically involved and then split up, just as Alvy and Annie do. If one needed the clincher, Diane Keaton's real name was Diane Hall. When she joined Actors' Equity at the start of her career, she learned there was already a "Diane Hall" on the rolls. The rules forbade two actors using the exact same name, so she took her mother's maiden name, Keaton. Despite these autobiographical similarities, Allen made it clear that he thought people were on the wrong track. "The stuff people insist is autobiographical is almost invariably not, and it's so exaggerated that it's virtually meaningless to the people upon whom these little nuances are based."

Keaton allowed a little more connection to reality. "It's not true, but there are *elements* of truth in it. It's about a relationship, and because Woody and I know each other well and have had a relationship, there's a quality of truth in it," she said. "My parents are not from Wisconsin but Balboa Island, California, and they're not at all like the parents in the film—but they are *goyim*."

Keaton—like Annie Hall—came to New York to break into show business, but it was to be an actress, not a singer. Her big break was in the stage production of *Hair*, in which she moved from the chorus to replace the female lead. She was told that if she wanted to keep the part she'd have to lose some weight, which she proceeded to do. On the other hand, she refused to strip for the show's famous (or infamous) nude scene, "It was optional. You'd get, like, $50 if you did it, but I passed on it." From *Hair* she moved on to *Play It Again, Sam*, where she and Allen met. He was concerned that she might be too tall for the role (that is, a lot taller than he); however, at five-foot-seven she had less than an inch on him, and she got the part.

Keaton made the transition to film with *Lovers and Other Strangers* (1970) and then won the role of Michael Corleone's non-Italian girlfriend (and then wife) in *The Godfather* (1972). She continued the role in both sequels. So even as she and Allen found their romance waning, their friendship and professional collaboration grew as she appeared opposite Allen on-screen in several films.

Keaton was a little nervous about the role of Annie. True, it was fiction, but she *had* been romantically linked with Allen and they had split and moved on, just like Annie and Alvy. Keaton wasn't sure how close to reality she could take the character, but she decided to go for it. "In the final analysis, working out my relationship with Woody was, and still is, great fun, and always a surprise and a revelation to me."

In the initial draft of the script, Annie was to be a neurotic New Yorker like Alvy, but Allen and Brickman decided to move her backstory to Wisconsin to add to the tension between the characters. Keaton brought her own ideas to the role, most memorably, perhaps, her clothing. In the film the characters meet at a tennis game set up by mutual friends, and afterward the two chat on their way out. Annie is dressed in a floppy hat, a vest, a tie, and slacks. It was what became known as the "Annie Hall look" and enjoyed a vogue, but when Keaton first showed up in this attire Allen's costumer, Ruth Morley, was aghast.

"Tell her not to wear that," Morley pleaded with Allen. "She can't wear that. It's so crazy."

"Leave her," Allen replied. "She's a genius. Let's just leave her alone, let her wear what she wants. If I really hate something, I'll tell her."

*

Annie Hall was also the first Allen movie in which casting became very important. No part was too small to be overlooked, and actors found

Diane Keaton displays what became known as the "Annie Hall look" while Woody Allen wonders how his stream-of-consciousness movie "Anhedonia" was transformed into a much-loved romantic comedy.

that a memorable moment in a small role in an Allen film could boost their professional reputation. Christopher Walken had only one big scene as Annie's brother Duane, who has a fantasy of driving his car into oncoming headlights and shares it with Alvy as a fellow "artist." Alvy's look as Duane drives them to the airport in the rain is priceless. The role provided a nice showcase for Walken relatively early in his acting career.

Other future stars have even smaller roles in the film. That's Jeff Goldblum on the phone at the trendy L.A. party complaining, "I forgot my mantra." And when Alvy bumps into Annie after they break up—she's taking her date to see *The Sorrow and the Pity*, the long documentary about the Nazi occupation of France that Alvy kept taking her to—Alvy's date is played by Sigourney Weaver, two years away from her star-making role in *Alien*. (Annie's date, by the way, is Walter Bernstein, the writer who had written *The Front*, in which Allen had appeared.)

Other roles amounted to stunt cameos. When Annie and Alvy are sitting in Central Park making fun of passersby, Alvy points to one flamboyant man as "the winner of the Truman Capote look-alike contest." The man is in fact Truman Capote. Earlier Annie and Alvy are on a date and waiting in a movie line when the man in the couple behind them begins pontificating on his theory of film and other media, citing Federico Fellini and Marshall McLuhan. When Alvy insists he pipe down because he doesn't know what he's talking about, the professor huffs that his insights have a great deal of validity. Alvy then pulls McLuhan himself out from behind a poster to put the blowhard academic in his place. (He then turns to the audience and asks, "Don't you wish real life was like this?") Allen had approached directors Fellini and Luis Buñuel to do the cameo, and for various reasons was turned down. He settled for McLuhan who, whatever his genius, was not one of the great film actors of our time. Another surprise appearance was by singer/songwriter Paul Simon, who was suggested for the part of record producer Tony Lacey by Marshall Brickman. Simon was no actor, but his former singing partner Art Garfunkel had done a few films (most notably *Carnal Knowledge*), so he took the chance. Allen encouraged him to ad-lib his few lines so he'd be more comfortable.

During the production of *Annie Hall*, Allen was open to new ideas from others. (He had built into his budget sufficient money to shoot additional scenes if he found them necessary.) One of the most famous bits in the movie was a total accident. Alvy who, like Allen, does not indulge in recreational drugs, is talking to some friends who are using cocaine, a fashion in some circles in the late seventies. When Alvy is invited to examine the powder he sneezes, setting the expensive drug flying. It was an unscripted moment left in the film because it got a laugh. In fact it got such a laugh that the editor had to extend the reaction footage so that people wouldn't miss the beginning dialogue in the next scene.

In another memorable moment we see Alvy's childhood home *beneath* the roller coaster at Coney Island. That was a real structure that still existed at the time, and it was discovered by production designer Mel Bourne, who told Allen, "I want to show you something that out-Fellinis anything Fellini has ever done."

Allen looked at the apartment and flipped. "This is where Alvy grew up," he told Bourne. "We're going to use this."

Most of all, *Annie Hall* showed that Allen was no longer just a gagmeister. Whether consciously or not, he was following in the footsteps of Orson Welles in his making of *Citizen Kane*. That movie was a catalog of virtually every technique that could be done on film at the time. *Annie Hall* did much the same. Allen gave many of the devices—animation, sub-titles, split screens—his own unique spin. The gags worked because they were, indeed, character driven. When we see Annie and Alvy at their separate therapists, it's not just the look of the contrasting scenes—with Alvy on a traditional couch and Annie seated facing her doctor—but what they are saying. Both are asked how often they have sex. "Hardly ever. Maybe three times a week," complains Alvy while Annie replies, "Constantly! I'd say three times a week."

Probably the most remarked-upon reimagining of a cinematic device was the use of sub-titles. After they first meet, Annie invites Alvy back to her place for a glass of wine. They're making small talk, getting to know each other. Meanwhile, the sub-titles are revealing what they're *really* thinking. While Alvy babbles on about the "aesthetic criteria" of judging photography, he's thinking, "I wonder what she looks like naked." Meanwhile she's thinking, "I hope he doesn't turn out to be a shmuck like the others."

Annie's use of the Yiddish "shmuck" (which, politely, might be taken as "jerk") says something not only about Woody Allen being Jewish but about how much American movies had changed. Although it's been widely noted that Hollywood was largely a creation of immigrant Jews (of the studio chiefs in the 1930s, only Walt Disney and Darryl Zanuck were not Jewish), Jewish characters disappeared from the screen even as Jewish actors and writers continued to find work. Over the decades this situation changed, and with the passing of the moguls of the immigrant generation—and the decline of American anti-Semitism after World War II—Jewish characters began emerging in the movies. To cite but one example, the great stage star Fanny Brice performed rarely in the movies, but Barbra Streisand won an Oscar and became a movie star playing her in *Funny Girl* (1968).

Allen had been using Jewish humor throughout his career, but it wasn't until *Annie Hall* that he identified his characters as Jewish. This led to a still ongoing debate among Jewish critics, thinkers, and movie fans as to whether his self-deprecating humor is, as they say, "good for the Jews." Allen himself has weighed in on this, noting, "I have frequently been accused of being a self-hating Jew, and while it's true I am Jewish and don't like myself very much, it's not because of my persuasion." In *Annie Hall* Alvy is constantly looking for evidence that he is being attacked because he is Jewish, whether it's a withering look by Annie's Grammy Hall (whom he describes as a "classic Jew hater") or it's Alvy's claim that the reason the rest of America hates New York is because they think "we're left-wing Communist, Jewish, homosexual pornographers."

How to read Allen's films in this context is difficult, particularly as his romantic opposites in the movies and in real life are obviously non-Jewish women like Keaton, Mia Farrow, and Soon-Yi Previn. But for those who are quick to dismiss him as a comic Jewish icon, it's worth noting that if he doesn't exactly celebrate his Jewish identity, neither does he run from it. As Lawrence J. Epstein notes in his book about American Jewish comedians, *The Haunted Smile*, "Allen was being bold putting his Jewishness directly in front of American audiences. In this, it is instructive to contrast Allen with a writer that Jewish audiences much more widely admired—Neil Simon—and to see how little overtly Jewish content was in Simon's plays and movies. Allen didn't smuggle his content in; he loudly proclaimed his Jewishness. However troubled his relationship to that Jewishness might have been, he refused to hide it."

*

Meanwhile, in the editing room, *Annie Hall* was an incoherent mess. Marshall Brickman was appalled. "To tell you the truth, when I saw the rough cut of *Annie Hall*, I thought it was terrible; completely unsalvageable. It was two and a half hours long and rambled and was tangential and just endless."

The original version was essentially Alvy free-associating about his life and his worries. Annie was seen briefly and then disappeared from the movie for fifteen minutes. Nothing was mentioned just in passing. Everything was an excuse for extended riffs, as if Allen was afraid of leaving something out. "It was like the first draft of a novel, like the raw material from which a film could be assembled, from which two or three films could possibly be assembled," recalled Brickman.

Even the scenes with Annie—they were already there, of course—led to fantasies and flashbacks galore. The sequence where Alvy, Annie, and Rob (Tony Roberts) head to Brooklyn originally ran ten to fifteen minutes and had many more scenes than the one or two we see in the final film. Alvy and his date from *Rolling Stone* (Shelly Duvall) spun off to a scene where they wound up in the Garden of Eden talking to God. When Alvy is arrested in Los Angeles (after playing bumper cars in the parking lot), there was a long scene of him interacting with the other prisoners in his cell.

Like the sculptor who chips away at the block so that the statue hidden inside can emerge, Allen and Rosenblum began hacking away at the movie to see if there was something in the material worth saving. "It was clear to Woody and me that the film started moving whenever present-tense material with him and Keaton dominated the screen, and so we began cutting in the direction of that relationship," Rosenblum later wrote. They tossed out entire sequences, tightened things up, and always kept the focus on Alvy and Annie. Even the scenes of flashbacks to Alvy's earlier marriages were greatly shortened. Some characters were eliminated altogether. Said Allen, "There was a lot of material taken out of that picture that I thought was wonderfully funny. . . . It wasn't what I had intended to do. I didn't sit down with Marshall Brickman and say, 'We're going to write a picture about a relationship.'"

One of the scenes cut was Duane's dark fantasy, but when the film started playing well at test screenings, they decided to put back some of the material they liked and missed. Christopher Walken's big moment was restored.

Finally whipping the film into shape, they still had two problems: the ending and the title. They tried a number of conclusions to the film, including ending it at the movie theater when Annie and Alvy meet with their respective dates, or showing an unhappy Alvy with a new girlfriend still trying to forget Annie. Instead Rosenblum instructed his assistant, Susan Morse (who would go on to edit most of Allen's films), to find footage of various romantic scenes between Alvy and Annie while Allen tried to come up with the right joke and narration to mirror the opening of the film. After some false starts, they arrived at the ending that now exists. Brickman, who thought the film was beyond repair (and described seeing the cuts as having his skin ripped off), saw the new ending and knew they had gotten it right. "I think every writer of comedy wants to send them out with something like that, to keep them laughing, extremely hysterical, for an hour and twenty-eight minutes, and then for the last two minutes turn it around and let them walk away with something they can chew on."

As for the title, Allen still wanted to call it "Anhedonia." When he first told the people at United Artists, the chairman Arthur Krim threatened—jokingly, one assumes—to jump out the window if they had to sell that. Brickman pitched other titles to Allen ("It Had to Be Jew" was one of them), but it was Allen's call. The UA publicity department began developing a teaser campaign to interest the public in this clinical title, which would have included ads declaring "Anhedonia

Strikes Cleveland!" Finally Eric Pleskow, another top UA executive, made it clear that Allen was being unreasonable. He had had a free hand making the film with none of the "suits" looking over his shoulder or ordering changes, but it was the suits who would have to sell the film, and a title that mystified and turned off viewers wouldn't sell tickets.

Pleskow told Allen, "For you and me, it will be "Anhedonia," but for the rest of the people we need to find a title."

So they came up with a few titles and tested them at screenings. Allen kept "Anhedonia" in the mix (where it was greeted with silence), but now tried out "Anxiety," "Annie and Alvy," and "Annie Hall." The last won the day and went on the finished film, now to be advertised as "a nervous romance."

When the film was released in the spring of 1977 it didn't take the world by storm, but critics heaped praised on the new Woody Allen, who had put some heart and soul into the jokes. It would be a major transition in his career. Two years later, in *Stardust Memories*, he played a director of comedies who wanted to get serious while his earlier successes were referred to as his "early, funny ones." Such was the case here. *Annie Hall* provided plenty of laughs, but Allen was now in a new league as a filmmaker. The New York *Daily News* called the movie not only funny but "so tinged with sadness it tends to encourage actual weeping." It was the show business trade paper *Variety* that may have summed it up best: "In a decade largely devoted to male buddy-buddy films, brutal rape fantasies and impersonal special effects extravaganzas, Woody Allen has almost single-handedly kept alive the idea of heterosexual romance in American films."

*

If moviegoers didn't realize the impact of *Annie Hall* upon its release, Hollywood set out to remind everyone when the Oscar nominations were announced early the next year. *Annie Hall* received nominations for best picture, best director, best original screenplay, best actor, and best actress. It was the first time since 1941—when Orson Welles had done it with *Citizen Kane*—that the same person was nominated for writing, directing, and starring in a film. Given the long tradition of studios campaigning for the Oscar with advertisements in trade publications offering up this nominee or that "for your consideration," it was expected that United Artists would back their horse in the race. As the film historian Tino Balio has pointed out in his history of United Artists, its management had snagged the previous two best-picture Oscars (for *One Flew Over the Cuckoo's Nest* and *Rocky*). To win three times in a row "would be the first time in the fifty-year history of the Academy of Motion Picture Arts and Sciences that a motion picture company had achieved this feat."

But Allen, unlike Jack Nicholson, was not part of the new breed of actors who reveled in the traditions of old Hollywood. Allen told UA to keep his name out of any ads they took for the Oscars. (Afterward he asked that they not include the film's Oscar wins in any advertising in New York City.) That was eccentric enough. It was not even surprising that Allen would not be attending the Oscars. Nominees had missed the award show for all sorts of reasons, but Allen's was unique. On the Monday night of the award show he would be in New York playing clarinet with the New Orleans Marching and Funeral Band at Michael's Pub, just as he did every Monday night. "I couldn't let down the guys," he was quoted as saying.

Annie Hall proved to be the big winner. Allen won best director and shared the best screenplay with Marshall Brickman, who did attend the ceremony and accepted the statuette in person. Keaton won best actress, confirming her stardom not just in Allen's films but in the industry. *Annie Hall* also won for best picture, joining *It Happened One Night*, *The Apartment*, and *Tom Jones* on the very short list of comedies that had won the top prize. The only award denied Allen was best actor, which went to Richard Dreyfuss for *The Goodbye Girl*, another romantic comedy, this one from Neil Simon.

While his movie was capturing all these honors, Allen was playing his clarinet. Around midnight he went home and read himself to sleep, without even bothering to find out how the film had fared at the Oscars. It wasn't until the next morning that he learned what had happened. His immediate remarks were gracious: "I felt good for Diane because she wanted to win. My friend Marshall and my producers Jack Rollins and Charles Joffe had a very nice time."

But how did he *really* feel about the Oscars? In other interviews he made it clear he wasn't impressed. "I have no regard for that kind of ceremony. I just don't think they know what they're doing. When you see who wins these things—or doesn't win them—you can see how meaningless this Oscar thing is."

It's hard to call this attitude sour grapes considering that he won, but part of his reaction might have been that as popular as Allen was at the height of his career—and *Annie Hall* was the start of a huge upswing—he was always an acquired taste. As he told the film critic Richard Schickel, "Only after it won the Academy Award did it start to make some money. Once the imprimatur of the Academy was put on it and it was reissued, then it started to glean bigger box office—never spectacular. If I'm not mistaken, it was the smallest-earning Academy Award–winning picture in history to that time, and maybe of all time, I don't know."

What's ironic is that people remember *Annie Hall* as one of the great love stories, even though it ends with Alvy and Annie going their separate ways. Yet it's such a celebration of love, right down to the corny joke Alvy tells at the end about why we keep going through it, that it's as much a tribute to romance as any other traditional romantic comedy. Alvy even gives us the unexpected side effect of a failed relationship when we see him rehearsing his first play, obviously modeled on his time with Annie, except that it ends with her coming back to New York with him. Alvy turns to the camera and remarks, "You know how you're always trying to get things to come out perfect in art because it's real difficult in life."

Alvy and Annie broke up, just as Allen and Keaton did, yet remained friends. The result was *Annie Hall*, a movie that audiences embraced and that paved the way for the new generation of romantic comedies to come.

11

ARTHUR

IF REAL LIFE were like the movies, the aftermath of *Arthur* should have been fame, fortune, and great success to everyone involved. It didn't work out that way, but we're left with a movie that charmed moviegoers in the summer of 1981 and still works more than two decades later. Pointing the way to those who would follow in trying to reinvigorate the romantic comedy in more cynical and jaded times, it was the work of writer-director Steve Gordon, a first-time director who came out of the worlds of advertising and television.

Taking a stab at the theater, Gordon wrote a play called *Tough to Get Help* and got it produced on Broadway, directed by Carl Reiner. It closed on opening night. But Gordon persevered and, having now made a connection with Reiner, worked his way into television. Over the course of the 1970s he sold scripts to shows like *Chico and the Man* and *Barney Miller*, and created two series of his own. The more successful one—it lasted into a second season—was called *The Practice* and starred Danny Thomas as a family doctor. A later series about a sportswriter, *Good Time Harry*, lasted all of six episodes in the summer of 1980. In short, Gordon's story was similar to that of many struggling writers. He had lots of talent and ideas, but managed to get little more than a toehold in the industry. Those who had achieved less might envy him, but his career had yet to take off.

In 1978 his first produced screenplay reached the screen, directed by his now old friend Carl Reiner. It was called *The One and Only* and starred Henry Winkler as someone who finds a measure of fame as a professional wrestler on television in the 1950s. It wasn't much of a success and was seen as a failed attempt by Winkler to break out from under the role he was associated with in the public mind, that of the leather-jacketed Fonzie on television's *Happy Days*. Still, it was a screen credit, and that opened some doors as Gordon tried to put his next project in play, this time with himself as director. It was the story of a lovable drunk named Arthur.

*

When *Arthur* was in development at Paramount, they couldn't find an actor who was willing to play the goofball alcoholic heir to the Bach family fortune. Names like Richard Dreyfuss, James Caan, Chevy Chase, and Ryan O'Neal were bandied about, to no avail. O'Neal saw one version of the script and turned it down. Indeed, everyone seemed to enjoy turning it down, including two of the people who eventually ended up in the cast, John Gielgud and Liza Minnelli. Gordon said he wasn't sure some of them even read the script.

"People said to me, 'The man is a rich drunk—I despise this!' People that I *loved* hated it," he recalled. "I felt so terrible."

The project moved from Paramount to Orion Pictures, and the name Dudley Moore came up for the title role. Moore was a British comedian who had first come to notice as part of *Beyond the Fringe*, a comedy show that included Alan Bennett, Jonathan Miller, and Peter Cook. They fell roughly in the gap between *The Goon Show* (which had brought Peter Sellers to prominence in the 1950s) and the late-sixties arrival of *Monty Python's Flying Circus*. A hit on stage in London and New York, *Beyond the Fringe* launched Moore and Cook as a duo who would do record albums, stage shows, and even movies together, notably the sixties cult hit *Bedazzled* with Cook as the devil offering Moore all his dreams, but always with a catch.

Moore was discovered by Hollywood in 1978 when he had a supporting role in the Goldie Hawn / Chevy Chase vehicle *Foul Play* and nearly stole the film from the two stars. The next year he had his break-out role in *10*, the Blake Edwards comedy about a man obsessed with a stunning woman played by Bo Derek, who then briefly enjoyed a vogue as the pinnacle of female beauty. As a comic actor, Moore was now hot, but he had not yet become a star. His turn in the mercifully forgotten *Wholly Moses* led nowhere. Then he was sent the script for *Arthur*.

His agent, Lou Pitt, recalled getting phone calls every few minutes from Moore as he was reading it. He couldn't believe how funny it was. It was the script he had been waiting for in order to make his mark. He wasn't halfway through when he called Pitt and said, "I've just got to do this. Who do I have to sleep with?" It was something Arthur Bach might have asked when he was in his cups—which is to say, almost any time. A meeting was arranged between Moore and Gordon at the Polo Lounge in Los Angeles. Moore wanted the part, and Gordon needed a star to get his film before the cameras.

Moore did his best to convince the director he was right for the movie. He noted that most scripts he saw had a laugh every ten pages. This one had ten laughs every page. He knew he could play the part. "I can walk out of the room and walk back in as Arthur," he told Gordon. Gordon was pleased with Moore's confidence, telling the actor, "That's good, because I don't know how to direct."

So Moore got the part, but Gordon and Orion Pictures remained nervous. Dudley Moore was a very funny guy, but he was, well, British. Arthur was American, and his family was American. Would he be able to do the part with an American accent?

Moore wouldn't be the first English speaker from overseas to be asked to lose his "accent," but he was one of the few who refused. For him trying to do an American voice would simply be too distracting. He was concentrating on the role and the drunk act (which he had already perfected in his stage comedy), and felt that if audiences bought the character, the accent wouldn't matter. Even as the film got under way, he and Gordon were still arguing over his voice, and couldn't he *please* do an American accent? Moore refused.

The powers that be decided they'd just have to live with it because, after all, he *was* very funny. The casting of Moore meant they had another shot at Liza Minnelli, who had previously turned down the part because she didn't think she had the right chemistry with the actors then being touted for the role. This time, though, she thought the chemistry was perfect. Minnelli had counted Peter Sellers among her serious romances over the years, so she was already comfortable with the British style of comedy acting that Moore brought to the table. The fact that Moore was also a serious musician gave them something else in common, since Minnelli had become the toast of Broadway, movies, and television as a musical star.

Minnelli, of course, was the daughter of the legendary actress/singer Judy Garland and the equally legendary film director Vincente Minnelli. Liza Minnelli made her screen debut at age three, appearing in the final scene of *In the Good Old Summertime* (1949) with her mother and Van Johnson. Her career took off while she was still in her teens and early twenties, in such Broadway shows as *Flora the Red Menace* (winning a Tony Award in the process) and movies like *The Sterile Cuckoo* (1969) for director Alan J. Pakula, which earned her her first Oscar nomination. She won the Oscar two years later for her performance in *Cabaret*, the film role for which she is best remembered. Perhaps the icing on the cake was her landmark television special (directed by *Cabaret* director Bob Fosse), entitled "Liza with a Z." Minnelli was on top of the world, but was beset by personal problems that included troubled marriages (she's been married four times) and substance abuse. Her subsequent film choices didn't help. *Lucky Lady* (1976) was a mess, and *New York, New York* (1977), while well regarded, had her secondary to the artistic relationship between the director Martin Scorsese and the actor Robert DeNiro. It was not the career boost she needed to show that she was in it for the long haul.

By the time *Arthur* came around she wasn't exactly a has-been; she was still a huge star on Broadway and in concert. But she had been off the screen for a few years and needed a hit to revitalize any movie career she intended to have. Here was a chance to work with Moore, whom she already knew from her London days with Peter Sellers in the sixties, and so she signed on. It wasn't a huge part, but it was an important one, and she wouldn't be carrying the weight of the movie. She and Moore became great friends off-screen, though strictly platonic ones. They were both romantically involved elsewhere, he with Susan Anton and she in her third marriage, to the sculptor Mark Gero.

As for the key role of Hobson, the butler, everyone wanted John Gielgud, whether the actor realized it or not. Moore had met Gielgud when he was doing *Beyond the Fringe*, and the Shakespearean actor was taken with the diminutive comic. Gielgud had come backstage to meet him one evening and later wrote a letter of introduction for him to the actress Lilli Palmer when he heard Moore was planning a trip to Italy. Gielgud referred to him as "Stanley Moon," and that became a standing joke, even becoming the name of Moore's character in *Bedazzled*.

Moore pushed Gielgud on Gordon, even though the actor had already turned down the part. "Dudley talked me into John Gielgud," he told *New York* magazine. "I wanted James Mason because I can imitate him. But Dudley said there's nobody funnier than John Gielgud."

Gielgud—who was embarrassed at having been talked into appearing in a couple of scenes of Bob Guccione's X-rated production of *Caligula*—saw *Arthur* as a broad comedy with some off-color humor, where he would be playing a stereotypical stiff-upper-lip British butler. He simply wasn't interested. He had no idea how his rejection was received by Hollywood. One of the giants of British theater in the twentieth century, occasionally appearing in British films, he was anything but a movie star. To his surprise, though, the studio figured he was playing hard to get.

"I thought it was rather smutty and a vulgar little film, so I refused it," he later recalled. "But each time they asked me they doubled my salary, so naturally I became reconciled to it."

Moore relocated to New York to begin filming in the hot summer of 1980. Here was a nervous first-time director working from his own script, a star who was obviously not American playing an American, a supporting player who had reluctantly taken the part because of the amount of money he was offered, and a female lead who hadn't been in a hit film in nearly a decade. *Arthur* was off to a fine start.

*

Gordon began the production uneasy and stayed that way throughout. That was not to say he didn't enjoy himself, but after years in advertising and then television, where in spite of some success the big break seemed always just beyond his grasp, this was the big time. He had the movie in his head and tried to convey it to his lead. Moore was having none of it. Gordon had a habit of acting out scenes to demonstrate how he wanted to see them played. Moore made it clear that if he did as Gordon instructed he would be doing a bad imitation of a wiry, nervous Jewish writer instead of finding his own voice for the character. Gordon realized that Moore was right and gave him the room to play the part within Gordon's conception of the film. It would turn into a very happy collaboration.

In one scene Arthur is meeting with his prospective father-in-law in a room dominated by a large moose head. Each time they shot the scene Moore had a different idea how to react. Only one could be used in the finished film, and Gordon would later say he wished he could have used them all. Gordon had given birth to the character on the page and written some hilarious dialogue. It was Moore's job to bring the character to life.

Gordon was constantly being surprised by his actors, not just by Moore. He recalled that watching Gielgud working was a revelation. "I never knew what he was doing until I saw the dailies. Then I would notice an eyebrow go up and I would get hysterical."

Even Minnelli took him unawares. At a read-through of the script, Gordon turned to the actress and told her she was quite funny, almost as if he was surprised she could play comedy. Moore, who had known Minnelli for years, replied, "No shit?" For her part Minnelli did her best to reassure the novice director, calling him "Boss" to let everyone know she acknowledged who was in charge. He appreciated it.

It was Gielgud who needed to be told how a scene was going and whether he was doing a good job. "John had a huge sense of humor, but he was never quite sure he was funny," said Minnelli. "He kept turning to Dudley and me and asking, 'Was that funny?'" Gielgud would get some of the biggest laughs of the film, but it was all in his droll delivery. Hobson was the father figure Arthur so desperately needed, but he was also a servant to an irresponsible lush. The comedy came from his sarcastic putdowns that were insolent without drawing blood, as in the famous moment when Arthur announces he thinks he'll take a bath and Hobson dryly replies, "I'll alert the media."

Moore loved the fact that Gielgud read his lines with the same seriousness he would use in declaiming Shakespeare, but he wanted to help the actor relax and get into the spirit of the film. "I tried to be Rabelaisian with him as much possible, to get him up and get him going." Moore claimed the public had the wrong idea about Gielgud: "I mean everyone thinks he reads Chaucer all day, and in fact he loves reading Harold Robbins."

Minnelli also did her part to make Gielgud feel at home on the film. "He hated being called Sir John, so I called him Uncle Johnny," she remembered. "And he seemed to like that, but he never knew just how funny he was: some of his lines were very raunchy, and to hear them spoken in that brilliant accent was magic."

There was a lot of laughing on the set. Moore had a built-in audience with the cast and crew, and his constant improvisations got laughs whenever he tried something new. It threatened to get out of hand. One scene took twenty-seven takes because of the laughing. One day the crew showed up with pieces of tape that they were planning to put over their mouths to stop the laughter. It was either that or get behind schedule.

Another problem, if it can be called that, is that Liza Minnelli shooting a film in Manhattan in the summer of 1980 became the buzz of the town. People couldn't resist shouting out to the actress or otherwise interfering with a scene. Gordon said the *Arthur* locations kept drawing crowds. "By mid-morning we were surrounded by thousands of people. We became a tourist attraction. People would say, 'Let's visit the Plaza Hotel and the Statue of Liberty and, on the way back, let's stop at *Arthur*.'" He was speaking only partly in jest. Minnelli may not have had a hit movie in a while, but she was a major figure in the world of entertainment. "People would fall down laughing at Dudley, but they wanted to reach out and touch Liza," Gordon said. "It's as if some bit of her magic would rub off on them."

Part of this was undoubtedly due to her own unquestioned talent, but there was no mistaking that Minnelli also had the show-business lineage. During a break in the shoot one day, an elderly woman appeared before Liza and declared, "Judy! I've seen all your movies. Is it really you?"

Minnelli might have reacted in a number of ways, but she told the woman, "No, my name's Liza, and I'm Judy's daughter. But I want you to know that's the nicest thing anyone has ever said to me."

Gordon remained a nervous wreck, but he expressed it comically so that his cast didn't share the burden of his anxieties. He'd loudly moan on the set, "*Oy vey*, this isn't going to work! What am I doing?" while taking his pulse and threatening to have a heart attack. Minnelli remembered one slapstick moment. ". . . It was dreadfully hot on the set and there was a fan next to Steve, who was sitting in his high director's chair. He was worried about a scene and he said, 'No, that's not quite right,' and started shaking his head, and he leaned back and his hair got caught in the fan."

As production went on, people began to feel a bit burned out, and that was when music came to the rescue. Moore had studied music and remained quite serious about it, composing as well as playing. Minnelli arranged for a piano to be installed in his dressing room, and Moore could be heard playing between takes, sometimes with Minnelli supplying vocals. When he learned that Jill Eikenberry—who played his prissy fiancée—also played the piano, he insisted she take her turn at the keyboard.

It was during production that Moore may have had his greatest moment as a pianist. He was visiting with his friends Robert and Lucy

Mann, who were well connected in New York's classical music world, at a party where musicians of international acclaim were on the guest list. Moore loved being part of this atmosphere but had no intention of putting himself on the line against such competition. On this fateful evening the guest of honor was violinist Itzhak Perlman, who was performing with a string quartet. When Mann suggested that Moore be invited to sit in at the piano, Perlman was surprised, assuming Moore was a comedian who, at best, noodled around at the keyboard.

But Mann insisted and suggested an especially difficult piece for Moore, one he had never seen before. Mann later recalled, "I could see Perlman smirking like mad while the others looked on very skeptically." Moore, however, had a gift that Mann knew about—and Perlman and the other guests did not. He could sight-read music and master even difficult compositions with little preparation. His playing that evening was a triumph. "Itzhak was dumbfounded—he couldn't believe anyone could read like that. They all burst into applause when he'd finished."

When the production finally wrapped, Gordon faced his biggest problem yet: how to take all the footage he had shot and turn it into a movie.

*

Susan E. Morse, who had become Woody Allen's editor after working with Ralph Rosenblum, was brought in to make sense of *Arthur*. When the cast saw the rough cut, Moore was appalled. For one thing, Gordon had shot several different endings for the movie and still hadn't figured out which one to use. For another, they apparently had been so taken by the relationship between Arthur and Hobson that they forgot this was supposed to be a romantic comedy. The film had turned into the story of a drunk forced to grow up when his only friend in the world dies. That was certainly one of the story strands, but now it had become the primary one, with the notion of whether

Would audiences buy British comedian Dudley Moore as a lush, a playboy, and an American? They did, thanks to a career-making performance and turns by Sir John Gielgud and Liza Minnelli (not shown).

Linda and Arthur could overcome their obstacles for true happiness decidedly on the back burner. Moore, who had stood up to Gordon on how he would play Arthur, now felt the director needed a big push once again.

"Who wants to see this drunken idiot for an hour and a half?" he declared at the end of the screening. He told Gordon that the director needed to go back to the story he had intended to tell in the first place, which was a romantic comedy. Later, some critics would have the same problem with the film, not understanding that without Linda there could be no redemption for Arthur. It's one thing for Arthur to recognize how much he owed Hobson and to finally show him some gratitude. It was another for Arthur to suddenly care for another person not out of a sense of obligation but because he truly loved her.

Gordon went back to the editing room. Minnelli credits Moore's outburst for rescuing her performance from the cutting-room floor, but there's no reason to think that Gordon wouldn't have eventually figured it out. The Arthur/Hobson relationship provides undeniable flavor and texture to the film, but Arthur needs to express the mature love he feels for Linda to show he's truly grown up. Linda's character, likewise, doesn't work if she's essentially Hobson's replacement, becoming Arthur's nursemaid. She has to validate the essential goodness of the character that Arthur's family—concerned primarily with their wealth—has largely ignored.

Gordon shot some new footage too. This included the scene in which Arthur is beaten up by his now father-in-law-not-to-be. Afterward Moore, in his tattered clothes and bloody makeup, was with his girlfriend Susan Anton in an elevator at the Waldorf-Astoria. With other people on the elevator he turned to her and said, "Susan, I *told* you I'd be home. *Why* wouldn't you believe me?" The other people looked at the blonde Anton towering over the cowering and bruised Moore and were aghast.

Arthur opened in the summer of 1981 to decidedly mixed reviews. Some faulted Gordon's direction, though Moore and Gielgud got generally good notices. Poor Minnelli took many of the hits, the low point being a cranky diatribe by John Simon in the *National Review*: "Miss Minnelli, though relatively restrained, still exudes her special brand of physical and spirited repulsiveness." But *Arthur* proved to be one of those movies where word of mouth is more important than any review. The movie became the surprise hit of the season, eventually taking in some $100,000,000 in domestic box office, highly unusual for a comedy in 1981.

Besides boosting the careers of the director and actors, the success of *Arthur* rubbed off on the people responsible for the film's music. The veteran composer Burt Bacharach wrote a bouncy score for the film, his first since the failed movie musical remake of *Lost Horizon* in 1973. He was also one of several hands involved in writing "Arthur's Theme (Best That You Can Do)" along with his then wife Carole

Bayer Sager, Liza Minnelli's ex-husband Peter Allen, and the singer Christopher Cross. Cross's recording of the song went gold.

But the top-of-the-line talent scored the biggest. Gordon's movie career was launched; Moore, who received a percentage of the profits, now had not only money but Hollywood clout, with script approval and big paydays for future projects. Even John Gielgud managed to cash in on the film's unexpected success. He had been paid only $100,000 for *Arthur* but now found himself in demand not only for small roles in other films but to succeed Orson Welles as the TV pitchman for Paul Masson wines, a gig that would make him rich.

Given its troubled history, *Arthur* had succeeded beyond anyone's dreams. Better yet, the Oscars were still to come.

*

In spite of the precedents of *It Happened One Night* and *Annie Hall*, no one expected *Arthur* to be a major Oscar contender. This was the year of *Reds, On Golden Pond, Ragtime, Atlantic City, Raiders of the Lost Ark*, and *Chariots of Fire*. So it was a pleasant surprise when *Arthur* received four nominations. Moore was nominated for best actor, Gielgud for best supporting actor, Gordon for original screenplay, and "Arthur's Theme" for best song.

When the nominations were announced, Moore made it clear that he had no expectations whatsoever. Henry Fonda had been nominated for *On Golden Pond*. It was only his second nomination in a long and distinguished career, and he had lost to Jimmy Stewart (*Grapes of Wrath* versus *The Philadelphia Story*) forty years earlier. It was highly unlikely he would be denied this time, and he wasn't. Fonda was too ill to attend, but his daughter Jane—who had also appeared in the film—accepted on his behalf. Fonda would die five months later. Gordon also lost, to the surprise British hit *Chariots of Fire*.

Arthur, however, did not go home empty-handed. "Arthur's Theme" won for best song, and Gielgud—who had also appeared in *Chariots of Fire*—won for best supporting actor. With Katharine Hepburn picking up her fourth best-actress Oscar (for *On Golden Pond*), it was clearly old-timer's night. Maureen Stapleton, who was then in her mid-fifties and won best supporting actress for *Reds*, was the youngster of the four acting honorees. Gielgud was not present at the ceremonies but was immensely touched by the honor. "It's extraordinary to have that Oscar after wonderful things like a knighthood. To think that people who've never heard of me now think of me as a kind of name," he said.

To show that success—even late in life—hadn't gone to head, Gielgud put the statuette in his bathroom, where it stayed the rest of his life. He was still doing serious work, and he was somewhat bemused—as Alec Guinness had been in the wake of *Star Wars* (1977)—to discover that what he had taken as a lark in a Hollywood film was now the strongest association he had in the minds of most people. "I got a new public all over the world who had never seen me play *anything*. They didn't know what to expect. They were just amused by my performance," he said. "That was why it was so satisfying."

The aftermath of the film, however, was not so happy for all concerned. Moore, now calling his own shots, made a series of films that ranged from mediocre to awful. He never enjoyed another film success like *Arthur*. Minnelli's well-publicized personal problems kept her off-screen. Several years later she and Moore reunited for *Arthur: On the Rocks* (1988), which even resurrected a ghostly Hobson (played again by Gielgud) for a few moments, but it failed to recapture the spirit of the original.

Moore's problems grew worse when he was diagnosed with progressive supranuclear palsy, an incurable disease. For a while he put up with being seen as Arthur and being offered similar roles, but as he was not a heavy drinker in private life, he was upset when the disease caused a slurring of his speech and people leaped to the wrong conclusion. "I'm doomed to become Arthur in real life," he said. He died in 2002 at the age of sixty-six.

But the saddest story is that of writer-director Steve Gordon, who had achieved success beyond his wildest dreams. He had taken a project that no one wanted to do and turned it into an Oscar-winning hit. The summer it came out he was already nervously looking ahead. "I haven't even started my next screenplay and already it doesn't work. I just think I fooled them once," he said. "This is a very scary business. . . . You're supposed to beat yourself every time. I have to beat *Arthur*."

He never got the chance. In November 1982, Gordon died of a heart attack. He was only forty-four.

Perhaps it's better to close on the final image of Arthur, grandly renouncing his fortune for true love and insisting that he'll get a job and turn his back on the never-ending party that's been his life. He walks over to the limousine to exchange final words with his grandmother (Geraldine Fitzgerald), who has declared that if he is cut off she will never take him back. When he returns to his own limo, Linda and his loyal chauffer Bitterman (Ted Ross) wonder what has transpired. Has he agreed to marry Linda on his grandmother's terms, taking the money?

There's a delicious pause, and then Arthur replies, "I'm not crazy." They get into the car, which then pulls out into traffic and heads off . . . somewhere between the moon and New York City.

12

WHEN HARRY
MET SALLY . . .

IN OCTOBER 1989, *Premiere* magazine acknowledged the success of the previous summer's hit romantic comedy by publishing a chart labeled "When Harry Met Woody." It noted that *When Harry Met Sally . . .* had numerous similarities to Woody Allen's films, particularly *Annie Hall* and *Manhattan.* Among these were that Harry (Billy Crystal) had an obsession with death, like Allen's protagonists; that *Annie Hall* and *When Harry Met Sally . . .* both had a key scene in which the woman made a late-night call for help to the man; that both *Manhattan* and *Harry* ended with the male lead running through the city to get to his lady love before it was too late; and that both *Annie Hall* and *Harry* made use of the romantic standard "It Had to Be You."

Nora Ephron, who wrote the screenplay to *Harry,* once reflected on the film and proposed that there are basically two sub-groupings of romantic comedy. The first she labeled the "Christian" romantic comedy, in which the couple must overcome some obstacle in order to make their relationship work. Most of the earlier films discussed in this book would fall into that category. The other she called the "Jewish" romantic comedy, which she acknowledged was "pioneered by Woody Allen." In these, the obstacle to be overcome consists of the neuroses of the male character. If *When Harry Met Sally . . .* is one of the best Woody Allen movies Allen never made, it is not so much a matter of being an homage or even of unwitting copying, but simply that, like Allen, Ephron, the director Rob Reiner, and Billy Crystal had all grown up with the same New York Jewish sensibility as Allen. It's like noting that Pierre Renoir and Claude Monet were both nineteenth-century French impressionists without claiming that one was imitating the other.

*

Rob Reiner was already famous as an actor and director when, nearing his fortieth birthday, he decided he wanted to do an adult romantic comedy. The son of the comedian/writer/actor/director Carl Reiner, he had grown up in a household where Mel Brooks was not only considered a very funny guy but someone who was a frequent visitor—a friend and often a partner of his father. Reiner had his first inkling that he would end up in a career in comedy when, at age sixteen, he came up with a joke for Brooks and his father to use in their famous "2000 Year Old Man" routine. It was about the invention of applause (Brooks explains they used to hit their faces to express approval but then started moving their heads to avoid the pain), and Reiner was thrilled when they used it.

He was in his mid-twenties when he was cast as Michael "Meathead" Stivic on *All in the Family*, Norman Lear's sitcom that changed American television with its frank discussion of politics, prejudice, sex, and other once-taboo topics. Reiner played the son-in-law of the blue-collar Archie Bunker (Carroll O'Connor), who was a graduate student and therefore living under Archie's roof. The debates between bleeding-heart liberal Mike and knee-jerk conservative Archie provided countless laughs and endless fodder for conversation around water coolers and dinner tables.

After he left the show Reiner moved toward what would become his ultimate career goal: becoming a movie director. His first film was the cult hit *This Is Spinal Tap* (1984), an uproarious "mockumentary" about a British heavy-metal rock band that never seems to make it. In test screenings audiences not clued in that it was a joke were puzzled why they had never heard of Spinal Tap. Reiner's reputation would grow with *The Sure Thing*, *Stand by Me*, and *The Princess Bride*. But shortly after the success of *Spinal Tap* he, his producer Andrew Scheinman, and the writer Nora Ephron began discussions about an idea he had for a romantic comedy that would be different from what people had seen. Reiner, who had married and divorced the actress/director Penny Marshall, had not been enjoying being a single adult and wanted to make a film that reflected his experience.

Ephron is the daughter of the classic Hollywood screenwriters Henry and Phoebe Ephron, whose screen credits include adaptations of *Carousel* and *Daddy Long Legs* and the Tracy/Hepburn comedy *Desk Set*. Nora Ephron went on to a career as a journalist and novelist before making her mark as a screenwriter in the 1980s with credits on *Silkwood* and *Heartburn*. (The latter was an adaptation of her novel based on the breakup of her marriage to the *Washington Post* reporter Carl Bernstein.) Ephron was not initially impressed with Reiner and Scheinman's suggestion for a movie about a lawyer, and she told them so. So they spent the rest of the lunch talking about themselves or, more particularly, Reiner and Scheinman told stories about being single in L.A. Reiner was divorced, Scheinman was unmarried; by the end of the meal they agreed to get together the next time they were all in New York. In November 1984 they met again and, as Ephron recalled, "Rob said he had an idea—he wanted to make a movie about a man and a woman who become friends, as opposed to lovers; they make a deliberate decision not to have sex because sex ruins everything; and then they have sex and it ruins everything. And I said, let's do it."

Ephron essentially interviewed the two men about their relationships and their feelings about love, sex, and women in general. Some of it was hilarious, some of it was appalling, and all of it was grist for the mill. Over the next few years they met periodically, and it wasn't only Reiner's and Scheinman's lives that provided material but Ephron's as well. It was a long process. Reiner explained, "Nora Ephron did a couple of drafts and then we'd all get together and work quite a bit. Then she'd go off and write some scenes, and then we'd come back together and rework those scenes. Then maybe she'd go off again."

By the time they finished, several years had gone by and other projects had come to fruition. But now the "Untitled Rob Reiner Project" was ready to begin casting. It was a movie that would require actors who were smart, talented, and could play real emotions as well as being funny. Most important, they had to be entertaining to listen to because the script was wall-to-wall talk. As Meg Ryan would later describe it, "It's about two neurotic, self-indulgent people who are madly in love with each other but don't know it . . . for twelve years."

This would be a movie about their romantic lives, and nothing else. Consider the other movies in this book. You have no problem identifying the jobs of Peter Warne in *It Happened One Night*, Sugar, Joe, and Jerry in *Some Like It Hot*, or Adam and Amanda in *Adam's Rib*. Not only is it spelled out, but their jobs are essential to their stories. Macaulay Connor shows up at the Lords' because he's been assigned to write a story about Tracy's wedding. The couples in *Trouble in Paradise*, *The Shop Around the Corner*, and *Pillow Talk* may initially connect in unconventional ways, but their workaday lives are crucial to understanding who they are. Even in *Annie Hall*, the fact that Alvy Singer is a comedian and Annie Hall is an aspiring singer is an important plot point.

Without checking, can you identify what Harry and Sally do for their livelihoods? It's a great trivia question because, except for passing references, we learn nothing at all about their work lives. We do not see them on the job. Their friends are unconnected with the office. Indeed, had their jobs been more prominent, it might have proved a needless distraction, because Sally is a journalist (we're told she writes for *New York* magazine) and Harry is a political consultant. A change of emphasis could have turned this into the forgettable 1994 comedy *Speechless*, with Geena Davis and Michael Keaton as the romantic couple who are working as speechwriters on opposing Senate campaigns. Said Reiner, "What I like about the film is that there's nothing going on in it. It was a real challenge, a high-degree-of-difficulty film, because there's no subplot."

One of the most difficult steps would be selecting the leads, and the fact that Billy Crystal was one of Rob Reiner's closest friends did *not* give him a leg up on the role. Quite the contrary.

*

Billy Crystal was also born into show business. His father, Jack Crystal, was a music promoter and a co-founder of Commodore Records. Young Billy met some of the top musical performers of the 1950s New York club scene. In one well-known story he recounted how he was once baby-sat by the legendary singer Billie Holliday. He was also touched early by tragedy when his father died at age fifty-four, when Crystal was only fifteen.

Although he had hopes of a baseball career, it never materialized. Instead, after college he went to Los Angeles to pursue a job in television, eventually landing a role in the new sitcom *Soap*, which was controversial before it even premiered. One of the reasons was Crystal's character Jodie, who was the first continuing gay character on a prime-time series. He also was chosen to play Mike Stivic's best friend for an episode of *All in the Family*. Reiner and Crystal connected off-camera as well, and they became close friends in real life.

By the time Reiner was casting *When Harry Met Sally . . .* , Crystal was a well-known comic actor, not only from *Soap* and a subsequent stint on *Saturday Night Live* but from hit movies like *Running Scared* and *Throw Momma from the Train*. Reiner, though, appeared fearful of risking their friendship by casting Crystal in his movie. Instead he sent the script around to other actors and told Crystal about all the problems he was having as a result. Albert Brooks turned it down, worried he would be typecast as a whiny misfit. Michael Keaton passed. Richard Dreyfuss was interested but wanted changes, to which Reiner wouldn't agree. Perhaps most curious is that Tom Hanks was given the opportunity to star in the film, which would have made this the first pairing of Hanks and Meg Ryan. Instead Hanks reportedly told Reiner that he didn't get it, and it wasn't for him. (Hanks and Ryan made their first film together the following year with *Joe vs. the Volcano,* and then more notably they teamed with Nora Ephron—who had graduated to directing—on *Sleepless in Seattle* and *You've Got Mail.*)

Crystal wanted the part, but he wasn't going to force the issue if Reiner wasn't interested. So he suffered in silence. "I was in pain the whole time. Doesn't he want me? Doesn't he trust me? I couldn't say anything to Rob. He had to go through the process. If he asked me, it should be on merit, not on friendship. It was just awful."

Reiner wasn't blind, but he had his own apprehensions about going to Crystal. "He knew what I was going through. And I knew what he was going through. I take a long, long time, especially before asking a friend. I don't want him to say no," said Reiner. There was another matter. At this point Reiner had a lot invested in the character of Harry. Much of the dialogue—whether written by him or by Ephron—had derived from their conversations and reflected his own experiences. Ephron understood and urged Reiner to play the part himself. Reiner, while still doing occasional acting (including in Ephron's films), didn't want the burden of being both director *and* star. Said Ephron, "From the beginning, Harry was Rob. He's a guy who's always telling you he's depressed while he makes you laugh."

That's where some of the Woody Allen comparisons come from, but in fact Allen, Reiner, Ephron, and later Crystal, when he started making his own contributions, were all drawing from a fatalistic strain of Jewish humor that Mel Brooks and many others have drawn from over the course of their careers. (It might be summed up by the song Brooks wrote for his 1970 film *The Twelve Chairs,* which advised: "Hope for the best, expect the worst.") As Ephron put it, "The point is that Rob was depressed; but he wasn't at all depressed about being depressed; in fact, he loved his depression. And so does Harry. Harry honestly believes that he is a better person than Sally because he has what Sally generously calls a dark side."

Can a man and a woman be friends without sex getting in the way? Harry (Billy Crystal) and Sally (Meg Ryan) call their married friends (Bruno Kirby and Carrie Fisher) after they think they've made a mistake.

Reiner finally offered the part of Harry to Crystal and made his peace with the notion that someone else would play him. In fact Crystal told Reiner he would have to let go of Harry and let Crystal find his own way into the character. There's some indication that the part of Jess, which went to Reiner and Crystal's friend Bruno Kirby, was inspired in part by Reiner's close relationship with Crystal. So on some level Reiner was directing Crystal playing Reiner while Kirby was playing Crystal. Or perhaps it was Meg Ryan playing Crystal. The scenes of Harry and Sally watching *Casablanca* in their separate apartments while talking on the phone came from Reiner and Crystal having done just that.

Casting the part of Sally was less of a problem. For one thing, although Ephron's life and attitude would be expressed through Sally, Sally was *not* Ephron's on-screen alter ego. She was a fictional character who was created to balance Harry. Harry is dark and cynical, advising a couple moving in together to start planning for their future breakup. Sally is sunny and optimistic; her darkest sex fantasy is an unknown stranger ripping off her clothes. When Harry asks if that's truly her only fantasy, Sally allows she sometimes varies it by imagining herself wearing different clothes. It was the old Hollywood cliché of opposites attracting given a fresh spin because it took so long them for them finally to be attracted to each other.

Sally's part was supposed to go to Elizabeth McGovern, whom Reiner had been dating. When their relationship ended, so did his interest in casting her. Instead the part went to Meg Ryan, not yet thirty, who had slowly been attracting attention in roles in mid-eighties movies like *Top Gun* and *The Presidio*. She met her future husband Dennis Quaid while making *Innerspace* with him, and now seemed ripe for stardom in the right role. Reiner was effusive in his praise for Ryan: "She's the best actress I've ever worked with. By far!" he told *Vogue* in 1989 at the time of the film's release. "She can do anything; she's equally adept at playing comedy and drama. Plus she's sexy and she's cute."

What he liked was that although Ryan was not a member of the Reiner/Crystal/Kirby "boys' club" on the film, she was able to get right into the rhythm of the comedy. Watch her in the scene at the museum when Harry starts talking with a strange accent and invites her to play along. It was something Crystal improvised without warning her in advance, and you can spot her looking quickly off camera at Reiner to see if he wanted her to go with it. He did and she did.

Principal casting was completed with the casting of Carrie Fisher and Kirby in the best friend roles. Yet as production neared they still had no settled ending for the story. And some of the most famous moments associated with the film had yet to be worked out.

*

"People who live in cities aren't in car chases. We don't get shot at. What we mainly do is talk on the phone and have dinner," Nora

Ephron explained about why *When Harry Met Sally . . .* is dialogue driven.

The film opens with an elderly couple talking about how they met. Different couples pop up in these interludes over the course of the film, culminating in Harry and Sally on the same couch telling their story. The implication is that beyond our learning that they have married, they have now joined the pantheon of other happily married couples whom we've seen throughout the film. Those couples were not part of the original conception for the film.

Reiner recalled visiting his friend Alan Horn (who later would become president and chief operating officer of Warner Bros. Entertainment) and seeing Horn's parents there. Horn's father, Sol, was in his eighties and didn't say a word. He just sat there. Reiner tried to think of some way to include him in the conversation and finally asked the older man how he and Mrs. Horn had met. Suddenly Sol Horn came to life, telling Reiner the story about seeing his future wife in a Horn and Hardart restaurant, and remarking to his dining companion how he was going to marry that woman. Reiner was charmed, and the story became the first one told in the movie. In the closing credits of the film, a special thank-you is given to Sol Horn for his "inspiration."

Once they had the idea to use the older couples as punctuation in the film, they began seeking out and filming people recounting how they had met. People had great stories, but Reiner discovered that once on camera they would become distracted or go off on a tangent. They were talking about their lives, not offering up pithy anecdotes for a movie. In the end, Reiner had the stories recorded, then hired professional actors to relate polished versions of them for the movie. The story of how Ephron's parents met is one of the stories told. Another—the one about the couple who were born and raised in the same neighborhood in New York but didn't meet until they got on an elevator together in a Chicago hotel—featured an actor named Bernie Hern, a family friend who had been best man at Reiner's parents' wedding.

Since, as Ephron noted, this wasn't an action film, many of the key scenes took place over meals, and there was a story behind almost every one of them. In the first section of the film, recent college graduates Harry and Sally are sharing a car ride from Chicago to New York. They stop for dinner at a diner where Sally proceeds to rewrite the menu as she places her order, asking for some things "on the side" and putting an option on other items ("only if it's real") that leaves Harry stunned. As it turns out, the notion for the scene was Ephron's, even though she didn't realize it.

Reiner watched Ephron order at one of their restaurant meetings, and it was just as you see Sally do in the movie. Ephron knew what she wanted and didn't think twice about it, but Reiner was amazed. "This is hilarious," he told her. "This has to be in the movie." That became one of Sally's signature traits, and it's notable that at the end of the film when the pair describe their wedding, Harry agrees with Sally about the importance of serving the chocolate sauce "on the side." He's adopted her point of view.

Sometime after the film was released, Ephron was on a plane when the stewardess came to take her food and drink order, and Ephron ordered as she usually did. The stewardess looked at her and asked, "Did you ever see *When Harry Met Sally . . .* ?"

Perhaps the most famous restaurant scene in the movie—maybe in any movie—is when Harry and Sally go to lunch at Katz's Deli. Ephron was again the inadvertent source for the scene. The premise of the movie is that, as Harry puts it, "Men and women can't be friends because the sex part always gets in the way." The rest of the film is about whether Harry can be part of a couple that first becomes friends, then has sex, and then has to figure out what it means to their relationship.

Much of Ephron's script was based on what she had learned from Reiner and producer Andrew Scheinman about how men think. Out of those conversations came such things as Harry explaining that after sex men began worrying about how long they have to hold their partner before they can leave (and whether thirty seconds is enough) while women want to be held all night. So they put it to Ephron to start offering up some of the things women think about and usually don't discuss with men, since if the film was going to work it had to have honesty from both sides. Ephron asked how men could be so selfish as to want to run right out the door after sex, and Reiner replied it wasn't really selfish. After all, the woman had had a good time too. Ephron asked Reiner how he knew that.

"I told Rob he couldn't be sure about a woman's satisfaction because women can fake orgasms," she said.

Reiner was surprised. He didn't believe anything like that had ever happened to him, or that this was something most women did. So he started asking the women in his office. More than half told him that, of course, at some time they had done just that. Reiner was shocked, but he realized that not only had Ephron told him the truth, but now they had to work that into the movie. Thus the genesis of the famous "fake orgasm" scene.

By the time the script was being read through by the cast—Reiner likes to give the actors plenty of rehearsal time—Ryan suggested that the scene would be even funnier if she demonstrated Sally's acting abilities in counterfeiting the throes of passion. This was immediately added in, but it was left to Billy Crystal to come up with the famous capper. He suggested that another patron in the restaurant who witnessed the scene tell her waiter, "I'll have what she's having." In passing out credit for what Reiner would call "the funniest line in any movie I've ever done," one can spot the fingerprints of the director, the screenwriter, and both the stars.

On the day of filming, Estelle Reiner, Rob's mother, arrived to be the person to deliver that line. Reiner wasn't sure how it would play, and he told his mother that if her line didn't get a big laugh in previews, he would cut it. That was fine with her. She was simply enjoying the opportunity to spend the day watching her son at work.

When they did the first take, Ryan, whose idea it was to act out the fake orgasm, seemed to be shy doing it front of a restaurant full of extras, plus the film crew. In a second take the problem was much the same. Reiner realized he would have to step in and demonstrate just how broadly he wanted her to play it if the scene was going to work. So the beefy, bearded director sat in the booth opposite Crystal and showed her how he wanted her to act it out. Crystal would later joke it was like being on a date with Sebastian Cabot. Reiner gave a big, sweaty, table-banging performance to make sure that Ryan saw how he wanted it. Only afterward did he remember that his mother was sitting at the next table, watching his orgasmic performance.

Ryan began pulling out the stops, as Reiner had wanted, and it became a great scene. The only problem was that they had to shoot the scene repeatedly in order to get different angles and cover mistakes. Crystal claimed to be having such a good time that he would blow a line just to watch her do it again. And, of course, the food on their table would have to be replaced every time they started anew. (Katz's still has a sign marking the table where "Harry met Sally," so they've been more than recompensed for their troubles that day.)

By the time Reiner finished shooting he had a scene that would enter cinema history, not only for the laughs it generated but for revealing a little-remarked-upon truth in the relationship of the sexes. It didn't hurt that Estelle Reiner's deadpan rendition of "I'll have what she's having" got an even bigger laugh, and drowned out the music for several moments into the next scene. Although she had sung when she was younger, her movie career, such as it was, consisted of brief bits in movies by her husband Carl and his friends Mel Brooks and Anne Bancroft. This time, however, she had a moment that would be remembered as long as people watched movies.

"My mother can never say I never gave her anything," Reiner said.

*

Reiner's motivation in making the film was to address the issues he had felt as a single man after his divorce from Penny Marshall. Of course he really hoped to meet someone himself. One day on the set he was looking at a picture of the actress Michelle Pfeiffer in a magazine, which noted she had recently been divorced. Reiner mentioned that he might see if she'd be interested in going out on a date. His cinematographer, Barry Sonnenfeld (who has since become a director himself), told Reiner he shouldn't date Michelle Pfeiffer; he should go out with a friend of the Sonnenfelds, a photographer named Michele Singer.

When Singer visited the set during the shooting of the film, Reiner asked her out. They went to dinner at the Café Lunenberg in New York. The next day he was back again, filming the scene where Harry and Sally try to fix each other up with their friends Jess (Bruno Kirby) and Marie (Carrie Fisher). That fix-up didn't work, but Reiner's date with Singer was a success. By the time the film was released, they had gotten married in Hawaii. As of this writing they're still living happily ever after. As Reiner puts it, "Our story could fit very nicely into the film."

Two other people had life-changing experiences during the making of the film, though not as intimate as Reiner's meeting the love of his life. Reiner wanted to use old musical standards to score the film. Woody Allen had been doing this, but the idea of having old songs on the soundtrack of a modern romantic comedy would not really take off until *When Harry Met Sally . . .* One of the reasons for the success of the idea was Marc Shaiman, whom Billy Crystal knew from his stint on *Saturday Night Live* where Shaiman had been the rehearsal pianist. Shaiman had an encyclopedic knowledge of the great American songbook, and with Reiner he began pulling out songs that were so perfect they could have been written for the film. Shaiman was particularly pleased with introducing Reiner to the Rodgers and Hart song "I Could Write a Book," which was used in the film. Reiner was so happy with the results that Shaiman became his composer/musical consultant on all his later films.

The other find was a twenty-year-old singer and jazz pianist named Harry Connick, Jr. Reiner's friend Bobby Colomby, a music executive and a former drummer with the group Blood, Sweat and

Tears, had suggested Reiner listen to the young talent who played many of the standards Reiner was considering for the film. Reiner eventually signed Connick to do several numbers for the film.

Connick's modern arrangements of such songs as "Our Love Is Here to Stay," "But Not for Me," and "I Could Write a Book" not only added immeasurably to the film's success, it brought Connick to the attention of a much wider audience than a young jazz musician might have reason to expect. The sound-track album went platinum, and Connick won his first Grammy for his vocal performance.

If the music fell into place, two other issues had to be resolved before the film could be completed. Both were more complicated than one might imagine, given the ease and rightness of the eventual solutions. The first was a title. Over the four years the script was in development, it had had many working titles. It had been called "Just Friends" and "Boy Meets Girl." Reiner, already knowing he wanted to use the song in the film, considered "It Had to Be You." Reiner even offered a reward on the set to whoever could come up with a title. "Blue Moon," "How They Met," and "Harry, This Is Sally" were considered, before they settled on "When Harry Met Sally . . ." (Who finally suggested the title with its ellipses is unreported.)

More difficult was a decision about the ending. In some versions, Harry and Sally did not get together at the end. If the whole point of the movie was that sex gets in the way of friendships between men and women, that was the logical outcome. But it became increasingly obvious that audiences would be satisfied only if they *did* get together—perhaps it was Reiner's new relationship that made him less cynical about romance—and the writers had to figure out just how the two of them would work out their differences. Harry's racing through the streets of Manhattan on New Year's Eve invited obvious comparisons to Woody Allen's doing much the same at the end of *Manhattan*. But Allen's film ended on an ambiguous note, with Mariel Hemingway's teenager telling Allen's middle-aged writer he would just have to have faith that she would remain unchanged by studying abroad. Here Harry and Sally would have to quickly work out their differences in a way that was both believable and satisfying to audiences. Thus Harry's heartfelt speech about just how much he loves Sally, which ends with, "I came here tonight because when you realize you want to spend the rest of your life with somebody, you want the rest of your life to start as soon as possible."

Reiner wasn't convinced. "It felt kind of phony to me," he said at the time—a feeling he would not have after he and Singer married.

*

When Harry Met Sally . . . not only marked the return of the romantic comedy in a big way, it set standards for innovations to the form, from the use of old standards to a new frankness about sex. It also made Meg Ryan a bona fide star. She would become America's sweetheart in a series of romantic comedies in the nineties. Among the most memorable ones were the two she did for newly minted director Nora Ephron, *Sleepless in Seattle* and *You've Got Mail*, both opposite Tom Hanks. Reiner himself took a small role in *Sleepless*.

Oddly, Billy Crystal's career took off, but not in an expected direction. In the immediate aftermath of the film, Crystal, more than a decade older than Ryan at forty-one and playing much younger, had been married for most of his adult life to the same woman (and still is). Suddenly he found himself being hailed as a "sexy" romantic star. Crystal found it amusing. "When people say I'm sexy, I go, 'What did I do? What did I say?'" But with the release of his next hit, *City Slickers*, two years later, his film career peaked. He would appear in other hits—he was paired with Robert DeNiro in *Analyze This*, as a psychiatrist treating a mobster, and with John Goodman in the animated smash *Monsters, Inc.* But his days as a leading man in romantic comedy were over. Yet he went on to great things as a perennial Oscar emcee and as star of his hit one-man stage show *700 Sundays*, which earned him a Tony Award.

Only Harry and Sally failed to thrive. While the film remains enshrined on numerous lists of the great American comedies, attempts to do sequels or spin-offs fizzled. Some foreign stage productions were attempted, notably one starring Luke Perry and Alyson Hannigan in London, but it's in the movie that we get the version of the story that audiences remember. As Nora Ephron summed it up in 2004, "The original script had a completeness. Anyway, romantic comedies are all about getting the couple together. After that, what else is there to say?"

13

PRETTY WOMAN

🦋 ROMANTIC COMEDIES are a great vehicle for launching or re-habilitating movie careers. Stars from Clark Gable in *It Happened One Night* to Doris Day in *Pillow Talk* found that a hit romantic comedy could transform their careers. Katharine Hepburn used *The Philadelphia Story* to scrub the stigma of "box office poison" from her name. Jack Lemmon in *Some Like It Hot* and Meg Ryan in *When Harry Met Sally . . .* saw themselves transformed from working actors into stars. *Pretty Woman* was a two-fer, making Richard Gere bankable again after a string of flops and turning twenty-three-year-old Julia Roberts into a star, a position she still holds almost two decades later.

Looking at the film today, that may not seem surprising. Nor does it seem odd that it performed almost equal wonders for the veteran character actor Hector Elizondo, who almost stole the film from the two stars with just a few minutes on-screen. What is surprising is that the film began life as a dark story more akin to *Leaving Las Vegas*, the 1995 drama about a suicidal alcoholic and a hooker. How *Pretty Woman* became not only a hit romance but a film from the family-oriented Disney studios to boot (from their Touchstone Pictures division) is a Cinderella story all by itself.

*

The screenplay credit for *Pretty Woman* notes that it was written by J. F. Lawton, but he was only the first of many writers on the project.

Indeed, if you look at his later credits—action movies like *Under Siege* and *Chain Reaction*—it's clear that *Pretty Woman* is not typical of Lawton's work. He was a writer in his late twenties and had written a number of scripts that had gotten nowhere when he found some interest in his screenplay entitled "3000." It contained the core idea for what became *Pretty Woman*, but little else. In it a businessman needs a female companion while in town on a business deal. He finds a streetwalker, and they agree on a price of $3,000 for a week's companionship. For that week the woman lives in a world of style and class, but at the end of the story she ends up back on the street.

"3000" was picked up by Vestron Video, a video company that was feeling flush from the success of its theatrical film release *Dirty Dancing* and was spending itself into bankruptcy looking for lightning to strike again. (To be fair, Vestron was also fighting the maturing of the home video market; the titles they were releasing were no longer a license to print money.) As Vestron's assets were sold off, "3000" was acquired by Disney. But they weren't interested in making a downbeat story about a prostitute who makes a big score but then returns to plying her trade. It's not clear what attracted them to the project in the first place, given their attitude, but now that they owned the property they wanted to get a return on it.

How downbeat was it? Julia Roberts later recalled seeing one of the early version of the script: "[It was] a really dark and depressing, horrible, terrible story about two horrible people . . . and [my] character was this drug addict, a bad-tempered foulmouthed, ill-humored, poorly educated hooker who had this weeklong experience with this foulmouthed, ill-tempered bad-humored very wealthy, handsome, but horrible man, and it was just a grisly, ugly story about these two people."

As a $3 million picture from an independent company, a gritty, downbeat film was not a problem. By the time it was in development at Disney the budget was now $17 million (modest for a major studio release, but still not small potatoes), and there were qualms about what a dark story it was. Garry Marshall had become attached as director, and though he had recently directed Barbara Hershey and Bette Midler in the "chick flick" drama *Beaches*, he still was best known for his comedies.

According to Lawton, Marshall remained committed to doing the film he had written. "Garry was a little nervous about making the ending too upbeat, because the script was well respected in Hollywood and he didn't want to be accused of being the guy who turned it into fluff."

That's not quite the way Marshall remembered it. He knew that in the world of television and movies, scripts may go through many hands. It's the rare project that is filmed according to the original writer's vision, unless that writer is also producing and/or directing. "On most films there are dozens of rewrites, which usually end up offending the original writer, and *Pretty Woman* was no exception. J. F. Lawton became disillusioned about the moviemaking process and its propensity for changing a writer's words," wrote Marshall in his memoirs. "Well, unfortunately, that's the way the movie business works."

Lawton left the project, not entirely of his free will, and other writers were brought in. He tried to be philosophical: "When you sell a script, it's theirs. You've got to accept what happens to it." Lawton had already tried out an ending in which the man and woman stay together, but there were still more changes to come, not all of them for the best. In one version Vivian, the prostitute, engages in a bondage scene with Edward, the businessman, and another storyline involved drug dealers.

As it slowly turned into the movie audiences would eventually see, Marshall figured out what the story really was: a fairy tale. This movie wasn't going to depict the real-life experiences of a Los Angeles prostitute. While there was a nod to concerns over sexually transmitted diseases, this was really a story of a modern-day Cinderella, a downtrodden woman who meets her prince and gets to escape her horrible existence. The film would open with a street entertainer singing about Hollywood as a place where dreams come true. "I fought to keep the two rap scenes in because they said, 'You're watching a fairy tale and we know it. We're not pretending to be anything else,'" Marshall explained. The film would be criticized just the same, but Marshall was comfortable that he had made what he was doing clear up front.

Without a title but with a certainty as to where the story was now going, Marshall had another issue to tackle. While Julia Roberts had agreed to do the movie when it was a Vestron project, the reaction at Disney was, "Who's Julia Roberts?" Marshall was in talks with Madonna to play the part. Ultimately she urged him to try someone younger.

*

Julia Roberts was just getting a toehold in the movies. Her parents, who were involved in theater in her native Georgia, had divorced when she was four. Her older brother Eric lived with her father in Atlanta and would eventually become a movie actor. Meanwhile she and her older sister lived with her mother in the suburb of Smyrna. There, she would later tell Marshall, she and her sister would sometimes pretend they were Laverne and Shirley, the title characters of one of his hit television sitcoms. It's not clear whether he was reassured by this.

By the time she was sitting down with Marshall to see if she would retain the part of Vivian, Roberts had achieved a few credits. She had played the young waitress in the ensemble cast for *Mystic Pizza*, about the love lives of three young women who work at a Connecticut pizzeria. She had completed her most notable role as the young bride who dies young in *Steel Magnolias*, as part of a powerhouse cast that included Sally Field, Dolly Parton, Daryl Hannah, and Olympia Dukakis.

Marshall and Roberts hit it off but weren't quite on the same wavelength. The script had gone through so many changes that Roberts was no longer certain who her character was. She had no clue how to show she could still play the part. Marshall knew the film would now be a comic fairy tale, and he went on a quest to find Roberts's "funny bone." He set up a series of screen tests in which she played opposite different actors, before finally doing one with the actor/writer Charles Grodin. Marshall told Grodin to pull out all the stops and told Roberts that Grodin was very funny and would blow her off the screen. They began playing the scene and Grodin began ad-libbing. If Roberts was thrown, she quickly found her footing, because she was soon giving as good as she got, and Marshall was persuaded that he wanted her for the film. He had found her funny bone.

As usual in the ways of Hollywood, studio executives were willing to indulge the director in casting provided there was a recognizable star in one of the leading roles. Although there's no proof that this tactic will turn a marginal film into a hit, it's an article of faith in the industry. But the part of Edward in *Pretty Woman* had already been turned down by a number of A-list actors, including Sean Connery, Al Pacino, and Richard Gere. Gere had seen the problem exactly: the story was about Vivian, not Edward. It was the same issue that had initially caused Gregory Peck to turn down *Roman Holiday* when it was offered to him four decades earlier, and the thinking of Hollywood stars had not changed. Said Gere, "It just was not the kind of movie that I do. In this film the wild exotic flower was the girl. Usually I'm the exotic flower."

The nearly forty-year-old Gere had another problem, though, that would leave him open to reconsidering his refusal. He had climbed the ladder of success in the 1970s—including a pivotal role as a hustler in *Looking for Mr. Goodbar*—before hitting the big time with *American Gigolo* (as another hustler) and the smash romantic drama *An Officer and a Gentleman*. He had incredible looks, stardom, and a keen mind not likely to grab at whatever brass ring was placed in front of him. Yet his collaborations with such leading directors as Francis Coppola, Bruce Beresford, and Sidney Lumet led to a string of disappointing flops: *The Cotton Club*, *King David*, *Power*. An actor can survive a few bad films, but by 1989 it had been seven years since *An Officer and a Gentleman*, and Gere was no longer hot.

Gere thought seriously about getting out of the movie business. "I looked around and asked, 'Why aren't you being offered certain movies?' And the hard answer was, 'You're not box office, pal.'" He decided to go around one more time on the Hollywood merry-go-round, looking for two or three projects that were commercial and could reignite his stardom. He decided on *Internal Affairs* and *Pretty Woman*. The former fizzled, but, as it turned out, that wouldn't matter.

First, though, Gere had to be convinced that this revamped project and its unknown female lead represented the right career move for him. Marshall took Roberts with him to New York, where they met with Gere in his apartment. According to Marshall, the chemistry of these two stunning actors next to each other was readily apparent. "They were bathed in this eerie light, and they looked so good together that I thought, *We just have to get Richard.* I told Julia she had to persuade him to come aboard."

Gere allowed himself to be persuaded, especially after Marshall promised they would beef up his part.

*

Compared to the horror shows of *Sabrina* or *Some Like It Hot*, the shooting of *Pretty Woman* was a largely happy experience, but that's not to say it was without its problems. Julia Roberts had the looks and the talent to carry off the part of Vivian in the now comedic script, but this was the first major Hollywood feature in which she was the star. In *Mystic Pizza* and *Steel Magnolias* she had been part of an ensemble cast. Now the whole movie was riding on her and Gere. Marshall believed she could do it. He had told the Disney executives that she could carry the film herself if a name star were not available for the part of Edward. Still, she would need a lot of care and tending.

Although much of the film was shot on studio soundstages, there was some location shooting, including scenes of Roberts in her street-walker getup out on real streets. She was not yet a famous face, and when she went outside she was taken for exactly what she was dressed as, a prostitute. Roberts was not really the hardened and experienced streetwise character she was playing, always ready with a comeback. She was a young actress from Smyrna, Georgia. She was mortified. "In fact at one point there were so many catcalls directed at me I went back to my trailer," she later recalled. "I felt hideous and just wanted to hide."

Then there was the matter of trying to explain her new movie to her mother without quite explaining it. Sight unseen, it still sounded rather lewd. "My mom works for the Catholic archdiocese in Atlanta," Roberts told *Rolling Stone*. "I mean, my mom's boss *baptized* me. So I called her at work, and was like, 'Hi, Mom. I got a job.' She said, "You did? What'd you get?' And I said, 'Oh, it's a Disney movie. I gotta go. I'll talk to you later. . . .'"

Some of her care and feeding was a consequence of her naiveté and inexperience. One night when the filming went into the early morning hours, Roberts passed out. Was she ill? Was it something more insidious, like a hidden drug problem? After she was revived, Marshall asked her a simple question. "Sweetheart, when was the last time you had anything to eat?" She allowed that she had had an avocado the day before, and nothing since. Whether it was concentration or a belief that she had to starve herself to look good on screen, Roberts had yet to learn how to prepare herself during a shoot. In spite of her experience, she was still a novice.

Roberts's actual love life would interfere with the production as well. She broke up with Dylan McDermott (her co-star from *Steel Magnolias*) during the shooting. After the breakup, which occurred late at night after a day's shooting, Roberts arrived on the set the next morning very out of sorts. Marshall sensed the situation and took Gere aside with an idea of how they might cheer her up. They were to shoot the scene in which Edward presents Vivian with a borrowed diamond necklace, so that she will look especially stunning for the occasion. On the page it was a pretty straightforward piece of business, but Marshall suggested that when Gere opened the jewelry case to

Edward (Richard Gere) presents a necklace for Vivian (Julia Roberts) to wear, but has a surprise in store. Her unrehearsed reaction would help make Roberts a star.

her, he should playfully snap it shut, as if it was trying to take a nip at her fingers. They didn't tell the actress about this change.

Roberts's reaction to this gambit has been preserved for the ages. It's her unexpectedly raucous laugh that became one of the signature scenes of the movie. "Now, in that situation, she could get annoyed, she could make a remark, but instead she burst out laughing," said Marshall. "Audiences loved her for that."

If there was a moment when Roberts became a movie star, that may have been it. Many beautiful actresses come and go in Hollywood, landing an occasional good part but failing to connect with viewers. That utterly honest and unself-conscious reaction marked Roberts as a real person beneath the glamour. That fit the character but, more important, it humanized the actress with whom most audiences were just beginning to get acquainted. After this it turned into a full-fledged love affair.

*

The Regent Beverly Wilshire was as much a character in the movie as any of the actors. It represented the elegance that Edward took for granted and of which Vivian (and most viewers) could only dream. Only the lobby of the hotel was used as a location, with the deluxe presidential suite recreated—and modified—on a soundstage. This allowed the filmmakers to add a terrace and the sunken tub that Vivian would enjoy so much. In spite of this unreality, moviegoers who could afford it specifically asked for the "Pretty Woman Suite" at the Beverly Wilshire after the movie became a hit. At $4,000 a night few could pay the tab, but those who could would sometimes be greeted upon their arrival with a bowl of strawberries and a video of the movie. A Texan wanted to know if the suite came with the red gown that Roberts wore in the film. When told it did not, he reserved the suite anyway and had one made up for his girlfriend.

"Guests do ask if Julia comes with the room," said a hotel spokeswoman. "They're joking . . . I think."

A small but equally important Garry Marshall touch was the casting of Hector Elizondo. A character actor who was discovered as a child by the famous blues musician W. C. Handy, he had come to early fame in the off-Broadway play *Steambath*, Bruce Jay Friedman's allegorical comedy in which he played a Puerto Rican towel boy who just might be God. Elizondo wanted to avoid playing strictly Latino parts, so he took a varied number of roles over the years, working steadily but never becoming a star. When Garry Marshall was making the leap from his small-screen successes like *Happy Days* and *Mork and Mindy* to the movies, his first film was a 1982 soap-opera spoof called *Young Doctors in Love*. Part of the gag of the movie is that a number of soap-opera performers appear in small roles (including Demi Moore). More important for Marshall's career was his decision to cast Elizondo as a mobster on the lam who must sneak into the hospital to see a sick family member. To do so, he disguises himself as a woman, which is how Elizondo spent most of the film. He was a good sport about it, and Marshall said he'd make it up to the actor. If he ever got to direct another film, he'd see to it that Elizondo was cast, and it would be in a part with great dignity.

Elizondo has appeared in every one of Marshall's films since, sometimes in a featured character role, like the father in *The Flamingo Kid* or the queen's trusted aide in *The Princess Diaries*. Sometimes it is just a few scenes, as in *Pretty Woman*. No one expected him to get the reaction he did. Marshall said the Disney studio balked at paying top-dollar to cast Marshall's friend in a nothing role, and Marshall paid Elizondo's salary out of his own pocket. (When they saw the finished film they apologetically reimbursed Marshall.)

It was interesting to see how audiences warmed to Elizondo's concierge, who became the "fairy godmother" of this Cinderella story. At first he is appalled at Vivian's presence in the hotel, but he says little because his job is to provide for the hotel's clientele. It is *his* approval of her transformation that confirms for the audience that Vivian's changes are real and heartfelt, and that she is ultimately redeemable. Said Marshall, "When we polled the early audiences, Julia and Richard Gere tested in the upper 25 percent in popularity, but Hector tested 65 percent—like a leading man." Gere, who had previously appeared with Elizondo in *American Gigolo*, said, "He made the character somehow British and Latin at the same time. Totally efficient and 'street,' with a big heart." Elizondo made such a mark that there was talk of creating a TV series about the character, and he was nominated for a Golden Globe. He had so little screen time that he wasn't sure he wanted to take screen credit, but he did—at the insistence of the studio, which now wanted to make sure people knew he was in the film.

Studio executives were not consistently a problem for Marshall. He had excellent relations with Jeffrey Katzenberg, then head of film production at Disney. During postproduction there was discussion over the scene in which Vivian accompanies Edward to the restaurant, where the conversation involves the complex business negotiations that brought his character to Los Angeles in the first place. After looking at an early cut of the film, Marshall was told that it was not at all clear what the business deal was about. The studio was willing to bring in another writer and budget some $100,000 for additional shooting to redo the scene. It's unusual for a director to turn down more money and a chance to reshoot, yet that's just what Marshall did.

Thinking about the scene, he realized that Edward's business deal is irrelevant to the story. We need to see him do the right thing at the end, but the details don't matter. Marshall asked for a meeting with Katzenberg and told him that he didn't need to reshoot the scene. "Jeffrey agreed with me. He said the audience wouldn't be on the edge of their seats trying to follow the financial discussion, but would be waiting to see if Vivian used the right fork in the fancy restaurant," he later wrote. So Marshall recut the scene, putting the focus on her nervousness and making the business conversation even more vague. It turned out to be the right—and thrifty—choice.

*

One shooting problem couldn't be avoided: Roberts was playing a prostitute, and the script called for at least two nude scenes. First was the scene in the bathtub where she accepts Edward's deal. Second was the expected bedroom scene. It's one thing to declare the movie an unrealistic fairy tale. It's quite another to have someone pay $3,000 for a prostitute and then not acknowledge that sex is part of the transaction.

Roberts had already decided she had no interest in doing nude scenes. "There are certain people in this life who should know what you look like naked, and I just don't think my high school algebra teacher is a person who should be privy to what my butt looks like," is the way she put it. Her attitude led to one of the strangest conversations of her still young movie career. She lacked the clout of a big star simply to refuse to do nude scenes, and she was in a heated discussion with her agent, Elaine Goldsmith of the William Morris agency, about how to handle the matter. In the middle of the meeting in walked Sue Mengers, then one of the biggest agents in Hollywood and one of the heavy hitters at William Morris. Roberts and Mengers had never met, and she had no idea who this imposing woman was. As Roberts recalled it, Mengers asked what the matter was, and Goldsmith said it had to do with Roberts not wanting to do nude scenes. Mengers looked at Roberts and said, "Oh, what's the big deal? We're not talking *beaver* here!" Roberts was shocked that this stranger was talking about her naked body and not stopping there: "If I had your body, you'd see me in [the supermarket] going down the frozen-foods aisle naked!"

Marshall did what he could to make Roberts comfortable, but he didn't want to use body doubles, and he had to get the shots. He joked he would put goldfish in the bathtub, but during rehearsals he saw that only made her more nervous. Instead he decided that she needed to know he respected her privacy. He did more than clear the set of unnecessary people, he cleared *everybody*. Without telling Roberts, he set up the shot for the bathtub scene where she dunks her head underwater, and then had everyone, including himself, leave. When Roberts emerged from the water she looked around and realized that the camera was running but no one was there. She laughed and thereby took some of the tension out of the scene.

The scene with Gere was not as easy. Roberts was so nervous she broke out in hives, and a vein in her forehead began visibly pulsing. It was impossible to shoot her in such a state. Marshall sent for calamine lotion for the hives, then climbed into bed with her and Gere to try to calm her. Gere and Marshall massaged her forehead and eventually got her calm enough to do the scene. "Love scenes might look glamorous on the screen," Marshall would later write, "but on the set they usually end up as high comedy."

Directors do what they have to do to get the performances they need for their films, but Marshall maintained a fatherly affection for his young leading lady even after he had what he needed. On the last day Roberts was shooting, she was already getting ready for her next film and was feeling anxious. Marshall came to her trailer for a chat. As she recalled, "He pulls this box from under his shirt, and tells me how young I am and how hard this business is. Inside this box is a necklace with a heart made out of diamonds. And he says to me, 'I give you this necklace so you know, wherever you go, somebody loves you.'"

Roberts was more than touched by the gesture. "I cried for a week," she recalled. Big stars eventually reach a place where they can be secure in their careers. For Roberts, knowing how many would-be stars *don't* make it, Marshall provided much-needed reassurance.

*

As production ended, two issues remained to be resolved. First was the ending, prompting numerous suggestions. Some had Roberts back on the street and Gere driving by in his car. In some versions he stopped, in others he kept going, but the focus would be on Roberts's smile, now recognized by the film crew—if not yet the rest of the world—as a major asset. Marshall, though, felt it would be too easy to end with a close-up on Roberts smiling. He wanted an ending that people would recognize as the perfect "they-lived-happily-ever-after" resolution that a fairy tale demanded.

On an October day in 1989, Marshall was filming the scene in which Edward comes to rescue Vivian from her life. As she comes down the fire escape and he climbs up, opera music is playing as an echo of an earlier scene when he takes her to the opera. But the scene wasn't working, and Marshall called it the worst day of the whole shoot. He would look at the crew after every take, and he could see from their reactions they weren't buying this cornball ending. Different ideas were added, including some pigeons who received minimal scale—some breadcrumbs thrown around to attract them. Now Marshall was going to shoot the scene one last time to see if he could get what he was missing.

The music played, the actors acted, the pigeons flew. At the end of the take the crew was as bored as ever, but Marshall noted that one of the policemen, hired to hold onlookers back, had tears in his eyes. Marshall went over to him and asked why. "Mr. Marshall, the opera music. The pigeons. The two lovers up there. It just gave me goose bumps." Marshall knew he had nailed it. He wasn't trying to impress a jaded Hollywood crew. He was trying to reach regular folks like that cop.

As he worked out various issues in postproduction, like the restaurant scene, it was also time to decide what to call the movie. "3000" was long since rejected, and "On the Boulevard" came and went. Finally Marshall and the studio decided they wanted a song title, since they could use a preexisting song's popularity to promote the film. This was a change for Marshall, who had boasted to critics a few years earlier that he had taken a song the studio insisted be used in *Nothing in Common* and played it during the closing credits.

No one will hear it, a stunned executive had said, they'll be leaving the theater.

So play it louder, Marshall replied.

Now there were three songs considered as potential title material: "The Lady Is a Tramp," "She's a Lady," and "Oh, Pretty Woman." Marshall went with Roy Orbison's "Oh, Pretty Woman" (losing the "Oh"), and the song was played during Vivian's transformation during her shopping spree. It was an inspired choice, providing a good hook for both the film and for Roberts, since she would thereafter be known as "Pretty Woman" rather than "Tramp." As Peter Lehman points out in his book on Orbison's life and work, however, the movie essentially makes use of the title and the musical beat and completely ignores the lyrics. Wrote Lehman, "The song is not really about the pretty woman of the title but rather the intense sexual longing of its feverishly daydreaming male protagonist. The film thus reverses the emphasis of the song's lyrics. . . ."

*

The success of *Pretty Woman* was beyond phenomenal. It was a worldwide hit eventually collecting some $460 million at the box office.

This made it the biggest Disney hit ever to that date, leading Marshall to suggest that Walt was spinning in his grave thinking that a movie about a prostitute was outgrossing his classic family films. It opened in March 1990, just a week before Roberts lost her first Oscar race. She had been nominated for best supporting actress for *Steel Magnolias*. A year later she'd be back, this time as a best-actress nominee for *Pretty Woman*. By the end of 1990 she would be ranked the number two star at the box office by the nation's theater owners, behind only Arnold Schwarzenegger.

Pretty Woman made Roberts a star, but it also gave Gere a certifiable hit. He may not have been the "exotic flower" of the story, but he was certainly the "Prince Charming," and that counted for something. Both actors would have their hits and misses in the years ahead, but Roberts would demonstrate that her stardom was not fleeting. She would eventually win her Oscar for the 2000 drama *Erin Brockovich*. Meanwhile Gere would surprise everyone and win a Golden Globe for showing his little-known singing and dancing skills in the 2002 musical *Chicago*.

Marshall's career might never make him a critic's favorite, but he scored often enough with audiences to keep working, and managed to get Roberts and Gere back together for another romantic comedy, *Runaway Bride*. It was fluff, but audiences didn't care, and it took in more than $150 million in domestic box office.

Gere, of course, was also known as an activist and a serious Buddhist, not simply a western show-biz figure dabbling in exotic Eastern religion. When he invited Marshall along to meet the Dalai Lama during one of the Buddhist leader's visits to the United States, he stunned the director with his introduction to the holy man, calling Marshall "one of the funniest men you'll ever meet." What could he possibly say to confirm such a buildup? Marshall was completely tongue-tied and greeted the Tibetan leader with the immortal words, "We're the same age."

The Dalai Lama replied, "And I think we've both done pretty well."

Meanwhile Roberts worked on dramas, thrillers, and comedies, proving herself adept in any form. Perhaps no film better demonstrated her growing sense of security than *My Best Friend's Wedding* (1997), which was structured like a modern screwball comedy. Roberts and an old friend (Dermot Mulroney) had vowed to marry each other if they were still single at thirty, and now, with the big birthday approaching, he's marrying someone else. In the traditional comic romantic triangle the other person would be little more than a joke, but instead the part was cast with a promising new actress, Cameron Diaz. It was Roberts's movie, even if it didn't end as audiences had been led to expect, but it's to her credit that Diaz was allowed to shine and that Roberts supported her along the way. In only her seventh film, it was clear that Diaz was on her way to stardom.

14

THERE'S SOMETHING
ABOUT MARY

THE RELEASE of *There's Something About Mary* in the summer of 1998 proved baffling to some film critics. It was a romantic comedy, yet it was also a collection of vulgar frat-boy humor, obsessed with bodily fluids and jokes in bad taste. For some critics this was too much. Romantic comedy was the world of Lubitsch and Cukor, of Noel Coward and Philip Barry, of Tracy and Hepburn. It was sophisticated, witty, smart. With jokes on subjects ranging from genital injuries to mental retardation, *There's Something About Mary* seemed utterly alien.

In fact it was quite different from most other romantic comedies, but not unprecedented. While Peter and Bobby Farrelly, the brothers who made the film, could not have gotten away with most of this half a century earlier, another writer-director, Preston Sturges, was being criticized for mixing romance with pratfalls and slapstick humor in movies like *The Palm Beach Story*, *The Lady Eve*, and *The Miracle of Morgan's Creek*. Some of the critics may have been baffled, but audiences weren't. In the first half of the 1940s, Sturges was one of the leading comedy directors in Hollywood. In the 1950s and early 1960s it was Billy Wilder who persuaded audiences to accept romantic comedies with attempted suicide (*Sabrina*), transvestism (*Some Like It Hot*), and adultery (*The Apartment*). In the seventies and eighties Woody Allen added his patented style of New York Jewish neuroticism to the mix. (His 1973 futuristic spoof *Sleeper* may not have had any jokes about hair gel, but it did introduce the world to the concept of the "orgasmatron," which allowed the impotent men and frigid women of this future society—meaning everyone—to have sex.)

So it wasn't so much that the Farrellys were destroying the romantic comedy as perfecting a new, hybrid sub-genre. Where traditional-style romantic comedies had come to be seen as "chick flicks"—something men might take a date to but not really want to see on their own—here was a movie with a hot babe, earthy humor, and a happily-ever-after romance that left everyone feeling good. It's a mix that would thrive in the coming years. Ironically, for the Farrellys themselves it was a combination they've been unable to make work in their own subsequent films as well as they did here. With *Mary* they hit the heights, then watched as others continued in the same vein with great success.

*

Peter and Bobby Farrelly were unlikely candidates to write one of the most popular and successful romantic comedies of recent times. They seemed unlikely to be very successful at all. Sons of a Rhode Island doctor and nurse, they worked in various jobs before setting out to write movies. As their father, Bob "Docky" Farrelly, told *Newsweek*, "Pete and Bobby were a couple of screw-offs." They held various sales jobs but quickly became bored. (Bobby, in a story that would become funny only in retrospect, lost a good deal of money on his invention of "round beach towels," allowing the user to move with the sun.)

They went out to Hollywood—first Pete, then Bobby—and worked on scripts with their friends. Over several years they wrote more than a dozen scripts, none of which were produced. They might get optioned or purchased, which brought the brothers some income, but nothing ended up on screen. Still, they persevered. They made each other as well as their friends laugh. Surely there was a place for them. A few years after writing *Dumb and Dumber*, and having it rejected everywhere they tried, they got lucky. Jim Carrey was interested. They didn't recognize the name. But by the time the film was made with, amazingly, these two novices as director, Carrey had appeared in *Ace Ventura, Pet Detective* and was the hot new comedy star. After years of rejection, the Farrellys found themselves in charge of the *next* film with this great property. However nervous they may have been, they saw the project through. *Dumb and Dumber* (1994) was an appalling collection of jokes focusing on bodily functions and stupidity, with the film's big scene featuring co-star Jeff Daniels grunting on a toilet. Reviews were mixed, but audiences who craved low-down humor weren't interested in the critics, they were too busy laughing at the bathroom jokes. The film made back its $16 million budget on opening weekend and finally earned more than $200 million in worldwide box office. It solidified Carrey's status as a comedy star and launched the Farrellys on their filmmaking careers.

Their next film, *Kingpin* (1996), was not a hit, but the "sophomore slump" is a well-known phenomenon, and the Farrellys were green-lighted to tackle their next project, a romance in which the hero was essentially stalking an old high school flame. If anyone could figure out how to turn that into an upbeat comedy, it would be them. Perhaps the key decision was that they deliberately set out to make an R-rated comedy. *Animal House* (1978) had been a favorite film of their formative years, and they noted that since then comedies had grown soft. Everything was now rated PG or PG-13 so that the all-important youth market wouldn't be cut off. The Farrellys came at it from the other direction. They wanted to do all sorts of outrageous jokes that would push the limits not only of the audience but also of the actors and even the props department. Hollywood may have finally noticed the Farrellys, but to the public the success of *Dumb and Dumber* was strictly Carrey's. This time their film was going to rise or fall on their own work.

"For us, this is the perfect movie," Peter Farrelly told interviewers. "We co-wrote it, we directed it, and we got everything we wanted into this movie—things that we never thought we'd be able to get away with."

Much of the casting for *There's Something About Mary* was done in the same haphazard manner used on all the Farrelly films. Friends and family were invited to participate. For the scene in which Ted (Ben Stiller) is mistakenly picked up at a highway stop that turns out to be a rendezvous for gay sex, most of the people hastily pulling up their pants and running were members of the film crew. Later, for the scene when Ted is released from jail, Cameron Diaz's father was visiting the set, and the Farrellys hastily got him into an orange jumpsuit and put him into the movie. He's the one with the long hair and beard yelling at the front of the other prisoners.

Audiences had not yet come to understand that in a Farrelly movie there would be plenty of jokes about people with physical or mental disabilities. At first this penchant seemed in the worst possible taste. But over the body of their work it became clear that they were in fact quite democratic. They weren't making fun of the disabilities; they were simply treating these characters in the same raucous manner they treated everyone else. Mary's brother Warren was played by actor W. Earl Brown, who would go on to greater fame as the oily henchman Dan Dority on the HBO series *Deadwood*. The character was based on a friend of the Farrellys since childhood, Warren Tashijan, who appears briefly in the film as Warren's friend Freddie. He also has had appearances in the Farrellys' *Kingpin*, *Me*, *Myself and Irene*, and *Fever Pitch*.

Cameron Diaz was an obvious choice for Mary, but only because the respective careers of the actress and the Farrellys happened to be in perfect synchronization. Diaz had begun modeling while in high school, but she was a working stiff, not a supermodel. Her stunning good looks, and her ability to come off as down to earth rather than as a diva, helped her move up the ranks from local store ads to national accounts. She got her break in the movies, as did the Farrellys, through Jim Carrey. She read for a small part in *The Mask* (1994) but made such an impression they kept calling her back to be considered for the female lead. After twelve auditions she finally won the part. It was a cartoonish movie that was essentially a vehicle for Carrey and a vast array of special effects, but Diaz got the screen time with him and made her mark.

Having launched a movie career with a hit film, Diaz made it clear to her newly acquired agents and managers that she was in it for the long haul, not just a series of ingenue roles. She took parts of varying importance in a wide range of films, some mainstream and some better suited for the art houses. These included *She's the One*, *Feeling Minnesota*, and a film with Julia Roberts, *My Best Friend's Wedding*. In that picture she came across as perfection, so sweet and so beautiful you just couldn't believe she would end up dumped at the altar, even if her putative rival was Julia Roberts. Even Roberts's character is won over by her, and audiences were too.

Thus in casting Mary the Farrellys felt they had struck gold with Diaz. "Mary is kind of the perfect woman. We rank Cameron in that category," said Bobby Farrelly. "She's like one of the guys except that she's a gorgeous babe." Indeed, during the shoot when she discovered the Farrellys and some of the crew members pitching quarters between takes, she joined in—and beat them.

Diaz's real-life boyfriend at the time, Matt Dillon, was cast as the sleazy detective Pat Healy, who's sent to track down Mary and ends up falling in love with her himself. Actors considered for the part included Bill Murray, Vince Vaughn, and Cuba Gooding, Jr. Dillon and Diaz had been together for a couple of years and had been looking for a movie to do together. "I guess I just imagined we would end up doing something a little more romantic," said Dillon, who was required to grow a pencil-thin moustache and keep it for the entire shoot. "I was on the fence about playing Healy. But Cameron said, 'Honey, you know how you're always lying to me? You'd be really good at this. You're such a pathological liar.'"

Dillon was one of the rare actors who had been able to make a successful transition from teen heartthrob to adult actor. His early films, like *My Bodyguard* and *Tex*, led to work with Francis Ford Coppola on *The Outsiders* and *Rumblefish*. He showed he could play both light and serious roles, and was often cast as a bad boy who might or might not be redeemed in the final reel. As he grew older he seemed more interested in character roles rather than playing the traditional leading man. He appeared in Garry Marshall's *Flamingo Kid*, where he played an older teen who must choose between his dull but respectable father (Hector Elizondo, naturally) or the well-heeled card sharp at the country club, played by Richard Crenna. Dillon convinced critics and audiences alike he was the real deal with *Drugstore Cowboy*, Gus van Sant's dark film about addiction.

Mary, though, would be something different. While Dillon was no stranger to comedy, this was much broader than anything he had done, and his character was a total sleaze. Instead of the romantic lead, he'd be playing the comic and unscrupulous rival. In some scenes he would have to make himself look ridiculous. Ben Stiller, who had far more experience with comedy than Dillon, found him up to the task. "It wasn't easy for Matt, I'm telling you. I saw him struggle with it, but his instincts were to go with it. I was very impressed."

For all his joking with Diaz, Dillon knew it was a good role. "I've never really done a broad comedy like this, but it's a really good story. And when I read the script, I laughed like crazy."

The toughest part to cast was that of Ted, whose quest to renew ties with Mary sets the story in motion. The way the Farrellys explained it, Ted may not be the focus of the characters in the story—clearly Mary is—but he is the focus of the comedy. The influence they credit for this approach is, of all things, *The Andy Griffith Show*, where Griffith played Sheriff Andy Taylor and Don Knotts was his comical sidekick, Deputy Barney Fife. In studying the show—they took a break to watch the reruns every day while their scripts were going nowhere—the Farrellys noticed how Griffith was given some comic shtick to do at the start of the series, but then he became the sensible center, leaving the comedy to others. Explained Peter Farrelly, "When Barney found his voice, Andy started being the straight guy, and that's why the show worked. Andy is Mary; Barney is Ted in our movie."

Given that the role would be the male lead, Twentieth Century Fox initially balked at the notion of Ben Stiller taking the part. The Farrellys agreed to look around and thought they found someone who could handle the part: Owen Wilson. This proved to be even more unacceptable to the studio, so they reluctantly went along with Stiller. Stiller was not yet a box office star (*Mary* would help make him one), but he wasn't exactly a novice. The son of the famous comedy team of Jerry Stiller and Anne Meara, he had been slowly building an impressive resumé that included winning an Emmy in 1993 for his short-lived variety series on the FOX network, *The Ben Stiller Show*. In addition to acting he had also directed the movies *Reality Bites* and *The Cable Guy* (the latter film being a rare Jim Carrey flop that proved too dark for audiences).

"The studio didn't want me at all," Stiller recalled about *Mary*. "Even going into the first day of shooting, I thought I might get fired."

Stiller proved to be a good choice—an Everyman type. Dillon's movie-star looks were hidden behind the mustache and, later, some fake teeth. Stiller, while certainly not unattractive, seemed more like a guy you might know at work or school. Since the film required Mary to fulfill Ted's fantasy (as well as that of all the male viewers) by picking Ted even over real-life football star Brett Favre, the fact that he could play Ted as a likable character was a plus. As Diaz put it, "Ben's funny. He's kind of geeky, but he's got a lot of good qualities. And Mary's now a mature woman, no longer in high school. She sees all those qualities."

All three actors knew they were taking a chance on *Mary*. Diaz had long discussions over what became known as the "hair gel" scene, not sure if it would be a career killer. Dillon would be playing an oily character part instead of the romantic lead. And Stiller's character would be put through a series of humiliations before finally winning the girl. Stiller said, "It was one of those scripts where if it works it could be really, really funny, and if it doesn't work it can be horrible and embarrassing." They were about to find out.

*

Although *Mary* would forever after be known as a Farrelly Brothers film, it didn't start out that way. The original script had been written several years earlier by Ed Decter and John J. Strauss. They received credit for the original story and shared screenplay credit with the Farrellys. Decter and Strauss went on to do some of the *Santa Clause* movies and *The Lizzie Maguire Movie*, so it is safe to assume that the more outrageous elements of the movie were not in the original script. What they had was the basic story: guy hires a detective to track down the whereabouts of a high school girlfriend.

The script had been sitting on a shelf for nearly a decade when Frank Beddor, a former actor and stuntman, decided he wanted to be a producer. He came across *Mary*, saw some possibilities, and pitched it to the Farrellys. The brothers had no problem taking on someone else's script as they had always worked in collaboration with others, but now they added their own sensibility to the mix. Among other things, they added the prologue, leading to the first of the big shock scenes in the film.

"In our script we didn't have the high school sequence," recalled Decter. "And, if you analyze it, that sequence is the single most brilliant, most lethal thing in the movie."

It served two purposes. First, it introduced Ted as the hapless but good-hearted character the audience would need to root for if the film were to work. After all, in some ways what he's doing is creepy. Several characters accuse him of being a stalker, and even Ted feels queasy about sending a detective out to find Mary. Yet when we see him as a dorky teenager not afraid to go up against a high school jock who is abusing Warren, Mary's mentally handicapped brother, he shows himself to be both just and brave. He's just working under his own handicaps, like his ridiculous eighties hairdo and a mouthful of wire.

Stiller showed his dedication to the film in this prologue, in terms of physical pain and of personal humiliation. The pain came from the fake braces he had to wear. The Farrellys sent him to an orthodontist who created a "biteplate," sometimes used to show teen patients what they will look like once the braces are in. "I had to sit there in the waiting room with three twelve-year-old kids," said Stiller, who was having his own first experience with such dental devices. In between takes he would remove the plate to soak in a dental solution. Stiller used his discomfort to feel the pain of his character. "The braces totally change how you talk, so you don't have to really act—you just talk with the braces in. They were like a gift from the Teenage Awkward God."

As the sequence plays out, Mary—taken by nerdy Ted's heroism in defense of her beloved brother—gets to talking with him and decides to give him a chance by asking him to take her to the senior prom. This leads to the sequence at Mary's house where Ted undergoes one humiliation after another. First her stepfather, played by Keith David, tells Ted that Mary has already left on her date, then laughs when poor Ted takes him seriously. Then Ted, thinking he's performing a kindness by bringing a gift for Warren, touches his ear, which, as we soon learn, sets the demented boy off in a violent rage. Ted is then relieving himself in the bathroom where, through the window, he inadvertently spots Mary and her mother (Markie Post) repairing her dress, making him look like a Peeping Tom.

The Farrellys, though, are building to what they know will be the second most talked-about scene in the movie: Ted getting his "frank and beans" caught in his zipper. The genesis of the gag came, incredibly enough, from real life. The brothers recalled that when one of their sisters had a twelfth birthday party, one of the boys disappeared for an unusually long time in the bathroom. Their father was dispatched to see what the problem was, and it turned out the boy had gotten caught in his zipper and could not extricate himself. Being a doctor, Dad called for ice to reduce the swelling and soon had the boy freed. The Farrellys took that and turned it into a scene where seemingly the whole world is aware of Ted's dilemma.

The quick shot of the "frank and beans" enmeshed in Ted's zipper was one of only many challenges for the people responsible for

Ted (Ben Stiller) goes through one of many humiliations in his pursuit of the sweet and irresistible Mary (Cameron Diaz), showing that romantic comedy could survive even frat-boy humor.

designing effects for *Mary*. Tony Gardner, who also created the "hair gel" for use later in the film, had to speak to the Farrellys to find out what precisely they were looking for in these effects. "It got to the point where they put me on speakerphone because they thought my questions were so funny," Gardner explained. On the other end of the conversation, things were so graphic that opening it up to others was the last thing he wanted. "I'm used to having business calls at home. But my wife, Cindy, and I have three kids, and any time I get on the phone with the Farrellys it's pretty much guaranteed that I have to talk in another room."

In another unintentional effect, a cast member took one for the team. Lin Shaye is a working actress whose credits go back to the 1970s. She found herself a member of the Farrellys' stock company.

(She's worked on five of their films, though her scenes for *Me, Myself and Irene* did not make the final cut.) She came to their attention when they were making *Dumb and Dumber* for New Line Cinema. Her brother, Bob Shaye, founded the company.

For *Mary* she was cast as Magda, Mary's much older, sex-driven neighbor, who is also devoted to her little terrier Puffy. This led to numerous gags in the film in which the poor dog was either being abused by Pat (who resuscitates the dog at one point with electrical wires from a lamp) or busily attacking Ted. In one scene Mary and Magda are discussing Mary's big plans for the evening while Magda lies on the couch playing with Puffy. The dog, it seems, developed a taste for the actress's lip-gloss and began heavily licking her mouth. The actress let it happen while she played the scene, and Diaz went right along with it, hoping she wouldn't burst out laughing and ruin the take. Said Diaz, "It was one of the funniest and most disgusting and disturbing things I've ever seen."

For once a gross-out moment took Peter Farrelly by surprise, and he loved it. Here was a scene that was essentially exposition—about Mary's plans for the evening—and suddenly it had people laughing and squirming quite apart from the information being conveyed. Dillon, who wasn't even in the scene, saluted Shaye for going beyond even what he was willing to do for the film. "I don't see myself lip-locking a dog the way she did."

Puffy was also a trouper. Played by a dog named Slammer, he was substituted for most of the action scenes with fake prop dogs, including one with an inflatable stomach, used when Pat tried to give Puffy mouth-to-mouth resuscitation. But the body cast featured the real dog in a removable head-to-toe cast that came apart quickly in sections. The dog would be placed in the fake cast, they'd get the shot, and he would be out again in a matter of seconds.

For the scene in which Puffy goes flying out the window, the Farrellys didn't think Diaz and Shaye were reacting with sufficient horror, so Bobby created additional motivation. Puffy and Ted are engaged in mortal combat, and when Ted dodges, Puffy leaps out the window. Mary and Magda run over, stick their heads out, and scream at the sight, and then rush to rescue the presumably injured dog. To get the appropriate reaction, they were told to run through the scene one more time, and when they stuck their heads out the window, Bobby was down below with his pants dropped, mooning them. Their screams of shocked surprise were real, and the Farrellys got their take.

The moment of truth for Cameron Diaz was the soon-to-be notorious "hair gel" scene, in which the Farrellys showed just how far they would go for a laugh. Ted's friend Dom (Chris Elliot) has advised him that he should masturbate before his big date with Mary so that he won't be going out with a "loaded gun." After the zipper scene this was nothing for Stiller, though thankfully his self-manipulation takes place off-camera. But when he looks for the product of the act he can't find it, until the now-arrived Mary notices it hanging from his ear, which she proceeds to wipe off and use to fix her hair.

This one gag probably led to more discussions than any other on the film. For Diaz it was a matter of dignity. She was more than willing to be in a raunchy comedy, but she didn't want to stigmatize a career that was just taking off by being forever associated with one crude moment. She was also concerned it would undercut the character. In an early meeting with the brothers she told them, "You guys, the one thing we have to keep is Mary's credibility. You don't want her to look like a numbskull." Diaz couldn't believe that Mary wouldn't notice that her inseminated hair was now standing straight up. Wouldn't she look in a mirror at some point? The Farrellys were convinced of the rightness of the gag but promised Diaz they could try different takes, and they would see whether it worked. In retrospect, however, Diaz saw that it was inevitable. "They humored me, but we all knew as soon as we did it straight up that there was only one way to go." As soon as Diaz left makeup and came out for the scene with her forelock sticking straight up, people began laughing, and many of them didn't even know the joke that set it up.

The special effects people had to create the fake semen, leading to the sorts of calls the Farrellys put on speaker phone. What color should it be? What texture? How much of it would they need? For his part, Peter Farrelly maintained he wanted people to laugh, not be disgusted, "A guy with a load hanging from his ear is funny because it's *unexpected*, not because it's gross." Audiences decided it was both, and roared with laughter.

One of the film's simplest gags was having musician Jonathan Richman narrate the film through song (accompanied by drummer Tommy Larkins). The Farrellys pitched him on the idea by asking if he was familiar with the 1965 western spoof *Cat Ballou*, where Stubby Kaye and Nat King Cole popped up throughout the film singing "The Ballad of Cat Ballou." Richman knew the film well and leaped at the chance, even though the Farrellys told him there was only a fifty-fifty chance he'd make the final cut. For every scene he was in, they shot an alternate version without the singer, just in case. Bobby Farrelly recalled what happened: "When we sent it to the studio, they said, 'Don't shoot any more! This is not working! Is he kidding?' But when we showed it to an audience, they loved him." This allowed them to have the shaggy-dog ending in which Ted wins Mary, but Magda's crazed lover announces he was only using her to get to Mary himself and takes a potshot at Ted, hitting Richman instead.

The film's end allowed for another type of stunt casting, by bringing in quarterback Brett Favre of the Green Bay Packers, playing himself as Mary's dream man whose relationship had been secretly broken up by Tucker (Lee Evans), who has been nursing his own crush on Mary. Favre had no idea what he was getting into, but his agent said it would be easy money for very little work, and they were willing to accommodate him by holding off his scenes until after the Packers' season ended. Diaz recalled that the day Favre showed up, the men in the cast and crew turned into a bunch of starry-eyed sports fans: "Not one of them didn't turn into a twelve-year-old boy. They're all like, 'Can I get my picture with you?'"

The joke of the film is that Mary chooses geeky Ted over Favre, but for the football star the real surprise came when he took his family to see the film months later, having no idea what to expect. While he came across all right, he was so mortified by some of the other high jinks in the film that he beat a hasty retreat before the houselights came up. He needn't have worried. Not only did audiences love the film, but the decision to end the movie with an infectious full cast sing-along of the seventies pop hit "Build Me Up Buttercup" ensured that audiences left the theater with a big smile.

*

In spite of challenges to the actors' dignity and to the creativity of the prop department, *There's Something About Mary* was a happy production. Stiller, who had already directed a couple of films himself, was amazed at the unfrenzied atmosphere the Farrellys maintained. "They're fun, open," he said. "It's 'We're going to finish early and play golf.' There was no stressing about what the camera angle was going to be. I really learned from that."

Unlike *Sabrina*, where Audrey Hepburn was supposed to fall in love with one character on-screen while falling in love with the actor playing the other character off-screen, there were no difficulties here. Bobby Farrelly described Diaz and Dillon: "On the weekend, they were arm in arm and fun to be around because they are in love, but on the set, they were just two actors going about their business." They eventually went their separate ways. After having posed for magazines with Dillon in promoting the film, and then seeing her love life publicly dissected, Diaz decided there were things the public did not need to know about her. Although her subsequent romances (notably with the former N'Sync member Justin Timberlake) would attract attention, she would no longer cooperate with that sort of publicity. Diaz said it was one of the things she had learned from working with Julia Roberts (the other being knitting).

"Everybody has their own way of dealing with fame, and I have to say that I learned how to deal with mine from Julia," said Diaz. "I had a little moment where it was all just overwhelming. I became really uncomfortable about people knowing my name, because before, people who called my name were people I knew." Now there were strangers shouting out at her, and Diaz quickly learned not to turn around.

The film was released in July 1998, and while it did well at the box office it was not an immediate smash hit. Instead it was the sort of film theater owners dream of: a movie that built by word of mouth as people brought friends and family to see it and gladly sat through it again. Usually a film opens big and then drops off in passing weeks. *Mary* hit number one at the box office in its *eighth* week of release. Twentieth Century-Fox ran thirteen different TV spots for the film during the course of its release (all preserved on the "special edition" DVD), some of them capitalizing on the public's embrace of the film by quoting real moviegoers or showing them singing "Build Me Up Buttercup."

Bob Harper, head of the movie studio's marketing arm, explained, "We expected it to be a big hit. We knew that this [was] a picture the audience was going to love." The promotional push included a greater than usual number of sneak previews and sending movie critics dog dolls encased in bandages. "We did everything we could to attract the word of mouth."

*

The biggest boost from the film went to the Farrellys, who had now shown they could not only push the edges of bad taste but could make moviegoers who would not ordinarily see such fare love it. *Mary* attracted women as well as men, and older viewers brushed off the bad taste because they saw the underlying sweetness.

Now the Farrellys had two new problems that they hadn't had to face before. First, as the old joke has it, Hollywood is a town where everyone is first in line to be second. Said Bobby at the time, "People are trained to think we'd never go as far as we have. So the surprise is funny. If everyone starts doing it, which I'm sure they will, it might not be as funny." The handwriting was already on the bathroom wall.

Mary made rude humor respectable and showed it could be combined with the elements of traditional romantic comedy. Adam Sandler was already doing much the same in his films, and found himself attracting new viewers when he was paired with Drew Barrymore that same year in *The Wedding Singer*. Sandler's frat-boy fans may have complained, but others found it a Sandler movie they could enjoy. Two other brothers, Paul and Chris Weitz, were soon upping the ante on *Mary* with the following summer's *American Pie*, which combined all sorts of rude antics with a story line in which four teenage boys learn the difference between love and sex. The movie was the surprise hit of 1999 and led to several sequels.

Perhaps no one has mined this new hybrid of earthy humor and romantic comedy more than Judd Apatow who, after several years in television and movies (including a stint on *The Ben Stiller Show*), hit the big time in 2005 with *The 40 Year Old Virgin*. In a star-making turn, Steve Carell plays a middle-aged man who has never gone to bed with a woman and lives like an overgrown twelve-year-old. His buddies do what they can to hook him up in a series of raucous scenes, but the message of the film is that love will ultimately prevail. The humor depends on the sex, but the story is one of two misfits (Carrell and Catherine Keener) finding true love together.

Apatow used a similar formula in 2007 for *Knocked Up*—a title the Farrellys should have already used—in which a fat, adolescent man (Seth Rogan) gets drunk, gets a woman (Katherine Heigl) pregnant, and only *then* do they start dating and falling in love.

Thus *Mary* spawned a whole new type of romantic comedy, even if some critics found it hard to accept. The Farrellys not only had competition now, they were expected to keep topping themselves. Unfortunately their subsequent films fell short. The balance that made *Mary* work was a fine one. *Me, Myself and Irene* was too harsh, with Jim Carrey's over-the-top portrayal of a state trooper with a split personality more annoying than amusing. *Shallow Hal* featured Jack Black as a selfish guy who is hypnotized into seeing only the "inner beauty" of people, including an obese woman (played by Gwyneth Paltrow in a fat suit). It was a sweet and sentimental film, too rude for some people and far too treacly for others.

"We'll laugh at our body fluids, our body sounds, our body smells," said Bobby Farrelly. "In our world a well-timed fart can be very funny, so why can't it be in the movies? We belong to the school that says farts are funny. But we don't want to be judged as Fart Guys. And that's how we're judged."

Fans of traditional romantic comedies may or may not appreciate *Mary* and what the Farrellys have wrought, but it's a modern trend that's not likely to go away soon. For those who preferred the more sophisticated approach, where you left the theater quoting the dialogue rather than cataloging the bodily fluids, it would take a television writer from New Zealand—by way of England—to save the day.

15

LOVE ACTUALLY

SEPTEMBER 11, 2001, is a date now permanently etched in history. The terrorist attacks on the World Trade Center and the Pentagon, and the fourth plane that crashed before reaching its intended target, stopped the world in its tracks. Historians will debate if, as was said at the time, the events of 9/11 "changed everything" or didn't really change anything at all, except for the families of those who perished that day. For the movie industry the more immediate, practical matter was what, if anything, would change on screen.

The teaser trailer for *Spider-Man*—featuring a web slung between two towers of the World Trade Center—was immediately pulled from theaters, as was the poster for a romantic comedy from Edward Burns, *The Sidewalks of New York*, that also featured the towers. The Arnold Schwarzenegger action thriller *Collateral Damage* was taken off the fall 2001 schedule since it was about Schwarzenegger's character seeking revenge on terrorists who were responsible for the death of his family. *Serendipity*, a romantic comedy with John Cusack and Kate Beckinsale, was put back into postproduction, and in every shot of the New York–based movie that featured the city skyline, the two towers were digitally removed. People were understandably nervous and upset and angry, and it wasn't clear what might prove distracting or set people off. The fact that even two romantic comedies needed alterations suggested that nothing was immune from the impact of that horrible day.

As time passed, the hypersensitivity of that period receded, and a variety of responses to the new post-9/11 environment appeared. No one would suggest that romantic comedies, or movies in general, or even the entertainment industry as a whole were the front line of that response. People use the means at their disposal to express what they have to say. For a New Zealand–born writer known primarily for his work on British TV shows and a handful of screenplays, his response was his first foray into film directing, and the result was arguably the first great romantic comedy of the twenty-first century.

*

Over a montage of real people hugging and kissing at London's Heathrow Airport, the voice of Hugh Grant notes, "Before the planes hit the Twin Towers, as far as I know, none of the phone calls on board were messages of hate and revenge—they were all messages of love." This was Richard Curtis's response to 9/11: to write and direct a mostly upbeat love story that in fact featured several stories about love in its various forms.

Richard Curtis established himself first in television, then the movies, as a highly successful comic scriptwriter. He wrote for the comic actor Rowan Atkinson, first on England's topical satirical show *Not the Nine O'clock News*, and then on the *Black Adder* series, in which Atkinson's character played through a series of historical periods trying, and failing, to get ahead. Curtis's first feature film was the hilarious but little seen *The Tall Guy* (1989), in which Jeff Goldblum is in London appearing in a stage musical version of *The Elephant Man*. He contends with an egotistical star (Atkinson) and has a torrid affair with a young Emma Thompson, making her film debut. Although it is very funny, the film was not a success, and Curtis returned to television as well as being one of the founders of the charitable "Comic Relief" benefit shows in England.

He finally made his mark on the big screen with the screenplay for the 1994 hit *Four Weddings and a Funeral*. It marked the first time

Curtis had worked with actor Hugh Grant, writing the part that propelled him to stardom. Like Atkinson, Grant became an important member of what would eventually become the Richard Curtis stock company, appearing in all his subsequent feature films to date. They reunited for *Notting Hill*, with Grant playing a bookstore owner who stumbles into a romance with a Hollywood star played, in all her glory, by Julia Roberts. Grant also appeared as the caddish Daniel Cleaver in the movies based on Helen Fielding's *Bridget Jones* novels, with Curtis one of several writers credited with the screenplay. The *Bridget Jones* movies allowed Curtis to cross paths with Colin Firth, who was emerging as a British heartthrob (especially after playing D'Arcy in a TV version of *Pride and Prejudice*), and who would also be included in what was soon to be the very large cast of *Love Actually*.

Curtis was inspired by Robert Altman's movies *Nashville* (1975) and *Short Cuts* (1993) as well as Wayne Wang's *Smoke* (1995) to do a movie that would combine several stories into one narrative. *Love Actually* consists of nine stories with a certain amount of intertwining. One story involves the new bachelor prime minister (Hugh Grant). Another involves his sister (Emma Thompson) whose husband (Alan Rickman) may be cheating on her. Another involves one of the husband's employees (Laura Linney) who is trying to kindle a love life while burdened with the care of a mentally disturbed brother. Viewers of earlier versions had trouble keeping all the characters straight, but in the final release version it really doesn't matter. The crossovers and connections are more of a joke than anything else, as when the prime minister is going door to door looking for a former employee, and the door opens at one residence to reveal the secretary who has been tempting his brother-in-law.

What matters is that Curtis made a movie that was a celebration of love even though not all the stories have happy endings and not all of them are romantic. Perhaps the easiest way to describe the film is to take the stories one at a time.

*

The film opens at the arrival gate at Heathrow. Those are real people hugging and kissing as they're reunited after whatever journeys they've been on. Curtis had a camera crew at the airport for a week with instructions to shoot whatever looked interesting. Then someone would run over to get the people to sign a release allowing their image to be used in the film. Unlike *When Harry Met Sally . . .* , where the old married couples told true stories but were played by actors, these are real people and real emotions.

The film then goes right into its first story. Curtis thought he could pare all his stories down to their bare essentials so there would be no downtime. He had no specific number of stories he was aiming for; some stories would end up on the cutting-room floor. At the time he spoke to *Premiere* magazine in the midst of production, there were apparently seven.

"I thought, 'Let's have seven good beginnings, seven good middles, and seven good endings, and cut the rest out.' I find it quite bizarre how we managed to string the other films out to such a length," he told the reporter.

The first story introduced was actually the least conventional. It focused on Billy Mack (Bill Nighy), an aging rock star well past his prime who has been convinced by his longtime manager Joe (Gregor Fisher) to do a Christmas version of one of his old hits. It's sentimental nonsense, to be sure, and as Billy keeps singing the wrong lyrics it's obvious it's not going well.

Audiences may be excused if they don't immediately pick up on the in-joke here. The song "Love Is All Around," now to be called "Christmas Is All Around," was originally done in the sixties and became a hit all over again when it was used in *Four Weddings and a Funeral*. The movie's joke is that Billy absolutely hates doing this; he doesn't take it seriously, and through the rest of the film—as Joe has him make appearances to help propel the song to the top of the charts—Billy is rude, crude, and brutally honest. During an appearance on a TV show he advises the young viewers, "Don't buy drugs—become a pop star and they give you them for free."

Billy was played in a bravura turn by Bill Nighy. He had been doing yeoman work in the theater, on British TV and film, and even voicing animation. This part would put him on the map, though he would be under a ton of makeup as a vampire in *Underworld* or as Davy Jones in *Pirates of the Caribbean* movies. Said Nighy, "Everybody knows these guys, guys like Keith Richards and John McEnroe, who seem to have a gift for saying the honest thing that cuts to the chase in a way that a lot of other people don't have." Gregor Fisher, a veteran British TV performer, was cast as Billy's loyal and long-suffering manager.

What made the story touching was Billy's realization of just how much he owed Joe, and what a good team they'd been. After his song improbably hits number one on the charts and Billy is invited to a swinging party at Elton John's on Christmas Eve, Joe is prepared to spend a quiet evening alone. Managers don't get to party with the stars and the groupies. Instead Billy shows up and says there's nowhere else he'd rather be, with Curtis's script showing he knows exactly how men *don't* ordinarily express affection like this. Joe looks at him and accuses him of being "gay as a maypole" after just a little while with Elton John. After a manly, platonic embrace, Billy suggests they celebrate Christmas in style: by getting drunk and watching porn. As Nighy put it, men don't express love to each other very well. "We usually kind of slap each other on the back briefly and leave the room. Then go to the football game and shout at the ref."

Curtis used this story to add a dash of comic fire to what soon becomes apparent is a highly sentimental movie. Whenever things get a little too sloppy, Billy can be counted on to tell an interviewer that if he has a hit with his new record he'll strip off his clothes on the air on Christmas Eve. When he does so, later in the film, it not only plays out that story but provides a much-needed distraction in another story when the image pops up on TV.

*

Several other characters and their stories are introduced in quick succession, and it takes a few scenes to get them sorted out. First is Jamie, played by Colin Firth. His story is about unlikely love on the rebound when he discovers his girlfriend is cheating on him—with his brother. Firth had been working steadily for years but had became a major romantic lead with the one-two punch of *Pride and Prejudice* on television and *Bridget Jones's Diary* in the movies. After playing these smoldering, inaccessible romantic heroes, it was a bit odd to see him here as the patsy. Yet, in the style of much British comedy, he must go through a period of embarrassment. After the humiliation at the beginning of the story, everything else that happens to him seems like a lark and only makes the audience yearn for the happy ending that this story has in store.

It is perhaps the most conventional of the stories in the film in following the classic "boy meets girl, boy loses girl, boy gets girl" plot, so Curtis gives it a fresh spin by ensuring that the two characters not only are from two different worlds but literally can't speak the same language. Jamie ends up at a house in France to work on his latest book. (Don't try to book the house for your next vacation. Unlike the *Pretty Woman* hotel suite, it no longer exists, having suffered a fire some time after the filming.) The "girl" in the story is Aurelia, a Portuguese housekeeper who doesn't speak English. She's played by Lúcia Moniz who, though unknown to American and British audiences, is a leading singer and television actress in her native Portugal. Indeed, that tattoo on her lower back—seen when she strips down to her underwear to dive into the pond and rescue Jamie's manuscript—is pictured on one of her albums.

The problem in shooting the story was not language differences, since Moniz does know English in real life; it was the work that had to go into that pond scene. To ensure a strong enough gust of wind to blow the manuscript away, a large fan was set up off camera. But fans make noises, which are then picked up by the microphones. The

dialogue in that scene all had to be dubbed in later in order to eliminate the noise. A problem like that would be all in a day's work for a
film crew. More difficult was the fact that the big pond they both must
dive into was only eighteen inches deep. Both Firth and Moniz had
to pad around on their knees to give the impression they were swimming in far deeper water.

The concluding section of the story has Jamie seek out Aurelia in
Portugal after having taken a language course so he can speak Portuguese . . . sort of. The subtitles in the story, showing the misunder-
standings and mangling of language, may be the funniest use of the
device since *Annie Hall*. Jamie must embarrass himself again by con-
veying to Aurelia's father and sister and, ultimately, a restaurant filled
with people that he is love with Aurelia and wishes to marry her. It's
exactly the kind of mixture of sweetness and unexpected comedy that
is Curtis's hallmark. As Firth put it, it's a delicate balancing act: "You
miss by an inch, and you've got something that's catastrophic. There's
a thin line between being deeply moved and the desire to vomit."

The day after shooting, it was Curtis's turn to be embarrassed. All
through the restaurant scene he kept instructing the actor playing Aurelia's father how he wanted the scene done. "I spent the two days we
were working giving him really pathetic notes, and acting how I wanted
it to be and saying, 'Louder, louder!' and 'Come on! Be better, better.'" While Curtis was eating breakfast at the hotel he was approached
by the actor, Helder Costa, who presented him with a four-hundred-
page coffee-table-sized book about his life and work. It turned out that
Costa was one of the most important theater directors in Portugal, not
the novice day player Curtis seemed to have assumed.

In spite of his embarrassment, Curtis let Jamie and Aurelia keep
their happy ending.

*

Daniel (Liam Neeson) is first seen in a brief phone conversation in
which we learn that his wife has just died. We then see the bittersweet

funeral scene and then finally the real story. Their son Sam (Thomas Sangster) is actually Daniel's stepson, so Daniel is coping both with a terrible loss and the awkwardness of not quite being sure how to deal with the moody Sam. When the boy finally emerges from seclusion in his room, it turns out that of course he misses his mother, but he's in love with the coolest girl in his grade school, and she doesn't know he exists.

This story line was aided immensely by the casting of Neeson and young Sangster. Curtis already had connections with Hugh Grant, Emma Thompson, and Colin Firth, but Neeson was a shot in the dark. He signed on but was locked into a tight schedule with other film commitments, and that's why some of his scenes may seem visually static. They were running out the clock on his availability, and they needed to make the most of it. The scene where we see the father and son lying head to head on a couch was set up that way because it was an easy way to get all the dialogue in a single shot.

They were even luckier with the talented and preternaturally adorable Sangster. Only twelve at the time, he already had several credits, including playing Adolf Hitler as a child in a few scenes of a television miniseries. He was much more innocent here and had the right bloodlines for the film. He is a distant cousin of Hugh Grant but, more important, his father is the actor Mark Sangster. It's important because when Sam decides the way to win the girl is to become a musician—in order to play at the Christmas concert where she'll be singing—he decides to take up the drums. Neither Sam—nor Thomas—knew how to play the drums, but Mark Sangster did, and he taught his son for the movie.

The scene of Daniel and Sam bonding was originally a much longer sequence involving Daniel getting his computer accidentally tied up with pop-ads for porn sites. But when the first cut of *Love Actually* came in at three and a half hours, Curtis began ruthlessly editing. The computer scene (in which Daniel bribes Sam to take the blame in front of his grandfather) was eliminated because the scene on the park bench where Sam reveals his secret love provided all the information the audience needed about the growing bond between the two. Curtis included the deleted scenes on the DVD release of the film.

The Christmas concert scene required the film finally to produce Joanna, the object of Sam's puppyish affections. This proved to be one of the most difficult casting searches for the film. Curtis listened to hundreds of audition tapes, looking for a girl who could believably belt out "All I Want for Christmas," a song Curtis had become attached to during the writing of the script. They were coming close to simply casting a young actress and dubbing in her voice. Then they found Olivia Olson, who does her own singing on the sound track. She was so good that they had to get her to add some rough edges to her performance, taking a few breaths here and there, so that there would be no question who was doing the singing.

The story culminates in a race to and through the airport so that Sam can profess his love before Joanna boards a plane to America. Here we see Curtis at his most manipulative, pulling coincidences out of thin air and ignoring the fact that after 9/11 airport security at Heathrow couldn't possibly be as loose as we see it here. The beauty of it is that we're much more interested in getting Sam to Joanna than in realism. Thus the appearance of Rowan Atkinson, who had popped up earlier as a prissy story clerk, and who now provides sufficient distraction for Sam to slip through the gate, seems heaven-sent, as does the appearance of Billy Mack stripping on TV in celebration of his Christmas hit status. Eliminated (but available on the DVD) is a sequence in which Sam proves to have Olympic-style gymnastic skills in eluding the pursuing security guards. These abilities hadn't been well established in the film, so most of the jumping and leaping was removed as well.

The result is easily one of the sweetest stories in the film. Said Neeson, "I think at a fundamental level [Curtis is] an incurable romantic. He loves romance and he likes turning it slightly askew." Curtis admits to being romantic but objects to those who claim he's writing autobiographical pieces. Strangely, he makes an exception in this case. "In fact, the most autobiographical may well be the little boy," he said, "because I was a very passionate little boy in terms of falling in love with girls."

The other story that begins in the first scene with Daniel is one of the saddest of the lot—a middle-class marriage that is heading to the rocks not by design but by neglect. Daniel's friend Karen (Emma Thompson) is a good wife and mother, but her husband Harry (Alan Rickman) seems bored. When his sexy secretary Mia (the German actress Heike Makatsch) makes it clear she is interested in him, he allows that interest to continue. It's left vague whether it ever gets beyond the flirting stage, but when Karen figures out what's going on, it's a betrayal all the same.

The part of Karen was written for Thompson, who had worked before not only with Curtis but with Rickman. They had appeared with Hugh Grant in *Sense and Sensibility* (Thompson won an Oscar for her screenplay adaptation of the Jane Austen novel), and Rickman had directed her in *The Winter Guest*, along with her mother, the actress Phyllida Law. So this was old home week. "We've got the Chekovian bit," Rickman told her when he read Curtis's script. "I enjoy the fact it has the most melancholy and the most regret. It's about how easily you can lose it, if you don't look after it."

It's mostly an actors' story, and Thompson and Rickman are two of the best, so it was basically a matter of stepping back and letting them work, as in the scene where Karen—knowing her husband has bought jewelry and expecting to receive it as a Christmas present—opens her gift from him and discovers a Joni Mitchell album. She excuses herself, allows her anger and tears to come out, then regains control and rejoins the family. By contrast Rickman's hardest moment may be waiting helplessly as Rowan Atkinson elaborately wraps the jewelry box that Harry had been hoping to pay for and slip quickly into his pocket. The scene was shot in Selfridges department store, and they could shoot only when the store was closed between 9 p.m. and 5 a.m. It took the crew more than seven hours to get the three-and-a-half-minute scene that appears in the film.

Rickman thought the story needed a bit more, and told Curtis so, which led to the addition of the brief confrontation scene following the Christmas pageant. It's classic British understatement: she knows, he knows she knows, and he admits he's been a fool. Nothing is resolved. When we see them reunited at the airport at the end, we find them still struggling to go through the motions. It's left to viewers to decide if this marriage is irretrievably over or if the struggle is just beginning.

*

Three of the shortest stories in the film are then introduced in quick succession. Two are essentially sketches while the third is a poignant and more elaborate story about unrequited love.

First there's goofy Colin (Kris Marshall), a delivery boy who decides that if he's going to score with the ladies he's got to go to America where all women are beautiful and everyone loves a Brit. It's a cartoonish fantasy that his friend (Abdul Salis) tries to talk him out of, to no avail. Colin takes all his money and uses it to go, seemingly at random, to Wisconsin. (It really was at random. Curtis had never been to Wisconsin and knew little about it.) The joke is that all of Colin's fantasies—filmed not in Wisconsin but back in England—come true. The three women he meets are played by rising young actresses who are knockouts: January Jones, Ivana Milicevic, and Elisha Cuthbert, the last probably most recognizable to audiences at the time from her work on the TV series *24* as Jack Bauer's constantly-in-trouble daughter. The punch line is the arrival of two more beauties. We hear that Colin will really hit it off with Harriet, referred to as "the sexy one" as compared to the three pinups he's already with, and when he returns to London, it is with Harriet, played by Shannon Elizabeth (from *American Pie*) who has brought her "friendly" sister Carla, played by Denise Richards (*Wild Things*, *The World Is Not Enough*). There's no deep message here, just a variation on the gag of someone seemingly delusional turning out, however improbably, to be right.

Equally light is the story of John and Judy, who are stand-ins for the unseen stars of some sort of erotic film. It's not clear if it's supposed to be soft-core porn or something artistically erotic, but the two are asked to mime increasingly explicit sex scenes while technicians check camera angles and lighting. As played by Martin Freeman (of the British television series *The Office*) and actress Joanna Page, the humor comes from how completely shy they are, hesitantly making small talk while miming oral sex. It is their ability to convey sincere and wide-eyed innocence, no matter what they're actually doing at the moment, that make this slight story work. Asked what his mother thought of his big-screen role in which he spends much of the time naked, Freeman replied, "She loved the film, but I'm sure there are better ways to pass the time as a mother."

A story of unrequited love has some of the most elaborate work in the film but tells us little about the characters except the situation they find themselves in. It works only in so far as the viewer has ever loved from afar and realized it was never meant to be—which means nearly everyone. The story opens at the wedding of Peter and Juliet. Whether by luck or design, Curtis and his people cast two performers on the verge of major stardom in the roles. Chiwetel Ejiofor had come to notice in Stephen Frears's *Dirty Pretty Things*, while Keira Knightley had been in the surprise hit *Bend It Like Beckham*. (By the time *Love Actually* was released, Knightley would be better known for *Pirates of the Caribbean*, a movie Curtis thought would be a mistake for her when she went off to make it. It was not one of his more astute predictions.)

Peter's best man, Mark (British film and TV actor Andrew Lincoln), has promised no surprises at the wedding, but in fact he has arranged for an incredible live performance of the Beatles' "All You Need Is Love" with the musicians and singers scattered all over the church. (Richard Curtis takes a Hitchcock-like cameo playing a trombone.) Curtis took his inspiration for this scene from, of all things, a funeral. Curtis recalled a memorial service for the Muppets creator Jim Henson at which various puppeteers brought their felt characters with them and, on cue, joined in a song in tribute to their fallen leader. The writer of *Four Weddings and a Funeral* had no problem taking an idea from one life-cycle event and applying it to another.

At the wedding reception, Mark looks so longingly at the couple that someone asks if he has a crush on Peter. This isn't a story of gay love. (Curtis had written one, but it was a victim to the need to get the film to a manageable length. The few scenes comprising that story are preserved on the DVD.) Instead, Mark's story is about why he is so cool to Juliet. When she asks to see the video he shot at the wedding, she discovers that all the footage is of her. Mark has been carrying a large torch for Juliet but can't possibly interfere in her marriage to his best friend. So he suffers quietly and appears distant. The video was shot by a second-unit cameraman who was told to get lots of glamour shots of Knightley, which did not prove to be a difficult task.

Now Curtis found he had painted himself into a corner. Knightley looks ethereally beautiful in the film, and it's not hard to see why Mark would have a painful crush on Juliet. Where, however, could the story go?

Curtis had different ideas for what Mark could do to make it clear that he would be moving on with his life—but not before he had the opportunity to express the depth of his love for Juliet. The director tried out various solutions on the women in his office to see which one they would find romantic and not, say, creepy or pathetic. That led to the scene that, in its own way, may be as much a fantasy as Colin's dream that he will be a "sex god" in America. It is heartbreakingly touching as Mark uses a boom box playing Christmas carols to get a moment with Juliet away from Peter. Through a series of placards he silently tells her how much he loves her, and how he has no agenda to take it any further. Few people get to make a clean break like that in such a nonrelationship. While it probably couldn't have sustained a film on its own, as a story in this collage it works beautifully. We don't know much more about these people, but it doesn't matter. As Curtis noted, "Her role relies so much just on her being gorgeous."

*

At the wedding we get our first glimpse of Sarah (Laura Linney), whose story of sibling devotion is the film's other sad story. Sarah works for Harry and has a long-standing crush on another person at the office named Karl. Everyone knows it except, apparently, Karl. In the course of the story Sarah will get her long awaited chance, only to have it dashed because of other obligations. She is the sole family for her institutionalized and disturbed brother (Michael Fitzgerald). When he calls, she drops everything for him. Just as she and Karl finally have their big night of passion under way, the phone rings. It's her brother, and she's off again.

Linney is the only American with a major role in the film. She was cast during a frustrating search to find someone for the part, when Curtis made it clear he wanted someone like Laura Linney instead of the English actresses they kept sending him. Linney had been quietly amassing an impressive list of acting credits since the early nineties when she had appeared in the television miniseries *Tales of the City*. Her one moment of unbridled joy in *Love Actually* is when she takes Karl back to her apartment and goes upstairs to quickly clean her bedroom. She stops on the stairs and does a little triumphant dance, not quite able to believe she's finally pulled it off. The apartment is an unusual one with a loftlike bedroom overlooking the rest of the living space. It is based on the apartment of Curtis's friend Helen Fielding, who had written *Bridget Jones's Diary*.

Curtis seems to have made an effort to give *Love Actually* an international cast, perhaps stung by a comment he heard in a nightclub one evening where a black performer suggested that *Notting Hill* deserved an award for best special effects because the movie had removed all the blacks from the racially mixed neighborhood. That musician was even given a brief appearance in *Love Actually*, as if Curtis wanted to make sure to deliver the message that there were no barriers on *his* films. The part of Karl went to Rodrigo Santoro, a Brazilian actor working primarily in television, and who in 2006 worked his way onto the U.S. series *Lost* (as Paulo).

During test screenings, audiences made it clear that they wanted Sarah and Karl finally to get together. She's a good person and doesn't deserve to be alone at the end, yet Curtis makes it clear that things will not change. For all the accusations that Curtis is a softie and a sentimentalist, at least a third of the film's stories end unhappily, including this one.

*

If any of the film's romances deserves primacy, it is the unusual office romance. Curtis gives it emphasis in several ways, making the boss the British prime minister, casting Hugh Grant in the role, and giving Grant's character the privilege of speaking the opening and closing narration. They also get the narrative's final moment on screen before the film reverts to the opening montage of real people embracing at the airport.

The casting of Grant underscored what was already widely remarked upon by film critics and astute viewers: the boyishly handsome British actor had become Curtis's on-screen alter ego, in much the same way that Jack Lemmon had served that role for Billy Wilder or, for many years, Robert DeNiro had done for Martin Scorsese. There is respect and friendship in these professional relationships. Each not only owes the other much for his success, each also recognizes that it really is a perfect match of director and actor. Grant had had a middling career as an actor when he auditioned for *Four Weddings and a Funeral*, wondering why he was putting himself through it again. Instead he found someone on the same wavelength. Recalled Curtis, "Suddenly in walked someone whose sense of humor was very similar to mine. It was a huge relief to find someone who actually got what the joke was meant to be." The movie went on to become the most successful British film released to that time, and it made Grant a star. Their on-screen partnership was cemented with *Notting Hill*.

The prime minister (Hugh Grant) and his tea lady (Martine McCutcheon) brazen out the discovery of their romance, providing one of nine different conclusions to Love Actually.

Both were in a different place in their careers by the time of *Love Actually*. Curtis was stepping up to directing while Grant had become tired of playing the cute, self-effacing love interest and was now playing cads in movies like *About a Boy* and *Bridget Jones's Diary*, the latter co-scripted by Curtis. Grant initially balked at playing the prime minister, telling Curtis, "I don't know that I really can go back to being that nice person—it maybe seems a little retrograde."

Grant made it clear that the character would have to change. Curtis, instead of pulling rank, accommodated him. "The one thing I was really keen on was not to make him too goody two-shoes," said Grant. "Originally, Curtis had written him as the ideal Prime Minister, incredibly charming, nice, amusing, and concerned with the right things. I said, 'It's all very well, but people are going to puke.' So we tried to put a bit of steel in there.'" Curtis would sometimes try to cajole Grant into an action or a line, but in the give and take between the two, each knew when to give in and when to stand firm. "It's very interesting to direct him because he is impossible to fool," said Curtis, "I'd say, 'Try the scene this way,' and he'd say, 'You're trying to make me softer; I won't do it.' He's not a puppy dog trying to please you."

Perhaps the real joke between them is that while the sweet-natured, easygoing characters Grant played for Curtis were presumed to be what Grant was really like—leading lazy critics to suggest he wasn't really acting—in fact they're a lot closer to what Curtis himself is like. Grant has said he figured out how to play his character in *Four Weddings* when he realized he was playing the writer. But he feels more of a kinship to the cads of *Bridget Jones's Diary* and *About a Boy* than to the romantic leads he's played more often. As Grant puts it, "That's the whole joke of the film. The voice-over begins, 'Some people think the world is full of hatred and greed.' And I'm one of them."

In the scene when the prime minister makes a rousing speech on behalf of all that is good in England (including Harry Potter, the Beatles, and soccer star David Beckham's feet), Grant refused to utter a reference to actress Catherine Zeta-Jones's breasts, knowing that while it would get a laugh, it would be out of character. Yet he went along with Curtis's elaborate gag in which the prime minister goes door to door looking for the woman he loves, having the street but not the address.

To play his lady love—the "tea girl" Natalie—Curtis decided on an actress unknown to American viewers but very well known in England, Martine McCutcheon. She had spent four years as Tiffany on *EastEnders*, a long-running British soap opera. She then launched a successful career as a pop singer. Curtis was a fan of the show. "I watched her and loved her every day. She is a wonderful, boisterous, confident girl." Having done only one previous (and obscure) film, McCutcheon was nervous about appearing with an established star like Grant, and called Curtis before the start of production wondering if she would work out. Curtis replied, "Oh, shut up, Tini. I wrote the part for you." Until that moment she had no idea just how much Curtis wanted *her* for his film.

The casting of some of the other roles was relatively easy. When Grant, as the newly elected prime minister, arrives at 10 Downing Street, he's greeted by his staff. Pat, the housekeeper, is played by Jill Freud, mother of Curtis's longtime partner Emma. (Emma made sure Mom had a few more words to say than were in the script.) The role of the randy American president was a bit more difficult. Colin Firth had jokingly suggested giving it to former President Bill Clinton, who was now out of work. Curtis offered it to John Travolta, whom he had met at a party and who had said he would love to appear in a Curtis film. It's unknown whether Travolta ever saw the script. His agent turned it down.

Curtis then approached Billy Bob Thornton, who agreed to take the small role because, according to Curtis, he was impressed with the letter the director had sent asking him to consider the role. "And he fancied a trip to England," Curtis added. Thornton appears in only a few scenes, but he quickly sketches in the politically—and sexually—aggressive president. Curtis said he had no aspiration for political commentary here, and neither Thornton nor Grant were modeled on real political figures. The idea was to set up a situation where the prime minister would have Natalie reassigned since he assumed she had welcomed the American president's attentions.

Their reconciliation takes place at the Christmas pageant, where several stories come together. The prime minister's sister Karen is there with her kids. On-stage Sam is drumming in hopes of attracting Joanna's attentions while Daniel will meet a potential new love interest in the form of another mom played by the model Claudia Schiffer. (Earlier in the film Daniel mentions that his late wife had suggested Schiffer as his date for her funeral.) The prime minister and Natalie are kissing backstage when the curtain they are hiding behind goes up. Their "secret" is now out, leading them to smile and wave to the audience while gracefully trying to exit. Curtis later joked that when Grant died, the TV obituaries would close with that little wave and exit, to which Grant replied it would probably be the mug shot from his notorious arrest with a Hollywood prostitute.

*

Love Actually ends back at Heathrow as several of the stories conclude with various arrivals. It looks so neat and effortless, but the actors sweated during a hot day of shooting (while dressed for winter), and the selection of the music proved daunting. Alan Rickman recalled, "When we were finishing the film, the last words I said to Richard were 'Good luck in the editing room.'"

Curtis had nine stories plus a number of sub-plots, but when the first cut ran to three and a half hours he knew he would have to be utterly ruthless in editing. Scenes that he liked were cut because they were no longer necessary, like Daniel and Sam and the computer pop-ups, or the story of Karen and her son getting in trouble with the school headmistress. Curtis had even shot some scenes in Africa in an attempt to universalize his theme. There were to be posters in Harry's offices of African natives toiling under the sun, which would then transition to actual scenes in which the Africans would be talking about their personal relationships. Curtis was assured that material he really liked but had to eliminate would eventually be seen on DVD, where such deleted scenes were now considered "bonus" material.

More difficult was the selection of music for the film. Some of it was integral to the script, such as Joni Mitchell's "Both Sides Now" when Karen realizes that Harry may be cheating on her, or Joanna singing "All I Want for Christmas." For the scene of Peter and Juliet's wedding, "All You Need Is Love" was an obvious choice. But for the closing scenes at the airport, Curtis had wanted to use "The Loving" by the band XTC. When actually played under the footage for the closing sequence, Curtis realized it was far too loud and busy and would prove distracting. Needing a replacement, he promised his editing crew he would spend the evening going through his well-organized and alphabetized collection of albums, and arrive in the editing rooms the next day with numerous choices to consider. But when something came up that evening, he barely made it to the Bs. He came in the next day with a song from Abba and the song that would eventually be used, the Beach Boys' "God Only Knows." It was upbeat but subdued, and underlined the message of the film: there are love stories all around us, even if we remain unaware of them.

Love Actually was released in November 2003 and eventually earned more than $200 million in worldwide receipts. It topped out at just under $60 million in the United States, and was not considered a smash hit, but romantic comedies are rarely blockbusters. What it demonstrated was that, well into the twenty-first century, the romantic comedy is alive and well. People still need to believe in the power of love and happy endings.

ACKNOWLEDGMENTS

THE GENESIS of this project occurred ten years ago when I was invited to speak to a senior citizen's group on a classic film. From that one lecture grew a wholly unexpected sideline to my career as a film critic. I now regularly speak at a number of senior residences in Massachusetts in an ongoing film series. They watch a movie, then I give them a behind-the-scenes look at the making of the film.

Over the years I've built a library of many lectures, and in each case I've had to begin by pulling out numerous sources to collect the various stories that would make up the lecture. While there are some films with "making of" books, for the most part this information is scattered in studio histories, actors' and directors' memoirs, and biographies of a variety of people who are involved in the filmmaking process. I came across marvelous stories in diverse places, and my lectures became popular events. As I shared the occasional anecdote with friends and film critic colleagues, I discovered they didn't know the history of many of these films either.

Thus in planning this book I looked for films that exemplified romantic comedy, as described in the introduction, but that also shed light on how movies get made and the personalities involved in making them. I hope these stories will prompt the reader to see the films again or for the first time, and to view them with a new appreciation for how much effort goes into the process of putting a movie together.

I want to thank the residents and programming staff at Chestnut Park, Boston; Evan Park, Newton; and Orchard Cove, Canton, all in

Massachusetts, as well as the numerous other facilities where I have spoken over the years. Some of the chapters here began—in much shorter form—as lectures for these audiences. I'm grateful for their continued enthusiasm and interest, which has spurred me on in continuing to ferret out these stories and weave them together.

I was amazed how much I could accomplish as a member of the Public Library of Brookline from my home computer. Through its Minuteman Network I was able to search the collective catalogs of libraries throughout eastern Massachusetts, then order those volumes to be borrowed locally. I was constantly surprised at what I found not only in Brookline but also, through Minuteman, at other libraries. Some key books were available only in one location far removed from me, but with a few keystrokes I was able to obtain them. For access to its vast periodical collection, I'm also indebted to the Boston Public Library. Articles in magazines like *Cosmopolitan*, *GQ*, *Premiere*, *Rolling Stone*, and others might never have crossed my path but for the library's extensive holdings of decidedly nonacademic journals.

As usual I also extend thanks to my agent, Alison Picard, and to my publisher/editor Ivan R. Dee, who supported my interest in writing about romantic comedy.

Individuals who provided key support and advice include Robert Devney, Bill Jarosz, Denise Karlin, Ken Levine, James R. Parrish, and Nat Segaloff. Many of the movies herein I first saw with—or later introduced to—my wife Donna, who was smart enough to keep out of the way when I was surrounded by dozens of books and trying to keep numerous facts in my head while writing about each movie. My daughter Amanda, already an aficionado of old movies (even as she and her friends adore *High School Musical*) will soon be old enough to appreciate these movies as well. I look forward to seeing what the next generation brings as they discover, and eventually help advance, that most enduring genre, the romantic comedy.

D. M. K.

Brookline, Massachusetts
March 2008

NOTES

1. Trouble in Paradise

page

13 "Are you crazy . . . but with your face?" Herman G. Weinberg, *The Lubitsch Touch*, New York, 1968, pp. 4–5.

16 "I've been to Paris, France . . . Paris, Paramount is better." John Walker, *Halliwell's Who's Who in the Movies*, 4ᵗʰ ed., London, 2006, p. 300.

17 "MGM likes heroes who . . . have been around the world." Ethan Mordden, *The Hollywood Studios: House Style in the Golden Age of the Movies*, New York, 1988, p. 21.

18 "became a star *only* . . . on and off the screen." Jeanine Basinger, *A Woman's View*, New York, 1993, p. 151.

19 "It is in the script . . . in the first place." Scott Eyman, *Laughter in Paradise*, New York, 1993, p. 197.

20 "No use reading the play, Sem. It's bad." Ibid., p. 189.

20–21 "We met every morning . . . two other words before." Weinberg, *Lubitsch Touch*, p. 206.

21 "I wish to God . . . that would have been a great thing." Ibid., p. 207.

21 "He always had an actor in mind . . . Just a genius." Bernard Rosenberg and Harry Silverstein, *The Real Tinsel*, New York, 1970, p. 230.

22 "Lubitsch's art is one of omission . . . the two passions are inseparable." Gerald Mast, *The Comic Mind*, 2ⁿᵈ ed., Chicago, 1979, pp. 207–209.

23 "The passage of time . . . underlying much of the comedy." William Paul, *Ernst Lubitsch's American Comedy*, New York, 1983, p. 42.

24 "What the scene actually shows . . . with romance and respect." Richard Corliss, *Talking Pictures*, Woodstock, N.Y., 1974, p. 166.

2. It Happened One Night

27 "Your last picture wasn't very good . . . what the picture was!" Bob Thomas, *King Cohn: The Life and Times of Harry Cohn*, New York, 1967, p. 53.

28 "Harry, I really need a *hundred* . . . ask for to *get fifteen*?" Frank Capra, *The Name Above the Title*, New York, 1985 (reprint), p. 84.

29 "a gigolo with brass knuckles." Warren G. Harris, *Gable and Lombard*, New York, 1974, p. 36.

30 "Montgomery says there are too many . . . You can have Clark Gable." Capra, *Name Above the Title*, p. 164.

30 "I always wanted to see Siberia . . . *what* you do with it." Lyn Tornabene, *Long Live the King*, New York, 1976, p. 173.

31 "I thought, 'It can't be that good . . . It was still good." Chrystopher J. Spier, *Clark Gable*, Jefferson, N.C., 2002, p. 103.

31 "I never ask one of my little girls to play a part she doesn't want." Tornabene, *Long Live the King*, p. 172.

32 "I hear that French broad likes money." Capra, *Name Above the title*, p. 165.

32 "She made more in overtime than I made for the picture." Joseph McBride, *Frank Capra: The Catastrophe of Success*, New York, 1992, p. 304.

32–33 "One thing I liked about it . . . beat up Miss Colbert." Spier, *Gable*, p. 103.

34 "Get her out of here . . . That's not *my* leg." Ibid., p. 105.

34 "Really, that's the only picture . . . loved doing those scenes." George Stevens, Jr., ed., *Conversations with the Great Filmmakers of Hollywood's Golden Age at the American Film Institute*, New York, 2006, p. 99.

34 "Well, there seems to be a slight problem . . . *You guys!*'" McBride, *Capra*, p. 307.

36 "Don't worry about it . . . without interfering with the plot." Thomas, *King Cohn*, p. 92.

37 "I just finished the worst picture in the world." Jane Ellen Wayne, *Clark Gable: Portrait of a Misfit*, New York, 1993, p. 113.

38 "I'm still going to wear the same size hat." Spier, *Gable*, p. 184.

38 "Having it doesn't mean anything. Earning it does." Wayne, *Gable*, p. 124.

39 "But it's the Nobel Prize of motion pictures." Mason Wiley and Damien Bona, *Inside Oscar*, 10th ed., New York, 1996, p. 57.

39 "I was just an innocent bystander." Ibid., p. 58.

39 "I want to tell you . . . I wouldn't be here." Ibid., p. 58.

40 "Well, Mayer sent us over . . . Gable's salary after that." Leland Pogue, ed., *Frank Capra Interviews*, Jackson, Miss., 2004, p. 190.

3. My Man Godfrey

41 "one of the most glamorous and unlikely 'double dates' in the history of Hollywood." Charles Francisco, *Gentleman: The William Powell Story*, New York, 1985, p. 168.

42 "Greg was most off-the-cuff . . . on the wagon in the 1940s." Wes. D. Gehring, *Carole Lombard: The Hoosier Tornado*, Indianapolis, 2003, p. 138.

44 "No American novelist . . . as fascinating as Carole Lombard . . ." Andrew Sarris, *"You Ain't Heard Nothing Yet,"* New York, 1998, p. 459.

45 "I must like the man . . . we're still the best of friends." Frederick C. Ott, *The Films of Carole Lombard*, Secaucus, N.J., 1972, p. 24.

45 "To the finest actress I have worked with, bar none." Ibid., pp. 27–28.

47 "If, as Godfrey later insists . . . manliness for Depression-era America." Maria DiBattista, *Fast Talking Dames*, New Haven, 2001, p. 111.

49 "Godfrey, the butler . . . enjoying illegal U.S. citizenship." Clive Hirschorn, *The Universal Story*, New York, 1983, p. 244.

50 "should be honored as the definitive film performance of man imitating ape." DiBattista, *Dames*, pp. 349–350.

50–51 "When Lombard asked Brady . . . many details of that brief affair . . ." Warren G. Harris, *Gable and Lombard*, New York, 1974, p. 55.

51 "She is and always will be a star . . . nor cease to be grateful to." Ott, *Lombard*, p. 43.

4. The Shop Around the Corner

54 "Lubitsch lost his nerve . . . he could get established pros." Scott Eyman, *Ernst Lubitsch: Laughter in Paradise*, New York, 1993, p. 264.

58 "She was protective, loving . . . indifferent, or contemptuous." Marc Eliot, *Jimmy Stewart*, New York, 2006, p. 78.

58 "I'll never marry until I find a girl like Margaret Sullavan." Ibid., p. 80.

61 "The other day he called me an idiot. . . . I'm no fool." Quoted in James Harvey, *Romantic Comedy*, New York, 1987, p. 395.

61 "Never did I make a film . . . than in this film." Jonathan Coe, *Jimmy Stewart: A Wonderful Life*, New York, 1994, p. 60.

61 "This ode to the modesty . . . and the economic recovery thereof." Sarris, *"You Ain't Heard Nothing Yet,"* New York, 1998, p. 305.

62 "To assure authenticity . . . from Budapest as a guide." Paul, *Lubitsch's American Comedy*, New York, 1983, p. 169.

62 She found a dress . . . it would fade in the sun. Eyman, *Lubitsch*, p. 277.

62 "Margaret had recently had a child . . . the story required them to have." Michael Munn, *Jimmy Stewart: The Truth Behind the Legend*, Fort Lee, N.J., 2006, p. 202.

62–63 "Stop and contemplate the lanky . . . great performances in cinema history." Coe, *Stewart*, p. 60.

63 "She'd say, 'Stop, right there . . . I'd just crack up with laughing." Munn, *Stewart*, p. 103.

63 "For some reason I couldn't say . . . So we did more takes." Brooke Hayward, *Haywire*, New York, 1977, p. 195.

64 "Well, no more Lubitsch. . . No more Lubitsch movies." Eyman, *Lubitsch*, p. 361.

5. The Philadelphia Story

66 "I'd be quite interested in . . . Scarlett O'Hara first." Charles Higham, *Kate*, New York, 1975, p. 95.

66 "I called Howard . . . which insured my success later." Katharine Hepburn, *Me*, New York, 1991, p. 204.

67 "This is Indianapolis. This is Indianapolis." James Robert Parish, *Katharine Hepburn: The Untold Story*, New York, 2005, p. 192.

67 "An actress doesn't get many . . . and she doesn't need many." A. Scott Berg, *Kate Remembered*, New York, 2003, p. 151.

68 "I liked him and he liked me . . . I must say I did too." Hepburn, *Me*, p. 215.

69 "Why don't you come up sometime and see me?" Jerry Vermilye, *Cary Grant*, New York, 1973, p. 32.

70–71 "She enjoyed Cary Grant's pushing . . . trying to be your own stuntman,' she quipped." Higham, *Kate*, p. 103.

71 "When I first read the script . . . never completely understood." Donald Dewey, *James Stewart*, Atlanta, 1996, p. 217.

72 "Donald Ogden Stewart . . . didn't try to star himself." Gavin Lambert, *On Cukor*, New York, 1973, p. 126.

72 "*The Philadelphia Story* was . . . the easiest ever obtained." Donald Ogden Stewart, *By a Stroke of Luck!*, New York, 1975, p. 253.

73 "What was special about George was . . . he never got them into bed." Emanuel Levy, *George Cukor: Master of Elegance*, 1994, p. 131.

73–74 He complained about a pantsuit . . . left the studio the following year. Scott Eyman, *Lion of Hollywood: The Life and Legend of Louis B. Mayer*, New York, 2005, p. 264.

74 "Cary and I used to talk . . . went any smoother." Christopher Anderson, *An Affair to Remember*, New York, 1997, p. 132.

74 "If I appear in a bathing suit . . . end of the motion picture industry." Coe, *Stewart*, New York, 1994, p. 69.

74 "Just before he did it . . . Jimmy got a wonderful take." Dewey, *Stewart*, p. 218.

75 "She herself found . . . only *she* thinks it's tragic." Lambert, *Cukor*, p. 126.

76 "Jimmy simply mesmerized me . . . he misses his triangle." Nancy Nelson, *Evenings with Cary Grant*, New York, 1991, p. 120.

76 "It doesn't take much imagination . . . as an 'independent woman.'" Coe, *Stewart*, p. 67.

76 "I want to assure you . . . amid shouts and applause." Mason Wiley and Damien Bona, *Inside Oscar*, 10th anniversary ed., New York, 1996, p. 110.

76–77 "Where'd you get that thing—Ocean Pier Park?" Donald, *Stewart*, p. 220.

77 "What'd they give you, a plaque?". . . Stewart replied. Gary Fishgall, *Pieces of Time: The Life of James Stewart*, New York, 1997, p. 153.

77 "Whatever success the picture is having . . . general hysteria at Kate's comeback." Nelson, *Evenings*, p. 120.

6. Adam's Rib

80 "Mr. Tracy, you're not as tall . . . set the record straight. Berg, *Kate Remembered*, New York, 2003, p. 167.

80 "Kate and Spence fell into . . . anyone like Kate." Bill Davidson, *Spencer Tracy: Tragic Idol*, New York, 1987, p. 84.

80 "In a town where nothing was sacred . . . a special category." Larry Swindell, *Spencer Tracy*, New York, 1969, p. 243.

81 "Oh, I'm too old to be carrying grudges." Berg, *Kate Remembered*, p. 300.

82 "The superficially outspoken . . . postwar sexist ideology." McBride, *Capra*, New York, 1992, p. 537.

82 "Tell me something interesting . . . That's pretty interesting." Garson Kanin, *Tracy and Hepburn*, New York, 1971, p. 157.

84 "It was the first time . . . immediately, without changes." Higham, *Kate*, New York, 1975, p. 135.

84 The published version of the script . . . nothing substantial. Ruth Gordon and Garson Kanin, *Adam's Rib*, New York, 1972.

84 "Adultery is not a proper subject . . . court system as well. Levy, *Cukor*, New York, 1994, p. 175.

84 "I may even go out . . . wouldn't have far to go, either." Gordon and Kanin, *Adam's Rib*, p. 60.

85 "There shouldn't be even the slightest indication that Kip is a pansy." Levy, *Cukor*, p. 178.

86 That evening as they gathered . . . to rename the character Amanda. Kanin, *Tracy and Hepburn*, pp. 163–165.

86 "I think the nicest thing . . . I am devoted to her." Charles Schwartz, *Cole Porter*, New York, 1977, p. 240.

87 "By now, it was customary . . . until she knew it inside out." James Robert Parish, *Katharine Hepburn: The Untold Story*, New York, 2005, p. 225.

87 "You know, Spencer, I think . . . I never see you do it." Levy, *Cukor*, p. 177.

87–88 "I gradually understood . . . I hadn't known that." Higham, *Kate*, p. 136.

88 "I can't see either of you. I really can't!" Patrick McGilligan, *George Cukor: A Double Life*, New York, 1991, p. 200.

88 "Didn't you ever hear of 'ladies first'?". . . listed first in the credits. Higham, *Kate*, p. 137.

88 "Chocolates broadened me . . . lest you forget." Christopher Andersen, *An Affair to Remember*, New York, 1997, p. 197.

89–90 He called her a "fat, Jewish broad" . . . not on a movie screen. Will Holtzman, *Judy Holliday*, New York, 1982, p. 133.

90 "She was not simply flattered . . . she was floored." Ibid., p. 134.

90 "Is that all?. . . They know lots of words." Anderson, *Affair*, p. 196.

91 When it was suggested . . . the way it's supposed to be." Lambert, *Cukor*, p. 196.

92 "I think doing it without them . . . something special with it." George Stevens, Jr., *Conversations with the Great Moviemakers of Hollywood's Golden Age at the American Film Institute*, New York, 2006, p. 284.

7. Sabrina

97 "This girl single-handedly may make bosoms a thing of the past." Edith Head and Patty Calistro, *Edith Head's Hollywood*, New York, 1983, p. 103.

97 "She gives the distinct impression she can spell schizophrenia." Charles Higham, *Audrey*, New York, 1984, p. 63.

97 ""I very much wanted Cary Grant . . . Maybe it was my accent." Robert Horton, *Billy Wilder Interviews*, Jackson, Miss., 2001, p. 187.

98 "When Cary retired . . . I'm not going to do it anymore.'" Nelson, *Evenings*, New York, 1991, p. 269.

98 "Fine, we'll use it as a doorstop." Ed Sikov, *On Sunset Boulevard*, New York, 1998, p. 363.

101 "It was good in case I talked in my sleep." Charlotte Chandler, *Nobody's Perfect*, New York, 2002, p. 171.

101 "Look, Billy, don't tell me the story . . . I have your handshake." A. M. Sperber and Eric Lax, *Bogart*, New York 1997, p. 491.

102 "Please get the electricians . . . the dialogue written yet." Horton, *Wilder*, p. 26.

102 "But it is so logically . . . Holden was getting only \$125,000." Tom Wood, *The Bright Side of Billy Wilder, Primarily*, Garden City, N.Y., 1970, p. 109.

103 "That talk I shouldn't get the girl . . . tombstone's already up." Joe Hyams, *Bogie*, New York, 1966, p. 167.

103 "Those Paramount bastards didn't invite me?" he'd say. "Well, fuck them." Stephen Humphrey Bogart, *Bogart: In Search of My Father*, New York, 1995, p. 180.

103 "You want me to kill him now or later?" Sperber and Lax, *Bogart*, p. 494.

103–104 "It's very simple . . . the usual roll-down-the-board-table shot." Bob Thomas, *Golden Boy*, New York, 1984, p. 99.

104 "the scariest experience I've ever had in my life." Alexander Walker, *Audrey: Her Real Story*, New York, 1994, p. 87.

104 "You can tell Mr. Wilder to come out now." Sikov, *Sunset Boulevard*, p. 115.

105 "How do you like working . . . like to do thirty-six takes." Ian Woodward, *Audrey Hepburn*, New York, 1984, pp. 116–117.

105 "I don't even need my hairpiece; the guy's shooting me from behind." Sperber and Lax, *Bogart*, p. 492.

106 "a strange mixture of the laziest and most conscientious actor." Jonathan Cox, *Humphrey Bogart: Take It and Like It*, New York, 1991, p. 176.

106 "Bogart had a peculiar sense of humor . . . wittier to be good and mean." Wood, *Wilder*, p. 76.

106 "They were standing a foot apart . . . happening between them." Diana Maychick, *Audrey Hepburn*, New York, 1993, p. 99.

106–107 "People on the set told me . . . I still don't know." Chandler, *Nobody's Perfect*, p. 174.

107 "That's all. 'Oh, Bill.'. . . What a waste." Woodward, *Audrey Hepburn*, p. 120.

107 "He was very brave . . . held him in the highest esteem." Horton, *Wilder*, p. 187.

108 "Her figure and flair told me . . . any actress since [Marlene] Dietrich." Edith Head and Jane Kesner Ardmore, *Dress Doctor*, Boston, 1959, p. 118.

108 "Hepburn said that . . . even thirty years later." David Chierichetti, *Edith Head*, New York, 2003, p. 114.

108 "My first impression was . . . so extraordinarily slender, so thin." François Mohrt, *The Givenchy Style*, New York, 1998, p. 82.

109 "She knew exactly what she wanted," Warren G. Harris, *Audrey Hepburn*, New York, 1994, p. 104.

109 "I depend on Givenchy in the same way American women depend on their psychiatrists." Robyn Karney, *Audrey Hepburn: A Star Danced*, New York, 1993, p. 55.

109 "I lied. So what? . . . gave them credit too?" Chierichettei, *Edith Head*, p. 136.

110 "Audrey Hepburn . . . made my house . . . essentially Anglo-Saxon." Chierichetti, *Edith Head*, p. 136.

110 "I miss them very much . . . It was all out of turn." Chandler, *Nobody's Perfect*, p. 174.

8. Pillow Talk

112 "Sing each song as if . . . You're acting." Tom Santopietro, *Considering Doris Day*, New York, 2007, p. 17.

112 "I never did like it. Still don't. I think it's a phony name." A. E. Hotchner, *Doris Day: Her Own Story*, New York, 1976, p. 46.

114 "I would like to do a movie about the beautiful people." William J. Mann, *Behind the Screen*, New York, 2001, p. 349.

115 "She just looked at me . . . she wasn't impressed." Tom Clark with Dick Kleiner, *Rock Hudson: Friend of Mine*, New York, 1989, p. 54–55.

115 "I knew Doris Day before she was a virgin," Santopietro, *Day*, p. 121.

115 "Doris hadn't a clue to her potential . . . it's about time you dealt with it.'" John Parker, *Five for Hollywood*, New York, 1991, p. 163.

115–116 "The plot, for 1959 . . . I had ever played before." Hotchner, *Day*, p. 194.

116–117 "All of the jokes about Doris Day's . . . men in her life." Santopietro, *Day*, p. 151.

117 "Actually it is the comical obstacle course . . . of Ingmar Bergman's women." Molly Haskell, *From Reverence to Rape*, New York, 1974, pp. 266–267.

117–118 "I was astonished . . . *you* thought I was a virgin." Rock Hudson and Sara Davidson, *Rock Hudson: His Story*, New York, 1986, p. 116.

118 "If you allow me to get Jean Louis . . . I can do the same thing.'" Hotchner, *Day*, p. 200.

118 "Doris gave the best acting lessons . . . my eyes open and copied her." Parker, *Five*, p. 164.

119 "Just treat it like the most tragic story . . . nobody else will." Hudson and Davidson, *Hudson*, p. 111.

119–120 "What are you trying to do? . . . the rest of his life." Tony Randall with Michael Mindlin, *Which Reminds Me*, New York, 1989, p. 71.

121 "I have certain misgivings about it . . . An amusing picture, though, no question." Oppenheimer and Vitek, *Idol*, p. 73.

121 ". . . Doris managed to combine . . . a pleasant ally in their bewilderment . . ." Marjorie Rosen, *Popcorn Venus*, New York, 1973, p. 304.

122 "If someone said that . . . a way of harming someone's reputation. . ." Boze Hadleigh, *In or Out*, New York, 2000, p. 122.

123 "All the women in America . . . seem any different than James Garner." Hudson and Davidson, *Hudson*, p. 117.

124 "The public found it was starved . . . where bonanzas count the most." Hotchner, *Day*, p. 201.

125 "I am trapped downstairs . . . thank you upstairs for this great honor." Mason Wiley and Damien Bona, *Inside Oscar*, New York, 1996, p. 312.

125 "Forget it, Sonny Boy . . . It could never happen." Clark, *Hudson*, p. 100.

126 "Rock's illness helped give AIDS a face." Oppeheimer and Vitek, *Idol*, p.220.

126 "Forget it. I came here . . . to come from this experience." Santopietro, *Day*, p. 325.

9. Some Like It Hot

128 "Thank you, I. A. L. Diamond . . . Thank you, Billy Wilder." Wiley and Bona, *Inside Oscar*, New York, 1996, p. 328.

128–129 "It was quite poor . . . latching on to an all-girl's band." Kevin Lally, *Wilder Times*, New York, 1996, p. 278.

129 "When everybody's dress . . . peculiar than anyone else." Sikov, *Sunset Boulevard*, p. 409.

130 "They thought that Wilder had lost his marbles . . . Everybody's in drag." Michael Freedland, *Jack Lemmon*, New York, 1985, p. 57.

131 "Joe E. Brown had been out of sight . . . while we were making *Hot*." Chandler, *Nobody's Perfect*, p. 000.

133 "If we held them up . . . our muscles disappeared." Tony Curtis and Barry Paris, *Tony Curtis*, New York, 1993, p. 154.

133 "He told Wilder that Curtis was fine but Lemmon was totally impossible." Don Widener, *Lemmon*, New York, 1975, p. 169.

135 "I didn't want to come out first . . . talking in a high voice." Chandler, *Nobody's Perfect*, p. 210–211.

135 "The only way to play it was . . . if it got out of bounds." Lally, *Wilder Times*, p. 280.

135 "You know, Tony's ass . . . in case there was any doubt. Curtis and Paris, *Curtis*, p. 169.

136 "I told her, 'I guess he's okay.' She's never let me forget that one." Widener, *Lemmon*, p. 167.

136 "Within three to four weeks . . . wanted to work with him again." Sikov, *Sunset Boulevard*, p. 411.

136 "I was upset with the crazy maracas . . . how wise Billy was." Maurice Zolotow, *Billy Wilder in Hollywood*, New York, 1977, p. 247.

136 "It was the most outrageous . . . three of us dancing into the film." Lewis Yablonsky, *George Raft*, New York, 1967, p. 219.

139 "What can you do?". . . something else that sounded "rich." Curtis and Paris, *Curtis*, p. 160.

139–140 "A lot of men have wanted . . . two friends who are girls." Donald H. Wolfe, *The Last Days of Marilyn Monroe*, New York, 1998, p. 315.

140 "I have an old aunt in Vienna . . . But who would go see her?" Tom Wood, *The Brighter Side of Billy Wilder, Primarily*, Garden City, N.Y., 1970, p. 161.

140–141 "Late? Look if we had a 9 a.m. . . . we came back from lunch." Maurice Zolotow, *Marilyn Monroe*, New York, 1990, p. 331.

141 "Tony and I suffered the tortures of the damned in those high heels," Freedland, *Lemmon*, p. 65.

141 "How was that for you, Paula?" Curtis and Paris, *Curtis*, p. 168.

142 "I took her aside . . . 'Worry? About what?'" Chandler, *Nobody's Perfect*, p. 213.

142 "Don't talk to me now . . . I'm going to play this scene." Wood, *Brighter*, p. 152.

142–143 "It's like kissing Hitler . . . and see how you feel." Zolotow, *Marilyn*, p. 333.

143 "We were in mid-flight and there was a nut on the plane." Anthony Summers, *Goddess*, New York, 1985, p. 177.

143 "Look, Arthur. It's now four o'clock . . . but at noon." Wood, *Brighter*, p. 159.

144 "I have discussed this project . . . too rich to go through this again." Zolotow, *Marilyn*, p. 339.

144 "Had you, dear Arthur . . . I had a nervous breakdown." Sikov, *Sunset Boulevard*, p. 425.

144 "I have never met anyone . . . and that includes Garbo." Zolotow, *Wilder*, p. 272.

145 "Nice little pictures . . . I wasn't getting a percentage of the gross." Wood, *Brighter*, p. 77.

145 "contains material regarded as too disturbing for Kansans." Anthony Holden, *Behind the Oscars*, New York, 1993, p. 224.

145 "The subject matter of 'transvestism'. . . in costuming was obvious." Leonard J. Leff and Jerold Simmons, *The Dame in the Kimono*, New York, 1990, p. 233.

145–146 "The one I liked? . . . No dear, the other one." Sikov, *Sunset Boulevard*, p. 427.

146 "We were set to film . . . Who knew it would become so famous?" Horton, *Wilder*, p. 191.

10. Annie Hall

157 "the clown tradition . . . the central comic performer . . ." Gerald Mast, *The Comic Mind*, Indianapolis, 1973, p. 280.

158–159 "walking up and down . . . talking and talking and talking." Douglas Brode, *The Films of Woody Allen*, New York, 1991, p. 157.

159 "We'd shovel it back and forth. . . and ask for $4 million." John Baxter, *Woody Allen*, New York, 1998, p. 241.

160 "Maybe you need a fresh mind . . . working on this for months." Stig Bjorkman, *Woody Allen on Woody Allen*, New York, 1993, p. 33.

161 "The whole thing just came to life . . . between living and dying." Eric Lax, *Woody Allen*, New York, 1991, p. 261.

161 "When you edit . . . throw them in behind the scenes." Bjorkman, *Woody Allen*, p. 34.

162 "The stuff people insist . . . these little nuances are based." Baxter, *Woody Allen*, p. 244.

162 "It's not true but . . . but they are *goyim*." Lee Guthrie, *Woody Allen*, New York, 1978, pp. 162–163.

162–163 "It was optional . . . but I passed on it." "Diane Keaton" in *Newsmakers 1997*, issue 4, Farmington Hills, Mich., 1997.

163 "In the final analysis . . . a revelation to me." Baxter, *Woody Allen*, p. 244.

163 "Tell her not to wear . . . If I really hate something, I'll tell her." Bjorkman, *Woody Allen*, p. 85.

166 "I want to show you something . . . we're going to use this." Baxter, *Woody Allen*, pp. 242–243.

166 "Hardly ever. Maybe three times a week . . . Constantly! I'd say three times a week." Woody Allen, *Four Films of Woody Allen*, New York, 1982, p. 80.

166 "I wonder what she looks . . . turn out to be a shmuck like the others." Ibid., pp. 39–40.

167 "I have frequently been accused . . . not because of my persuasion." Leonard J. Epstein, *The Haunted Smile*, New York, 2001, p. 196.

167 "we're left-wing Communist, Jewish, homosexual pornographers." Allen, *Four Films*, p. 30.

167–168 ". . . Allen was being bold . . . he refused to hide it." Epstein, *Smile*, pp. 202–203.

168 "To tell you the truth . . . tangential and just endless." Baxter, *Woody Allen*, p. 250.

168 "It was like the first draft . . . possibly be assembled," Ralph Rosenblum and Robert Karen, *When the Shooting Stops*, New York, 1979, p. 278.

168–169 "It was clear to Woody . . . cutting in the direction of that relationship," Ibid., p. 281.

169 "There was a lot of material taken out . . . about a relationship.'" Ibid., p. 283.

169 "I think every writer of comedy . . . something they can chew on." Ibid., p. 289.

170 "For you and me, it will be *Anhedonia* . . . we need to find a title." Marion Meade, *The Unruly Life of Woody Allen*, New York, 2000, p. 111.

170 The New York *Daily News* . . . heterosexual romance in American films." Wiley and Bona, *Inside Oscar*, p. 538.

171 "would be the first time . . . company had achieved this feat." Tino Balio, *United Artists*, Madison, Wisc., 1987, pp. 338–339.

171 "I couldn't let down the guys," Mason and Bona, *Inside Oscar*, p. 546.

172 "I felt good for Diane . . . Joffe had a very nice time." Brode, *Films*, p. 156.

172 "I have no regard . . . how meaningless this Oscar thing is." Anthony Holden, *Behind the Oscar*, New York, 1993, p. 72.

172 "Only after it won . . . maybe of all time, I don't know." Richard Schickel, *Woody Allen*, Chicago, 2003, pp. 113–114.

172 "You know how you're always . . . it's real difficult in life." Allen, *Four Films*, p. 102.

11. Arthur

174 "People said to me . . . I felt so terrible." Cynthia Heimel, "If You Loved 'Arthur,' You Ought to Meet Steve," *New York*, August 24, 1981, p. 28.

175 "I've just got to do this. Who do I have to sleep with?" Barbara Paskin, *Dudley Moore*, London, 1997, p. 216.

175 "I can walk out of the room . . . I don't know how to direct." Heimel, "If You Loved 'Arthur,'" p. 28.

177 "Dudley talked me into . . . nobody funnier than John Gielgud." Heimel, "If You Loved 'Arthur,'" p. 29.

177 "I thought it was rather smutty . . . I became reconciled to it." Jonathan Croall, *Gielgud: A Theatrical Life, 1904–2000*, New York, 2000, p. 505.

178 "I never knew what he was doing . . . and I would get hysterical." Heimel, "If You Loved 'Arthur,'" p. 29.

178 "No shit?" Paskin, *Moore*, p. 217.

179 "John had a huge sense . . . and get him going." Croall, *Gielgud*, p. 506.

179 "I mean everyone thinks he reads . . . loves reading Harold Robbins." Wiley and Bona, *Inside Oscar*, p. 600.

179 "He hated being called Sir John . . . in that brilliant accent was magic." Sheridan Morley, *John G*, London, 2001, p. 408.

179–180 "By mid-morning we were surrounded . . . her magic would rub off on them." George Mair, *Under the Rainbow*, Secaucus, N.J., 1996, p. 200.

180 "Judy! I've seen all your movies . . . nicest thing anyone has ever said to me." Woody Leigh, *Liza: Born a Star*, New York, 1993, p. 217.

180 "*Oy vey*, this isn't going to work! . . . his hair got caught in the fan." Paskin, *Moore*, p. 219.

181 "I could see Perlman smirking . . . burst into applause when he'd finished." Ibid., p. 220.

183 "Susan, I *told* you I'd be home. *Why* wouldn't you believe me?" Ibid., p. 234.

183 "Miss Minnelli, though relatively restrained . . . physical and spirited repulsiveness." Mair, *Rainbow*, p. 201.

185 "It's extraordinary to have . . . think of me as a kind of name," Wiley and Bona, *Inside Oscar*, p. 612.

185 "I got a new public . . . it was so satisfying." Croall, *Gielgud*, p. 507.

185 "I'm doomed to become Arthur in real life." Rena Fruchter, *Dudley Moore*, London, 2004, p. 141.

186 "I haven't even started . . . I have to beat *Arthur*." Heimel, "If You Loved 'Arthur,'" p. 29.

12. When Harry Met Sally . . .

187 In October 1989 . . . "It Had to Be You." "When Harry Met Woody," *Premiere*, October 1989, p. 31.

187 The first she labeled . . . the neuroses of the male character. "How Harry Met Sally," produced and directed by Jeffrey Schwarz, Metro-Goldwyn-Mayer Home Entertainment, 2000.

189 "Rob said he had an idea . . . And I said, let's do it." Nora Ephron, *When Harry Met Sally*, New York, 1992, p. viii.

189–190 "Nora Ephron did a couple of drafts . . . Then maybe she'd go off again." April Bernard, "Reiner's Reason," *Interview*, July 1989, p. 70.

190 "It's about two neurotic, self-indulgent people . . . for twelve years." "View," *Vogue*, July 1989, p. 46.

191 "What I like about the film . . . there's no subplot." Bernard, "Reiner's Reason," p. 71.

192 "I was in pain the whole time . . . It was just awful." Bruce Beschel, "Crystal Bawls," *Gentlemen's Quarterly*, August 1989, p. 203.

192 "He knew what I was going through . . . he's depressed while he makes you laugh." Ibid., p. 256.

192 "The point is that Rob was depressed . . . what Sally generously calls a dark side." Ephron, *Harry*, p. ix.

194 "She's the best actress; she's equally adept at playing comedy and drama. Plus she's sexy and she's cute." "View," *Vogue*, July 1989, p. 46.

194–195 "People who live in cities . . . talk on the phone and have dinner," Richard Corliss, "When Harry Met Sally . . .," *Time*, July 31, 1989. p. 65.

196 "This is hilarious. . . . Did you ever see 'When Harry Met Sally . . .?'" "How Harry Met Sally."

196 "Men and women can't be friends because the sex part always gets in the way." Ephron, *Harry*, p. 14.

197 "I told Rob he couldn't be sure . . . because women can fake orgasms," Beschel, "Crystal Bawls," p. 256.

197 "the funniest line in any movie I've ever done." "How Harry Met Sally."

198 "My mother can never say I never gave her anything." Commentary track, "When Harry Met Sally.. . ."

199 "Our story could fit very nicely into the film." "Harry and Sally meet a big squeeze in Beverly Hills," *People Weekly*, July 31, 1989, p. 24.

201 "I came here tonight . . . as soon as possible." Ephron, *Harry*, p. 97.

201 "It felt kind of phony to me." Commentary track, "How Harry Met Sally."

201 "When people say I'm sexy, I go, 'What did I do? What did I say?'" "Billy Crystal. (The 25 Most Intriguing People of the Year)," *People Weekly*, December 25, 1989, p. 75.

202 "The original script had a completeness . . . what else is there to say?" "Love at its wit's end." London *Times*, February 16, 2004, p. 16.

13. Pretty Woman

204 "[It was] a really dark and depressing . . . ugly story about these two people." James Spada, *Julia*, New York, 2004, p. 113.

205 "Garry was a little nervous about . . . being the guy who turned into fluff." Ibid., p. 114.

205 "On most films there are dozens . . . the way the movie business works." Garry Marshall with Lori Marshall, *Wake Me When It's Funny*, Holbrook, Mass., 1995, p. 115.

205 "When you sell a script . . . what happens to it." Wiley and Bona, *Inside Oscar*, New York, 1996, p. 783.

205–206 "I fought to keep the two rap scenes . . . not pretending to be anything else,'" Marshall, *Wake Me*, p. 246.

207 "It just was not the kind . . . I'm the exotic flower." Paul Donnelly, *Julia Roberts Confidential*, London, 2003, p. 84.

208 "I looked around and asked . . . 'You're not box office, pal.'" Kevin Sessions, "Richard Gere Shifts to High Gear," *Cosmopolitan*, July 1990, p. 133.

208 "They were bathed in this eerie light . . . persuade him to come aboard." Spada, *Julia*, p. 116.

209 "In fact at one point . . . just wanted to hide." Donnelly, *Julia Roberts*, p. 57.

209 "My mom works for the Catholic archdiocese . . . I'll talk to you later. . . .'" Steve Pond, "Pretty Woman Indeed," *Rolling Stone*, August 9, 1990, pp. 46, 49.

209 "Sweetheart, when was the last time you had anything to eat?" Marshall, *Wake Me*, p. 194.

210 "Now, in that situation . . . Audiences loved her for that." Johanna Schneller, "Barefoot Girl with Cheek," *Gentleman's Quarterly*, February 1991, p. 158.

211 "Guests do ask if Julia . . . They're joking . . . I think." Cindy Pearlman, "Suite Dreams," *Premiere*, October 1992, p. 24.

212 "When we polled the early audiences . . . with a big heart." Tim Allis, "As *Pretty Woman*'s Good-hearted Hotelier, Hector Elizondo Finally Checks into Suite Success," *People*, May 14, 1990, p. 77.

213 "Jeffrey agreed with me . . . fork in the fancy restaurant," Marshall, *Wake Me*, p. 237.

213–214 "There are certain people . . . frozen-foods aisle naked!" Spada, *Julia*, p. 119.

214 "Love scenes might look glamorous . . . end up as high comedy." Marshall, *Wake Me*, p. 241.

215 "He pulls this box from under his . . . I cried for a week." Fred Graver and Terri Minsley, "Garry Marshall Is Asking for It," *Esquire*, March 1990, p. 174.

216 "Mr. Marshall, the opera music . . . It just gave me goose bumps." Marshall, *Wake Me*, p. 254.

216 This was a change . . . So play it louder, replied Marshall. Garry Marshall told this story to the Boston film critics—and presumably those in other cities—when promoting his 1986 film *Nothing in Common*.

216 "The song is not really . . . reverses the emphasis of the song's lyrics. . ." Peter Lehman, *Roy Orbison*, Philadelphia, 2003, p. 113.

217 "We're the same age . . . And I think we've both done pretty well." Marshall, *Wake Me*, p. 191.

14. There's Something About Mary

220 "Pete and Bobby were a couple of screw-offs." "Wild Ride: The Farrelly Brothers, Perpetrators of 'There's Something About Mary,' Unleash 'Me, Myself and Irene,' a Raucous Oral History of Their Life and Crimes," *Newsweek*, July 3, 2000, p. 54.

221–222 "For us, this is the perfect movie . . . we'd be able to get away with." Kendall Hamilton and Devin Gordon, "Sibling Ribaldry," *Newsweek*, July 20, 1998, p. 64.

223 "Mary is kind of the perfect woman . . . she's a gorgeous babe." Chris Mundy, "A Fine Romance," *Harper's Bazaar*, August 1995, p. 114.

223 "I guess I just imagined . . . You're such a pathological liar.'" Ibid.

224 "It wasn't easy for Matt . . . I was very impressed." Ibid.

224 "I've never really done . . . I laughed like crazy." Margot Dougherty and Robert Maxwell, "King of Heart," *Los Angeles Magazine*, August 1998, p. 62.

224 "When Barney found his voice . . . Barney is Ted in our movie." John Brodie, "Gross Prophets," *GQ*, June 2000, p. 150.

225 "The studio didn't want me at all . . . I thought I might get fired." Chris Mundy, "The Evolution of Ben," *Rolling Stone*, November 12, 1998.

225 "Ben's funny. He's kind of geeky . . . She sees all those qualities." Robert Hofler, "The Year of Living Famously," *Premiere*, December 1998, p. 96.

225 "It was one of those scripts . . . it can be horrible and embarrassing." "Exposing Themselves," *There's Something* More *About Mary*, Widescreen Collections Edition DVD, 20th Century-Fox Home Entertainment, 2003.

226 "In our script we didn't have . . . most lethal thing in the movie." Brodie, "Gross Prophets."

227 "I had to sit there . . . gift from the Teenage Awkward God." "Brace Yourself," *People*, July 13, 1998, p. 128.

228 "It got to the point where . . . they thought my questions were so funny," "Puffy, Boobs and Balls," *There's Something* More *About Mary*.

228 "I'm used to having business calls . . . I have to talk in another room." "Wild Ride."

229 "It was one of the funniest and most disgusting and disturbing things I've ever seen." "Kissing Fool," *People*, September 14, 1998, p. 210.

229 "I don't see myself liplocking a dog the way she did." "Getting Behind Mary," *There's Something* More *About Mary*.

230 "You guys, the one thing we have to keep . . . was only one way to go." "Wild Ride."

231 "A guy with a load . . . not because it's gross." Brodie, "Gross Prophets."

231 "When we sent it to the studio . . . they loved him." "Baby, You're a Richman," *Entertainment Weekly*, July 24, 1998, p. 74.

231 "Not one of them didn't turn . . . 'Can I get my picture with you?'" "Getting Behind Mary," *There's Something* More *About Mary*.

232 "They're fun, open . . . I really learned from that." Mundy, Chris, "Evolution of Ben."

232 "On the weekend . . . going about their business." "There's Something About Cameron," *People*, August 17, 1998, p. 74.

233 "Everybody has their own way . . . called my name were people I knew." Jennifer Kasle Furmaniak, "Being Cameron Diaz," *Cosmopolitan*, January 2000, p. 144.

233 "We expected it to be a big hit . . . attract the word of mouth." William Spain, "'There's Something About Mary' Bob Harper," *Advertising Age*, June 28, 1999, p. S35.

234 "People are trained to think . . . it might not be as funny." A. J. Jacobs, "7 Peter + Bobby Farrelly," *Entertainment Weekly*, December 25, 1998, p. 32.

235 "We'll laugh at our body fluids . . . And that's how we're judged." Mim Udovith, "The Fabulous, Funny, Freak Farrelly Brothers," *Rolling Stone*, July 6, 2000, p. 94.

15. Love Actually

237 "Before the planes hit . . . they were all messages of love." Richard Curtis, *Love Actually*, New York, 2003, p. 9.

239 "I thought, 'Let's have seven good . . . other films out to such a length," Mark Salisbury, "In the Name of Love," *Premiere*, December 2003, p. 52.

240 "Don't buy drugs—become a pop star and they give you them for free." Curtis, *Love Actually*, p. 55.

240 "Everybody knows these guys . . . a lot of other people don't have." Kevin Maynard, "Bill Nighy: Love Actually (Eye on the Oscars the actor/supporting)," *Daily Variety*, January 7, 2004, p. S28.

240 "We usually kind of slap. . . and shout at the ref." Ibid.

242 "You miss by an inch . . . and the desire to vomit." Josh Tyrangiel, "Pouring on the Charm," *Time*, November 3, 2003, p. 62.

242 "I spent the two days we working . . . 'Come on! Be better, better.'" Curtis, *Love Actually*, p. 4.

244 "I think at a fundamental level . . . in love with girls." Salisbury, "In the Name."

245 "We've got the Chekovian bit . . . if you don't look after it." Ibid.

247 "She loved the film . . . pass the time as a mother." Robin Sayers, "Martin Freeman," *In Style*, May 1, 2005, p. 292.

248 "Her role relies so much just on her being gorgeous." Dave Karger, "The 'Love' Connection," *Entertainment Weekly*, November 7, 2003, p. 14.

250 "Suddenly in walked someone . . . the joke was meant to be." Sarah Lyall, "Four Comedies and a Collaboration." *New York Times*, Arts and Leisure section, November 2, 2003, p. 3.

251 "'I don't know that I really . . . seems a little retrograde." David Kamp, "Runaway Bachelor," *Vanity Fair*, May 2003, p. 170.

251–252 "The one thing I was really keen on . . . a puppy dog trying to please you." Johanna Schneller, "Nothing Compares to Hugh," *Premiere*, October 2003, p. 36.

252 "That's the whole joke . . . I'm one of them." Lyall, "Four Comedies."

252 "I watched her and loved her . . . boisterous, confident girl." "Hugh Grant's Cup of Tea: Brit TV star Martine McCutcheon tries Hollywood," *People Weekly*, November 24, 2003, p. 132.

253 "Oh, shut up, Tini. I wrote the part for you." "Martine McCutcheon, Slipping into Stardom," *USA Today*, November 7, 2003, p. 6E.

253 "And he fancied a trip to England," *Love Actually*, commentary track, Universal DVD, 2004.

254 "When we were finishing the film . . . 'Good luck in the editing room.'" Karger, "'Love' connection."

BIBLIOGRAPHY

BOOKS

Allen, Woody, *Four Films of Woody Allen*, New York, Random House, 1982.

Anderson, Christopher, *An Affair to Remember*, New York, William Morrow, 1997.

Balio, Tino, *United Artists*, Madison, University of Wisconsin Press, 1987.

Basinger, Jeanine, *A Woman's View*, New York Alfred A. Knopf, 1993.

Baxter, John, *Woody Allen*, New York, Carroll & Graf, 1998.

Berg, A. Scott, *Kate Remembered*, New York, G. P. Putnam's Sons, 2003.

Bjorkman, Stig, *Woody Allen on Woody Allen*, New York, Grove Press, 1993.

Bogart, Stephen Humphrey, *Bogart: In Search of My Father*, New York, Dutton, 1995.

Brode, Douglas, *The Films of Woody Allen*, New York, Citadel Press, 1991.

Capra, Frank, *The Name Above the Title*, New York, Vintage Books, 1985.

Chandler, Charlotte, *Nobody's Perfect*, New York, Simon and Schuster, 2002.

Chierichetti, David, *Edith Head*, New York, HarperCollins, 2003.

Clark, Tom, with Dick Kleiner, *Rock Hudson: Friend of Mine*, New York, Pharos Books, 1989.

Coe, Jonathan, *Jimmy Stewart: A Wonderful Life*, New York, Arcade, 1994.

Corliss, Richard, *Talking Pictures*, Woodstock, N.Y., Overlook Press, 1974.

Cox, Jonathan, *Humphrey Bogart: Take It and Like It*, New York, Grove Weidenfeld, 1991.

Croall, Jonathan, *Gielgud: A Theatrical Life 1904–2000*, New York, Continuum, 2000.

Curtis, Richard, *Love Actually*, New York, St. Martin's Press, 2003.

Curtis, Tony and Barry Paris, *Tony Curtis*, New York, William Morrow, 1993.

Davidson, Bill, *Spencer Tracy: Tragic Idol*, New York, E. P. Dutton, 1987.

Dewey, Donald, *James Stewart*, Atlanta, Turner Publishing, 1996.

DiBattista, Maria, *Fast Talking Dames*, New Haven, Yale University Press, 2001.

Donnelly, Paul, *Julia Roberts Confidential*, London, Virgin Books, 2003.

Eliot, Marc, *Jimmy Stewart*, New York, Harmony Books, 2006.

Ephron, Nora, *When Harry Met Sally*, New York, Alfred A. Knopf, 1992.

Epstein, Leonard J., *The Haunted Smile*, New York, Public Affairs, 2001.

Eyman, Scott, *Laughter in Paradise*, New York, Simon and Schuster, 1993.

Eyman, Scott, *Lion of Hollywood: The Life and Legend of Louis B. Mayer*, New York, Simon and Schuster, 2005.

Fishgall, Gary, *Pieces of Time: The Life of James Stewart*, New York, Scribners, 1997.

Francisco, Charles, *Gentleman: The William Powell Story*, New York, St. Martin's Press, 1985.

Freedland, Michael, *Jack Lemmon*, New York, St. Martin's Press, 1985.

Fruchter, Rena, *Dudley Moore*, London, Ebury Press, 2004.

Gehring, Wes D., *Carole Lombard: The Hoosier Tornado*, Indianapolis, Indiana Historical Society Press, 2003.

Gordon, Ruth, and Garson Kanin, *Adam's Rib*, New York, Viking Press, 1972.

Guthrie, Lee, *Woody Allen*, New York, Drake Publishers, 1978.

Hadleigh, Boze, *In or Out*, New York, Barricade Books, 2000.

Harris, Warren G., *Audrey Hepburn*, New York, Simon and Schuster, 1994.

Harris, Warren G., *Gable and Lombard*, New York, Simon and Schuster, 1974.

Harvey, James, *Romantic Comedy*, New York, Alfred A. Knopf, 1987.

Haskell, Molly, *From Reverence to Rape*, New York, Penguin Books, 1974.

Hayward, Brooke, *Haywire*, New York, Alfred A. Knopf, 1977.

Head, Edith, and Jane Kesner Ardmore, *Dress Doctor*, Boston, Little, Brown, 1959.

Head, Edith, and Patty Calistro, *Edith Head's Hollywood*, New York, E. P. Dutton, 1983.

Hepburn, Katharine, *Me*, New York, Alfred A. Knopf, 1991.

Higham, Charles, *Audrey*, New York, Macmillan, 1984.

Higham, Charles, *Kate*, New York, W. W. Norton, 1975.

Hirschorn, Clive, *The Universal Story*, New York, Crown Publishers, 1983.

Holden, Anthony, *Behind the Oscars*, New York, Simon and Schuster, 1993.

Holtzman, Will, *Judy Holliday*, New York, G. P. Putnam's Sons, 1982.

Horton, Robert, *Billy Wilder Interviews*, Jackson, University Press of Mississippi, 2001.

Hotchner, A. E., *Doris Day, Her Own Story*, New York, William Morrow, 1976.

Hudson, Rock, and Sara Davidson, *Rock Hudson: His Story*, New York, William Morrow, 1986.

Hyams, Joe, *Bogie*, New York, New American Library, 1966.

Kanin, Garson, *Tracy and Hepburn*, New York, Viking Press, 1971.

Karney, Robyn, *Audrey Hepburn: A Star Danced*, New York, Arcade, 1993.

Lally, Kevin, *Wilder Times*, New York, Henry Holt, 1996.

Lambert, Gavin, *On Cukor*, New York, Capricorn Books, 1973.

Lax, Eric, *Woody Allen*, New York, Alfred A. Knopf, 1991.

Leff, Leonard J., and Jerold Simmons, *The Dame in the Kimono*, New York, Grove Weidenfeld, 1990.

Lehman, Peter, *Roy Orbison*, Philadelphia, Temple University Press, 2003.

Leigh, Woody, *Liza: Born a Star*, New York, Dutton, 1993.

Levy, Emanuel, *George Cukor: Master of Elegance*, New York, William Morrow, 1994.

Mair, George, *Under the Rainbow*, Secaucus, N.J., Birch Lane Press, 1996.

Maltin, Leonard, *Movie Guide*, New York, Plume Books, 2007.

Mann, William J., *Behind the Screen*, New York, Viking Press, 2001.

Marshall, Garry, with Lori Marshall, *Wake Me When It's Funny*, Holbrook, Mass., Adams Publishing, 1995.

Mast, Gerald, *The Comic Mind*, 2nd ed., Chicago, University of Chicago Press, 1979.

Maychick, Diana, *Audrey Hepburn*, New York, Birch Lane Press, 1993.

McBride, Joseph, *The Catastrophe of Success*, New York, Simon and Schuster, 1992.

McGilligan, Patrick, *George Cukor: A Double Life*, New York, St. Martin's Press, 1991.

McNeil, Alex, *Total Television*, New York, Penguin Books, 1997.

Meade, Marion, *The Unruly Life of Woody Allen*, New York, Scribners, 2000.

Mohrt, Francois, *The Givenchy Style*, New York, Vendome Press, 1998.

Mordden, Ethan, *The Hollywood Studios: House Style in the Golden Age of the Movies*, New York, Afred A. Knopf, 1988.

Morley, Sheridan, *John G*, London, Hodder & Stoughton, 2001.

Munn, Michael, *Jimmy Stewart: The Truth Behind the Legend*, Fort Lee, N.J., Barricade Books, n.d.

Nelson, Nancy, *Evenings with Cary Grant*, New York, William Morrow, 1991.

Oppenheimer, Jerry, and Jack Vitek, *Idol: Rock Hudson*, New York, Villard Books, 1986.

Ott, Frederick, *The Films of Carole Lombard*, Secaucus, N.J., Citadel Press, 1972.

Parish, James Robert, *Katharine Hepburn: The Untold Story*, New York, Advocate Books, 2005.

Parker, John, *Five for Hollywood*, New York, Lyle Stuart, 1991.

Paskin, Barbara, *Dudley Moore*, London, Sidgwick & Jackson, 1997.

Paul, William, *Ernst Lubitsch's American Comedy*, New York, Columbia University Press, 1983.

Pogue, Leland, ed., *Frank Capra Interviews*, Jackson, University Press of Mississippi, 2004.

Randall, Tony, with Michael Mindlin, *Which Reminds Me*, New York, Delacorte Press, 1989.

Rosen, Marjorie, *Popcorn Venus*, New York, Coward, McCann and Geoghegan, 1973.

Rosenberg, Bernard, and Harry Silverstein, *The Real Tinsel*, New York, Macmillan, 1970.

Rosenblum, Ralph, and Robert Karen, *When the Shooting Stops*, New York, Viking Press, 1979.

Santopietro, Tom, *Considering Doris Day*, New York, Thomas Dunne Books, 2007.

Sarris, Andrew, *"You Ain't Heard Nothing Yet,"* New York, Oxford University Press, 1998.

Schickel, Richard, *Woody Allen*, Chicago, Ivan R. Dee, 2003.

Schwartz, Charles, *Cole Porter*, New York, Dial Press, 1977.

Sikov, Ed, *On Sunset Boulevard*, New York, Hyperion, 1998.

Spada, James, *Julia*, New York, St. Martin's Press, 2004.

Sperber, A. M., and Eric Lax, *Bogart*, New York, William Morrow, 1997.

Spier, Chrystopher J., *Clark Gable*, Jefferson, N.C., McFarland, 2002.

Spignesi, Stephen J., *The Woody Allen Companion*, Kansas City, Andrews and Mc-Meel, 1992.

Stevens, George Jr., ed., *Conversations with the Great Filmmakers of Hollywood's Golden Age at the American Film Institute*, New York, Alfred A. Knopf, 2006.

Stewart, Donald Ogden, *By a Stroke of Luck!*, New York, Paddington Press, 1975.

Summers, Anthony, *Goddess*, New York, Macmillan, 1985.

Swindell, Larry, *Spencer Tracy*, New York, World Publishing, 1969.

Thomas, Bob, *Golden Boy*, New York, Berkeley, 1984.

Thomas, Bob, *King Cohn: The Life and Times of Harry Cohn*, New York, G. P. Putnam's Sons, 1967.

Tornabene, Lyn, *Long Live the King*, New York, G. P. Putnam's Sons, 1976.

Vermilye, Jerry, *Cary Grant*, New York, Pyramid, 1973.

Walker, Alexander, *Audrey: Her Real Story*, New York, St. Martin's Press, 1994.

Walker, John, *Halliwell's Who's Who in the Movies*, 4th ed., London, HarperCollins Entertainment, 2006.

Wayne, Jane Ellen, *Clark Gable: Portrait of a Misfit*, New York, St. Martin's Press, 1993.

Weinberg, Herman G., *The Lubitsch Touch*, New York, E. P. Dutton, 1968.

Widener, Don, *Lemmon*, New York, Macmillan, 1975.

Wiley, Mason, and Damien Bona, *Inside Oscar*, 10th ed., New York, Ballantine Books, 1996.

Wolfe, Donald H., *The Last Days of Marilyn Monroe*, New York, William Morrow, 1998.

Wood, Tom, *The Bright Side of Billy Wilder, Primarily*, Garden City, N.Y., Doubleday, 1970.

Woodward, Ian, *Audrey Hepburn*, New York, St. Martin's Press, 1984.

Yablonsky, Lewis, *George Raft*, New York, McGraw-Hill, 1967.

Zolotow, Maurice, *Billy Wilder in Hollywood*, New York, G. P. Putnam's Sons, 1977.

Zolotow, Maurice, *Marilyn Monroe*, New York, Harper Perennial, 1990.

MAGAZINES AND NEWSPAPERS

Allis, Tim, "As *Pretty Woman*'s good-hearted hotelier, Hector Elizondo finally checks into suite success," *People*, May 14, 1990, p. 77.

"Baby, You're a Richman," *Entertainment Weekly*, July 24, 1998, p. 74.

Bernard, April, "Reiner's Reason," *Interview*, July 1989, p. 70.

Beschel, Bruce, "Crystal Bawls," *Gentlemen's Quarterly*, August 1989, p. 203.

"Billy Crystal. (The 25 Most Intriguing People of the Year)," *People Weekly*, December 25, 1989, p. 75.

"Brace Yourself," *People*, July 13, 1998, p. 128.

Brodie, John, "Gross Prophets," *GQ*, June 2000, p. 150

Corliss, Richard. "When Harry Met Sally . . .," *Time*, July 31, 1989, p. 65.

Dougherty, Margot, and Robert Maxwell, "King of Heart," *Los Angeles Magazine*, August 1998, p. 62.

Furmaniak, Jennifer Kasle, "Being Cameron Diaz," *Cosmopolitan*, January 2000, p. 144.

Graver, Fred, and Terri Minsley, "Garry Marshall Is Asking for It," *Esquire*, March 1990, p. 164.

Hamilton, Kendall, and Devin Gordon, "Sibling Ribaldry," *Newsweek*, July 20, 1998, p. 64.

"Harry and Sally Meet a Big Squeeze in Beverly Hills," *People Weekly*, July 31, 1989, p. 24.

Heimel, Cynthia, "If You Loved 'Arthur,' You Ought to Meet Steve," *New York*, August 24, 1981, p. 28.

Hofler, Robert, "The Year of Living Famously," *Premiere*, December 1998, p. 96.

"Hugh Grant's Cup of Tea: Brit TV Star Martine McCutcheon Tries Hollywood," *People Weekly*, November 24, 2003, p. 132.

Jacobs, A. J., "7 Peter + Bobby Farrelly," *Entertainment Weekly*, December 25, 1998, p. 32.

Kamp, David, "Runaway Bachelor," *Vanity Fair*, May 2003, p. 170.

Karger, Dave, "The 'Love' Connection," *Entertainment Weekly*, November 7, 2003, p. 14.

"Kissing Fool," *People*, September 14, 1998, p. 210.

"Love at Its Wit's End," *The Times*, London, February 16, 2004, p. 16.

Lyall, Sarah, "Four Comedies and a Collaboration," *New York Times*, Arts and Leisure section, November 2, 2003, p. 3.

"Martine McCutcheon, Slipping into Stardom," *USA Today*, November 7, 2003, p. 6E.

Maynard, Kevin. "Bill Nighy: Love Actually (Eye on the Oscars the actor/supporting)," *Daily Variety*, January 7, 2004, p. S28.

Mundy, Chris, "The Evolution of Ben," *Rolling Stone*, November 12, 1998.

Mundy, Chris, "A Fine Romance," *Harper's Bazaar*, August 1995, p. 114.

Pearlman, Cindy, "Suite Dreams," *Premiere*, October 1992, p. 24.

Pond, Steve, "Pretty Woman Indeed," *Rolling Stone*, August 9, 1990, p. 46.

Salisbury, Mark, "In the Name of Love," *Premiere*, December 2003, p. 52.

Sayers, Robin, "Martin Freeman," *In Style*, May 1, 2005, p. 292.

Schneller, Johanna, "Barefoot Girl with Cheek," *Gentlemen's Quarterly*, February 1991, p. 158.

Schneller, Johanna, "Nothing Compares to Hugh," *Premiere*, October 2003, p. 36.

Sessions, Kevin, "Richard Gere Shifts to High Gear," *Cosmopolitan*, July 1990, p. 133.

Spain, William, "'There's Something About Mary' Bob Harper," *Advertising Age*, June 28, 1999, p. S35.

"There's Something About Cameron," *People*, August 17, 1998, p. 74.

Tyrangiel, Josh, "Pouring On the Charm," *Time*, November 3, 2003, p. 62.

Udovith, Mim, "The Fabulous, Funny, Freak Farrelly Brothers," *Rolling Stone*, July 6, 2000, p. 94.

"View," *Vogue*, July 1989, p. 46.

"When Harry Met Woody," *Premiere*, October 1989, p. 31.

"Wild Ride: The Farrelly Brothers, Perpetrators of 'There's Something About Mary,' unleash 'Me, Myself and Irene,' A raucous oral history of their life and crimes," *Newsweek*, July 3, 2000, p. 54.

INTERNET

"Diane Keaton." *Newsmakers 1997*, Issue 4. Gale Research, 1997. Reproduced in *Biography Resource Center*. Farmington Hills, Mich., Thomson Gale, 2007. *http://galenet.galegroup.com/servlet/BioRC*.
Internet Movie Database, *http://www.imdb.com*.
Worldwide Box Office, *http://worldwideboxoffice.com/*.

DVD (EXTRAS)

"Love Actually," Universal DVD, 2004.
"There's Something *More* About Mary," Widescreen Collections Edition DVD, 20th Century Fox Home Entertainment, 2003.
"When Harry Met Sally . . . ," MGM Home Entertainment, 2000.

INDEX

A NOTE ON THE AUTHOR

Daniel M. Kimmel is a Boston-area film reviewer and past president of the Boston Society of Film Critics. He reviews films for the *Worcester Telegram and Gazette* and is the Boston correspondent for *Variety*. He has also written for the *Boston Globe*, *Film Comment*, the *Jewish Advocate*, the *Christian Science Monitor*, and the Internet Review of Science Fiction. He currently teaches film at Suffolk University. His history of the FOX television network, *The Fourth Network: How Fox Broke the Rules and Reinvented Television*, received the Cable Center Book Award.